MW01008859

Abbreviated Guide
Pneumatic Conveying Design Guide

Abbreviated Guide
Pneumatic Conveying Design Guide

David Mills PhD
Centre for Industrial Bulk Solids Handling,
Glasgow College,
Glasgow,
UK

Butterworths
London   Boston   Singapore   Sydney   Toronto   Wellington

 PART OF REED INTERNATIONAL P.L.C.

First published 1990

© **Crown Copyright, 1990.** Published by permission of the Controller of Her Britannic Majesty's Stationery Office
Warren Spring Laboratory. All rights reserved

ISBN 0 408 04719 4 (Main guide)
ISBN 0 408 04731 3 (Abbreviated guide)
ISBN 0 408 04707 0 (Combined set)

British Library Cataloguing in Publication Data

Mills, David
    Abbreviated guide: pneumatic conveying design guide
    1. Pneumatic conveying equipment. Design
    I. Title
    621.8′672

ISBN 0-408-04731-3

Library of Congress Cataloging in Publication Data applied for

Any queries should be addressed to:

The Director
Department of Trade and Industry
WARREN SPRING LABORATORY
Gunnels Wood Road
STEVENAGE
Hertfordshire
SG1 2BX

quoting reference 153/10/02

Photoset by KEYTEC, Bridport, Dorset
Printed in Great Britain at the University Press, Cambridge

Preface

During the late 1970's, Warren Spring Laboratory (WSL) was funding research into pneumatic conveying by means of an extra mural research award to Thames Polytechnic. By the beginning of the 1980's, government funding for such awards was curtailed and, with much work still to be done, WSL initiated a multi-client project to fund the continuation of the work. UK-based users and manufacturers joined the project, paying a membership fee, and the Department of Industry provided the remaining funds, up to fifty per cent of the project costs.

In 1982, a detailed programme for a two-year project was drawn up and agreed by members. The information and results were presented in a series of confidential reports to members. As part of the programme, a comprehensive test facility was built at Thames Polytechnic, funded by the project. The project was extended to three years with most of the member companies continuing to support it for the third year.

Each report included background explanations and derivations of formulae, etc and the complexity of some of the information led to a decision to produce an Abbreviated Guide which provided the project engineer with all the information required to design, or check the design, for a system but including only essential mathematics.

The project administration was carried out by WSL under the guidance of the then Head of Materials Handling Division, Dr Peter Bransby. The majority of the test work and report writing was carried out by Professor David Mills, then of Thames Polytechnic, under the supervision of the Head of Department, Dr Stanley Mason.

Because each report had to be complete in itself, the total of fifteen reports and appendices included some repetition in both text and diagrams as well as extensive cross-referencing. The difficult job of editing all the information to produce this book was carried out by Dr Pauline Hornsby, a freelance technical writer, with the technical guidance of Mr Chris Duffell of WSL.

The project was supported by the following companies:

Babcock Hydro-Pneumatics	Pedigree Petfoods
Blue Circle Industries	PIAB
British Gypsum	Portasilo
British Steel	Rank Hovis McDougal Research
Central Electricity Generating Board	Reckitt & Colman

Claudius Peters
Colmans of Norwich
Conoco
Doulton Industrial Products
Henry-Simon
Hepworth Iron
John Grist
Kemutec
National Coal Board
Neu Engineering

Redland Technology
Schlumberger Research
Shell Research
Sim-Chem
Simon-Carves
Simon-Solitec
Stb Engineering
Sturtevant Engineering
Tate & Lyle
Unilever
Vac-U-Max

It is through the efforts of the individuals and companies mentioned above and others who were involved in the project that this book can be produced now the project confidentiality period has expired. Having only had the responsibility of ensuring its publication, I am particularly indebted to Pauline Hornsby and Chris Duffell for producing a book which will undoubtedly enhance the understanding and application of pneumatic conveying.

This *Abbreviated Guide* for the *Pneumatic Conveying Design Guide* brings together all the essential elements in the selection, design and specification of conventional pneumatic conveying systems. The design procedure is based on the use of test data or on previous experience with the material to be conveyed. Consideration is given to system economics and operating costs, the choice of the most appropriate system and components, and system control and flexibility for possible future changes and alternative requirements. Reference is made to the chapters and sections of the *Pneumatic Conveying Design Guide* for more detailed explanations of each aspect.

Maurice Webb
Head, Marine Pollution and Bulk Materials
Warren Spring Laboratory, 1989

Contents

Note: Chapters in brackets [ ] indicate the part of the *Pneumatic Conveying Design Guide* where full details of the subject may be found.

1.1. Introduction   1
    1.1.1. Decision Stages   1
    1.1.2. System Selection [Ch. 2, 4, 10, 14]   1
    1.1.3. Pipeline Design [Ch. 5, 9]   2
    1.1.4. Specification of Components   2

1.2. System Selection [Ch. 2, 4, 10, 14]   2
    1.2.1. General   2
    1.2.2. Closed Systems   3
    1.2.3. Open Systems [Ch. 12]   3
    1.2.4. Positive Pressure Systems [Ch. 2]   3
    1.2.5. Negative Pressure (Vacuum) Systems [Ch. 2, 3]   3
    1.2.6. Combined Negative and Positive Pressure Systems [Ch. 6]   4
    1.2.7. Dual Negative and Positive Pressure Systems   4
    1.2.8. Innovatory Systems [Ch. 2, 12]   4

1.3. Pipeline Design   5
    1.3.1. General   5
    1.3.2. Conveying Air Velocity [Ch. 6]   5
        1.3.2.1. Conveying Line Inlet Air Velocity   5
        1.3.2.2. Volumetric Air Flow Rate   6
        1.3.2.3. Conveying Line Inlet Air Pressure   6
        1.3.2.4. The Influence of the Conveying Variables   6
    1.3.3. Logic Diagrams [Ch. 5]   7
        1.3.3.1. Material Conveying Characteristics [Ch. 4, 7]   7
    1.3.4. Using a Logic Diagram [Ch. 5]   7
        1.3.4.1. Specify Mass Flow Rate of Material ($\dot{m}_p$)   8
            1.3.4.1.1. Batch Operating Systems [Ch. 3, 10, 14]   8
            1.3.4.1.2. Choice of System [Ch. 4, 14]   8
        1.3.4.2. Specify Conveying Distance [Ch. 9]   9
            1.3.4.2.1. Pipeline Routing   9
        1.3.4.3. Material Conveying Characteristics [Ch. 7, 9]   9
            1.3.4.3.1. Conveying Limits   9
            1.3.4.3.2. Non-availability of Conveying Limit Data [Ch. 8]   10
        1.3.4.4. Scale to Distance and Geometry [Ch. 9, 14]   11
            1.3.4.4.1. Horizontal Conveying   11

1.3.4.4.2. Conveying Vertically Up   11
1.3.4.4.3. Conveying Vertically Down   11
1.3.4.4.4. Pipeline Bends   11
1.3.4.4.5. The Scaling Model   12
1.3.4.4.6. Scaling Requirements   12
1.3.4.4.7. Empty Line (Air Only) Pressure Drop Datum (Single-phase Flow)   13
1.3.4.4.8. Results of Scaling   13
1.3.4.4.9. Conveying Limit Changes   13
1.3.4.5. Can Material Mass Flow Rate be Achieved?   14
1.3.4.6. Calculate Power Requirements of Air Mover [Ch. 5, 6, 14]   14
1.3.4.7. Scale to Different Pipeline Bore [Ch. 5, 9, 14]   15
1.3.4.7.1. The Scaling Model   15
1.3.4.7.2. Scaling Requirements   15
1.3.4.7.3. Empty Line (Air Only) Pressure Drop Datum (Single-phase Flow)   16
1.3.4.7.4. Results of Scaling   16
1.3.4.7.5. Conveying Parameters   16
1.3.4.7.6. Cautionary Note   16
1.3.4.7.7. First Estimate of Pipeline Bore   16
1.3.4.8. Specify Pipeline Bore   17
1.3.4.8.1. Stepped Pipelines [Ch. 6, 9]   17
1.3.4.9. Specify Air Requirements [Ch. 6]   17
1.3.4.9.1. Volumetric Flow Rate [Ch. 7]   17
1.3.4.9.2. Air Leakage/Ingress Across Feeding Device Allowance   17
1.3.4.9.3. Specification for Air Mover (Flow Rate)   17
1.3.4.10. Delivery Pressure [Ch. 1, 3, 9, 10]   17
1.3.4.10.1. Pressure Drop in Air Lines   18
1.3.4.10.2. Pressure Drop Across Feeding Device   18
1.3.4.10.3. Pressure Drop in the Conveying Line   18
1.3.4.10.4. Pressure Drop Across Gas–Solid Separation Device   18
1.3.4.10.5. Specification for Air Mover (Air Supply Pressure) [Ch. 11]   18
1.3.5. Choice of Air Mover [Ch. 6]   18
1.3.5.1. Power Requirements   19
1.3.6. Other Considerations   19
1.3.6.1. System Uprating [Ch. 11]   19
1.3.6.2. Alternative Conveying Distances [Ch. 5]   20
1.3.6.3. Alternative Materials [Ch. 5]   20
1.4. Specification of Components [Ch. 2, 3, 6]   20
1.4.1. General   21
1.4.2. Economic Considerations [Ch. 14]   21
1.4.3. Mode of Operation   21
1.4.4. Material Feeding Devices [Ch. 3]   22
1.4.4.1. Selection Considerations [Ch. 10]   22
1.4.4.2. Types of Feeding Device [Ch. 2, 3]   22
1.4.4.2.1. Rotary Valves   22
1.4.4.2.2. Screw Feeders   22
1.4.4.2.3. Venturi Feeders   22
1.4.4.2.4. Gate Lock Valves   23
1.4.4.2.5. Blow Tanks   23

1.4.5.   Air Mover [Ch. 6]   24
    1.4.5.1.   Specification of Air Requirements   24
    1.4.5.2.   Choice of Air Mover   24
    1.4.5.3.   Control Requirements   24
    1.4.5.4.   Use of Plant Air   24
    1.4.5.5.   Positive Pressure Systems [Ch. 2]   24
    1.4.5.6.   Negative Pressure (Vacuum) Systems [Ch. 2]   25
    1.4.5.7.   Combined Negative and Positive Pressure Systems [Ch. 2]   25
1.4.6.   Gas–Solid Separation System [Ch. 3]   25
    1.4.6.1.   Choice of Gas–Solid Separation System   25
    1.4.6.2.   Gravity Settling Chambers   25
    1.4.6.3.   Cyclone Separators   25
    1.4.6.4.   Fabric Filters   26
    1.4.6.5.   System Considerations   26
        1.4.6.5.1.   Continuously Operating Systems   26
        1.4.6.5.2.   Batch Conveying Systems   26

Appendix   27
A.1.   Reference   27
A.2.   Nomenclature   27
    A.2.1.   Symbols   29
    A.2.2.   Prefixes   29
    A.2.3.   Subscripts   29
    A.2.4.   Non-dimensional Group   29
A.3.   Conversion Factors   29
A.4.   Formulae   30
A.5.   Illustrations   31

Pneumatic Conveying Design Guide Index   41

Index   73

Abbreviated Guide

1.1. Introduction

Note: Cross references in parentheses ( ) are located in this Abbreviated Design Guide. Cross references in brackets [ ] are located in the *Pneumatic Conveying Design Guide*.

1.1.1. Decision Stages

a) Decide on the basic type of conveying system to be used.
b) Design the pipeline (this determines the conveying parameters).
c) Specify plant components to be used.

   This order is not fixed but it is the preferred one if no constraints are imposed on the selection of plant components and should result in the most economical and suitable system for a given duty. If outside influences dictate that certain components must be used, the number of possible systems will be limited and the order of decision stages will be changed.

1.1.2. System Selection

A wide variety of systems are available and the majority of systems are capable of meeting any specified demand in terms of material flow rate and distance conveyed. This makes the process of total system selection very difficult. This is illustrated in Figure 1 which shows the combinations that are possible for conventional systems with a single air source. Only system types are presented in detail, with positive pressure, negative pressure, and combined positive and negative pressure systems considered, in relation to both open and closed systems. Air requirements are given in terms of a high or low operating pressure. The selection of air mover, from the wide range available, comes at this point. Material feed into the conveying line is expressed in terms of mode of operation; it is here that the selection of the feeding device is made, in conjunction with information on air supply pressure. The choice of gas–solid separation device is made in terms of system type and mode of operation. [System Selection and System Selection Considerations are discussed in Chapter 2, Types of Pneumatic Conveying System, Section 2.4.; Chapter 4, Selection of a Pneumatic Conveying System for a Particular Application; Chapter 10, Design of the Total Conveying System; Chapter 14, Case Study.]

The properties of the material to be conveyed have a significant influence on the decision to be taken at several stages. Personal preferences for a particular type of system, feeder or air mover automatically limit the choice. Site constraints of space and headroom need to be taken into account. Simplicity of operation may be a requirement for a plant destined for developing countries. Capital cost is probably a major consideration, although operating cost, plant maintenance and reliability can also be very important. Logic diagrams provide a means by which decisions could be ordered and processed but the wide variety of plant layouts required, systems and components available, and specific conditions which can be applied to selection, make their use far too complex to be of any general value.

1.1.3. Pipeline Design

Pipeline design is the most complex and critical step in conveying system design. The entire success of the plant depends upon the correct specification of the pipeline bore and the air requirements in terms of delivery pressure and volumetric flow rate. Since the application and reliability of mathematical models for pipeline design is very limited the design process is based entirely upon the use of available test data for a material obtained either from previous experience with the material or from conveying trials carried out with the material. [See Chapter 5, Pneumatic Conveying Design Procedures, and Chapter 9, Design of the Conveying Line Layout.]

1.1.4. Specification of Components

Once the pipeline design parameters have been established, an appropriate system must be selected. This generally means that the operating expenses and capital cost of the plant should be a minimum. The design procedure for the pipeline is specifically directed towards selecting parameters to achieve minimum power requirements. It is with the specification of the plant components, for a given mode of operation and pipeline design, that the capital cost can be established.

1.2. System Selection

1.2.1. General

The first stage in the overall design process requires two decisions to be made. One is to decide whether an open system is satisfactory or whether a closed system [see Section 2.4.5.] is required. The properties of the material to be conveyed [see Sections 10.4.1. to 10.4.12. and 13.6.1. to 13.6.10.] feature significantly in this decision. The type of system to be used also has to be selected [see Chapter 2]. The requirements of the system, in terms of plant layout and material properties, have to be considered here. [System Selection and System Selection Considerations are discussed in Chapter 2, Types of Pneumatic Conveying System, Section 2.4.; Chapter 4, Selection of a Pneumatic Conveying System for a Particular Application; Chapter 10, Design of the Total Conveying System; Chapter 14, Case Study.]

1.2.2. Closed Systems

For certain conveying duties it is necessary to convey the material in a controlled environment [see Section 2.4.8.]. If a dust cloud is potentially explosive, nitrogen or another inert gas can be used to convey the material. In an open system environmental control can be very expensive but in a closed system the gas can be recirculated. If the material to be handled is radioactive it may be possible to use air for conveying. Very strict control must be maintained over emissions making a closed system essential.

1.2.3. Open Systems

Where strict environmental control is not necessary an open system is generally preferred to a closed system because the capital cost of the plant is less, the operational complexity is reduced, and a much wider range of systems are available. Most pneumatic conveying pipeline systems can ensure totally enclosed material conveying, therefore, with suitable gas–solid separation and venting, the vast majority of materials can be handled quite safely in an open system. Many potentially combustible materials are conveyed in open systems by incorporating safety features [see Sections 12.6.1. to 12.6.4.].

1.2.4. Positive Pressure Systems

Positive pressure systems [see Section 2.3.1.] are probably the most common type of pneumatic conveying system. A wide range of material feeding devices can be used from venturis [Sections 2.3.2. and 3.2.5.] and rotary valves [Sections 2.3.2. and 3.2.3.] to screws [Sections 2.3.2. and 3.2.4.] and blow tanks [Sections 2.3.7. and 3.2.7.].

With the use of diverter valves, multiple delivery to a number of reception points can be arranged very easily. Although multiple point feeding into a common line can also be arranged, care must be taken, particularly in the rotary valve feeding of the pipeline, because the air leakage through a number of such valves can be significant in relation to the total air requirements for conveying [see Section 3.2.3.1. and Figure 17].

1.2.5. Negative Pressure (Vacuum) Systems

Negative pressure systems are commonly used for drawing materials from multiple sources to a single point [see Section 2.3.5.]. There is little or no pressure difference across the feeding device in a negative pressure system and multiple point feeding into a common line with rotary valves [Sections 2.3.2. and 3.2.3.] is quite satisfactory. As a result the rotary valve can be a cheaper item in a negative pressure system than in a positive pressure system. However, the filtration plant [Section 3.3.3.3.] has to be much larger as a larger volume of air has to be filtered under negative pressure conditions. The exhauster must be protected from the ingress of material.

Negative pressure systems are widely used for drawing materials from open storage and stockpiles and for off-loading ships, where an open surface of the material is accessible. Recovery is achieved by using suction nozzles [see Section

3.2.8.]. They are also particularly useful for cleaning processes, such as the removal of material spillage and dust accumulations.

Negative pressure systems have the particular advantage that all gas leakage is inward so that injection of dust into the atmosphere is virtually eliminated. This is a great advantage in the handling of toxic and explosible materials, making use of a closed system unnecessary, provided that adequate safety measures are taken [see Sections 12.6.1. to 12.6.4.], particularly with regard to exhaust venting.

1.2.6. Combined Negative and Positive Pressure Systems

Combined negative and positive pressure systems [Section 2.3.6.] represent a very versatile type of pneumatic conveyor, combining many of the features of the negative pressure [Section 2.3.5.] and positive pressure [Section 2.3.1.] systems. They can be used to transfer material from multiple sources to multiple discharge locations thereby extending negative pressure systems over much longer distances.

The exhauster must be protected from the ingress of material. It should be noted that the available power for the system has to be shared between the two sections and the pipelines for the two parts have to be carefully sized to take account of different operating pressures and possible losses through rotary valves [see Section 3.2.3. and Figure 17; Section 6.2.: Sub-sections 6.2.1. to 6.2.6.].

1.2.7. Dual Negative and Positive Pressure Systems

If the conveying potential of a system requiring negative pressure pick-up of a material needs to be improved beyond that capable with a combined negative and positive pressure system [Section 2.3.6.], particularly in terms of conveying distance, then a dual system should be considered. In this, the two conveying elements are separated and two air movers are provided. By this means the most suitable air mover can be dedicated to the negative pressure system and the most appropriate positive pressure system can be used for the onward transfer of the material.

1.2.8. Innovatory Systems

For materials which are either friable or abrasive, alternatives to conventional systems may have to be considered, particularly if the materials are not capable of being conveyed in the dense phase mode and hence at low velocities. Considerable particle degradation of friable materials [see Sections 2.4.4., 3.3.2.3. and 12.2.1. to 12.2.3.] can occur in a high velocity dilute phase (suspension) flow. Erosion of pipeline bends [see Sections 2.4.5. and 12.3.1. to 12.3.9.] and other plant surfaces subject to particle impact will occur if an abrasive material is conveyed in dilute phase.

For a material which is only slightly hygroscopic, successful conveying can be achieved without the need for special air drying equipment if the material is conveyed in dense phase. Air quantities required for dense phase conveying can be significantly lower than those for dilute phase. Where food products may be subject to a loss in flavour from contact with air, dense phase conveying is automatically recommended.

Innovatory systems [Section 2.5.] include single-plug blow tank systems [Section 2.5.2.], pulse phase systems [Section 2.5.3.], and plug control systems [Section 2.5.4.]. The pulse phase system was developed for the handling of fine materials of a cohesive nature which are difficult to convey in conventional systems.

An innovatory system may also be chosen because such systems are capable of conveying materials in dense phase and reducing power costs compared with a conventional dilute phase system. The capital costs for the innovatory system are likely to be higher and an economic assessment of the alternative systems needs to be carried out.

Many innovatory systems are capable of being stopped and re-started during operation. With most conventional systems this is not possible. In any operation where this feature would be necessary, therefore, one of the innovatory systems should be considered.

1.3. Pipeline Design

1.3.1. General

For a given duty, a decision is required on the bore of the pipeline to be used and the air requirements in terms of delivery pressure and volumetric flow rate. The rating of the air mover is then based on this data. Any error in this data results in a system which is either over-rated or is not capable of achieving the desired material flow rate.

1.3.2. Conveying Air Velocity

To ensure that the required velocity is maintained, the volumetric flow rate of air available to convey the material must be correctly specified. Problems arise because air is compressible and the volumetric flow rate varies with both pressure and temperature. [The theory and use of compressed air in pneumatic conveying is discussed in Chapter 6.] The volumetric flow rate of 'free air' required for conveying a material can be determined from:

$$\dot{V}_0 = \frac{13400 p_i d^2 C_i}{(t_i + 273)} \text{ m}^3 \text{min}^{-1} \tag{1}$$

where $\dot{V}_0$ = volumetric flow rate at 'free air' conditions $\text{m}^3 \text{min}^{-1}$
p_i = conveying line inlet air pressure   bar abs
d = pipeline bore   m
C_i = conveying line inlet air velocity m s^{-1}
t_i = conveying line inlet air temperature   °C

or

$$\dot{V}_0 = 2.23 \frac{p_i d^2 C_i}{(t_i + 273)} \text{ m}^3 \text{s}^{-1} \tag{2}$$

where $\dot{V}_0$ = volumetric flow rate at 'free air' conditions $\text{m}^3 \text{s}^{-1}$
p_i = conveying line inlet air pressure kN m^{-2}

1.3.2.1. Conveying Line Inlet Air Velocity
This is the superficial velocity of the air [see Section 1.6.1.8.] at the material

pick-up point. It is essential that this specified velocity is always maintained otherwise the pipeline may block. For this reason it is recommended that a conveying line inlet air velocity 20 per cent higher than the minimum conveying air velocity should be used for design purposes. A velocity greater than this is not generally recommended because of the increased power and filtration requirements, the adverse effect (for most materials) on material flow rate [see Section 6.1.3.], and the increase in erosive wear with abrasive materials and particle degradation with friable materials.

1.3.2.2. Volumetric Air Flow Rate
This is the volumetric flow rate of free air required to convey the material through the pipeline. The volumetric flow rate of air to be specified for the air mover must take account of air leakage across feeding devices in positive pressure systems, and possible air ingress in negative pressure systems.

1.3.2.3. Conveying Line Inlet Air Pressure
This is the pressure of the air at the material pick-up point at the start of the conveying line. The air supply pressure to be specified for the air mover must take into account the pressure drop across the feeding device. An allowance may also be needed for surges in material feed.

1.3.2.4. The Influence of the Conveying Variables
Since the conveying line inlet air velocity is such an important parameter it is essential that the influence of pressure, air flow rate and temperature are taken into account [see Chapter 6, Theory and Use of Compressed Air in Pneumatic Conveying]. An alternative arrangement of the model given in Equations (1) and (2) (Section 1.3.2.) in terms of the conveying line inlet air velocity is:

$$C_i = \frac{(t_i + 273)\dot{V}_0}{13400 p_i d^2} \, \mathrm{m\,s^{-1}} \tag{3}$$

or

$$C_i = \frac{(t_i + 273)\dot{V}_0}{2.23 p_i d^2} \, \mathrm{m\,s^{-1}}$$
$$= \frac{0.448(t_i + 273)\dot{V}_0}{p_i d^2} \, \mathrm{m\,s^{-1}} \tag{4}$$

It can be seen from Equations (3) and (4) that if the pressure is increased, then the conveying line inlet air velocity will fall. Therefore the volumetric flow rate of air which is specified must be sufficient to maintain the desired conveying line inlet air velocity at the maximum air supply pressure anticipated. Account must be taken of possible surges in material feed rate.

In positive pressure systems the volumetric flow rate of air supplied by the air mover must take into account air leakage across the feeding device. If this is not allowed for, the volumetric flow rate of air available could be significantly below that required to convey the material and lead to pipeline blockage.

It will be seen from Equations (3) and (4) that if the temperature is decreased, then the conveying line inlet air velocity will fall. The volumetric flow rate of air which is specified must be sufficient to maintain the desired

conveying line inlet air velocity at the lowest temperature anticipated. Account must be taken of cold start-up and winter operating conditions.

1.3.3. Logic Diagrams

Logic diagrams can be used to determine the alternative between pipeline bore and conveying line pressure drop for achieving a given material flow rate over a specified conveying distance [see Chapter 5, Pneumatic Conveying System Design Procedures]. Logic diagrams are available for design based on the use of mathematical models or on the use of test data. In this Abbreviated Guide system design is based only upon test data in the form of material conveying characteristics [see Chapter 7, Determination and Use of Conveying Characteristics in the Pipeline].

1.3.3.1. Material Conveying Characteristics
To illustrate some of the points in pipeline design procedure the conveying characteristics for two very different materials are presented. One is dicalcium phosphate, a material having very good air retention properties, a material type A, which can be conveyed in dense phase [see Chapter 4, Selection of a Pneumatic Conveying System for a Particular Application]. The other is sodium sulphate, a material having very poor air retention properties, a material type B, which can only be conveyed in dilute phase (suspension flow) in a conventional conveying system [see Chapter 4]. The relationship between the minimum conveying air velocity and the phase density at which they are conveyed is presented in Figure 2. The conveying characteristics for the two materials conveyed through a horizontal pipeline 100 m (330 ft) long, 81 mm (3.25 in) bore, having eight bends at 90 degrees are given in Figures 3 and 4[1].

Comparing the conveying characteristics it can be seen that, although both materials were conveyed through exactly the same pipeline with the same conveying line pressure drop values, the air requirements and material flow rates achieved are totally different.

The differences are emphasised by drawing single pressure drop lines from the conveying characteristics for seven different materials each conveyed through the same pipeline, 50 m (165 ft) long, 50 mm (2 in) bore, having a total of nine bends at 90 degrees ($D/d = 24$) [Pipeline No.1 shown in Figure 173]. These are presented in Figure 5. The conveying line pressure drop was 1.5 bar for each material. The granulated sugar, like sodium sulphate (Figure 3), could be conveyed only in dilute phase (suspension flow). All the other materials could be conveyed in dense phase (non-suspension flow), like dicalcium phosphate (Figure 4), although their material flow capabilities, with respect to air flow rate, are very different. This clearly illustrates the necessity for such data on the material to be conveyed if a reliable design for a pneumatic conveying system is to be obtained.

1.3.4. Using a Logic Diagram

Figure 6 is a logic diagram for system design based on available conveying characteristics for a material [see also Chapter 5, Pneumatic Conveying System Design Procedures, Section 5.3., The Use of Test Data in System Design: Sub-sections 5.3.2. to 5.3.2.9. and Figure 67]. The process is traced from the

specification of the fixed parameters, through the necessary scaling procedures, to the final specification of the most suitable pipeline bore and air requirements. The numbers adjacent to the boxes on Figure 6 correspond to the number of the section in which the relevant procedure is discussed.

1.3.4.1. Specify Mass Flow Rate of Material ($\dot{m}_p$)
This is generally a steady hourly rate, or a time averaged mean value. For continuously operating systems this value is the flow rate, which needs to be specified.

1.3.4.1.1. Batch Operating Systems. For batch operating systems a higher value than the steady hourly rate must be specified to allow for non-continuous conveying. The ratio between the value to be specified and the time averaged mean value depends upon the type of batch system to be used and the distance conveyed. Typical ratios would be about 0.80 for a twin blow tank system, and 0.65 for a single blow tank capable of conveying a 1 t batch. [See Chapter 3, Feeding and Discharging the Conveying Line, Section 3.2.7., Blow Tank Systems; Chapter 10, Design of the Total Conveying System, Section 10.5., Analysis of Blow Tank Cycles; Chapter 14, Case Study, Sections 14.4.3.2. and 14.4.3.3.]

If the ratio between the time averaged mean material flow rate, $\bar{\dot{m}}_p$, and the value to be achieved by a batch operating system, $\hat{\dot{m}}_p$, is χ then:

$$\hat{\dot{m}}_p = \frac{\bar{\dot{m}}_p}{\chi} \tag{5}$$

Thus if a steady material flow rate of $40\,\mathrm{t\,h^{-1}}$ is required and a single blow tank is used, for which the value of this ratio is 0.65, the steady flow rate to be achieved during the conveying cycle has to be about $61.5\,\mathrm{t\,h^{-1}}$.

1.3.4.1.2. Choice of System. If the choice of system required is pre-determined for some reason, then the appropriate value of material flow rate can be specified. If the investigation or survey is to cover a wide range of pipeline bores, then a wide range of conveying line pressure drop values will result [see Chapter 4, Selection of a Pneumatic Conveying System for a Particular Application, and Chapter 14, Case Study]. The ultimate value of conveying line pressure drop selected will, to a certain extent, dictate the choice of system.

A wide combination of conveying line pressure drop values and pipeline bores will be capable of achieving the required material flow rate [see Chapter 5]. If the conveying line pressure drop is below 1 bar ($100\,\mathrm{kN\,m^{-2}}$), then a continuously operating rotary valve system might be appropriate. If it is below 2.5 bar ($250\,\mathrm{kN\,m^{-2}}$) the choice could be between a continuously operating screw pump system and a blow tank system. Above 2.5 bar it would be a blow tank system, but the choice could be a twin blow tank system capable of continuous operation [see Section 14.4.2.2.]. Alternatively, if the material is abrasive, a low pressure blow tank system might be chosen because of feeder wear considerations. Approximate operating pressure ranges for conveying line feeding devices are given in Figure 12.

If a number of different systems are to be considered for the duty then material flow rates up to about 100 per cent in excess of the specified flow rate may need to be considered. It is necessary for the conveying characteristics for

the material to cover a reasonably wide range of pressure drop values and material mass flow rates, as well as air flow rates and phase densities.

1.3.4.2. Specify Conveying Distance
The conveying distance needs to be specified together with the routing and details of the pipeline. Actual distance, orientation of the pipeline and the number of bends and their geometry are equally important. Pipeline length has to be considered in terms of the individual lengths of horizontal, vertically up and vertically down sections. Bend geometry is considered in terms of the bend angle and the ratio of the bend diameter to the pipe bore (D/d). Pipe bore is an entirely separate variable and is not considered at this stage. [See Chapter 9, Design of the Conveying Line Layout.]

1.3.4.2.1. Pipeline Routing.
Careful consideration should be given to the routing of the pipeline. The conveying distance should be kept as short as possible and the number of bends should be kept to the absolute minimum. Although considerable flexibility is possible in the routing of pneumatic conveying system pipelines, unnecessary distance and bends add significantly to the line resistance. For a given air supply pressure, an increase in distance, or the number of bends, means that the material flow rate has to be reduced to compensate.

1.3.4.3. Material Conveying Characteristics
The conveying characteristics obtained for a material from conveying trials form the starting point in a design based on experimental data [see Chapter 7, Determination and Use of Conveying Characteristics in the Pipeline]. System design is simply based on the scaling of the conveying characteristics for a specified material from the test situation to the plant requirements. The scaling is in terms of the pipeline geometry. [See Chapter 9, Design of the Conveying Line Layout, Section 9.3., Material Conveying – Pipeline Scaling Parameters and Chapter 14, Case Study, Section 14.3., Sub-sections 14.3.1. to 14.3.5.3.]

Scaling is clearly critical in this process, and the closer the test line is to the plant situation the more accurate will be the analysis. Scaling, however, can be carried out with a reasonable degree of accuracy over a fairly wide range of pipeline bores and conveying distances. Conveying characteristics are presented for a number of different materials (barytes, bentonite, cement, coal, flour, fluorspar, pearlite, p.f. ash, polyethylene pellets, pvc resin, sand, granulated sugar) [Figures 145 and 187 to 224], together with details of the pipelines used [Figures 172 to 186]. These conveying characteristics could, therefore, be used as the starting point for a system design for the pneumatic conveying of any of the materials presented.

1.3.4.3.1. Conveying Limits.
The conveying characteristics presented in Figures 3 and 4 for sodium sulphate and dicalcium phosphate are typical of the data that is required for a comprehensive design study. It is important that the data should cover the entire conveying capability of the material. This means that the data must extend to the limits of conveyability [see Sections 7.5.6. and 8.2.3., and Figure 228] for the material so that minimum conveying air velocities and maximum phase densities are established.

Test data can be extrapolated with a reasonable degree of accuracy to regions

of higher flow rates and higher conveying line pressure drops on the conveying characteristics. It cannot be extrapolated down to lower air mass flow rates and up to higher phase densities unless it is definitely known that the material is capable of being conveyed under these conditions. It is for this reason that separate data on conveying limits, such as that presented in Figure 2, is so valuable, for this clearly defines the limits of conveyability for a material [see Sections 7.4.5. and 7.5.6., and Figures 138 to 141].

For the dicalcium phosphate, a material having very good air retention properties, a material type A [see Chapter 4], the conveying limits are defined approximately by:

$$C_{min} = 12 \qquad \text{for } \phi < 10$$
$$C_{min} = (33\phi^{-0.4} - 1) \qquad \text{for } 10 < \phi < 150 \qquad (6)$$
$$C_{min} = 3.5 \qquad \text{for } \phi > 150$$

and for the sodium sulphate, a material having very poor air retention properties, a material type B [see Chapter 4], the conveying limits are defined approximately by:

$$C_{min} = 12 \qquad \text{for all } \phi \qquad (7)$$

where C_{min} = minimum conveying air velocity $m\,s^{-1}$
ϕ = phase density

Design would generally be based on a conveying line inlet air velocity 20 per cent greater than the minimum conveying air velocity.

1.3.4.3.2. Non-availability of Conveying Limit Data.   If data on conveying limits, such as that presented in Figure 2, or in Equations (6) and (7) (Section 13.4.3.1.), is not available for a material, the data presented here could be used, but with extreme caution.

The first point is to establish whether the material is capable of being conveyed in dense phase (non-suspension flow), such as the dicalcium phosphate, a material having very good air retention properties, a material type A [see Chapter 4, Selection of a Pneumatic Conveying System for a Particular Application], or whether it can only be conveyed in dilute phase (suspension flow), such as the sodium sulphate, a material having very poor air retention properties, a material type B [see Chapter 4]. To establish this, tests have to be carried out with a sample of the material [see Chapter 8, Effect of Material Properties on Conveying Performance].

For materials such as pulverised fuel ash (p.f. ash), cement, barytes, bentonite and flour, materials having very good air retention properties, a material type A [see Chapter 4], the model presented in Equation (6) can be used quite reliably. For fine granular materials, materials having very poor air retention properties, a material type B [see Chapter 4], and materials having a wide particle size distribution with a bulk density below $1000\ kg\,m^{-3}$, the model presented in Equation (7) can be used quite reliably. For coarse granular materials, and materials having a wide particle size distribution with a bulk density greater than $1500\ kg\,m^{-3}$, materials having very poor air retention properties, a material type B [see Chapter 4], the model presented in Equation (7) has to be modified. A minimum conveying air velocity of 15 to $16\ m\,s^{-1}$ (50 to $53\ ft\,s^{-1}$) is more appropriate for these materials.

1.3.4.4. Scale to Distance and Geometry
Scaling of the data, or conveying characteristics, is carried out in two separate stages. In the first stage the data for the test line is scaled to the plant line. This takes into account differences in conveying distance, including horizontal and vertical lengths, and differences in the number of bends [see Chapter 9, Design of the Conveying Line Layout, Section 9.3., Material Conveying – Pipeline Scaling Parameters: Sub-sections 9.3.1. to 9.3.5.2.].

The second stage is to scale in terms of pipeline bore [see Section 9.3.6.]. This is necessary if the desired material flow rate cannot be achieved in the plant pipeline having the same bore as that of the test line. Additional scaling in terms of pipeline bore is necessary if the design is to consider alternative combinations of pipeline bore and conveying line pressure drop for the required conveying duty. This is considered in Section 1.3.4.4.9. [and in Chapter 14, Case Study, Sections 14.3.5. and 14.3.6.].

1.3.4.4.1. Horizontal Conveying.   Horizontal conveying is taken as the reference for scaling with respect to conveying distance, pipeline orientation and geometry. For this purpose vertical conveying and bends are expressed in terms of an equivalent length of horizontal pipeline. The starting point is to determine the length of horizontal pipeline on both the test line and the plant line.

1.3.4.4.2. Conveying Vertically Up.   The equivalent length of vertically up sections of pipeline can be taken to be twice that of the horizontal pipeline. This is a universal factor and applies over the entire range of conveying characteristics, regardless of phase density and conveying air velocity [see Section 9.3.5.1.].

1.3.4.4.3. Conveying Vertically Down.   The pressure drop over a vertically downward section of pipeline can be positive or negative, depending upon the conveying conditions, therefore no simple universal correlation applies. However, there is an approximate correlation with phase density and the transition from pressure loss to pressure gain in conveying vertically down occurs at a phase density of about 40 [see Section 9.3.5.2.].

This means that for materials conveyed at a phase density of about 40, no allowance need be made for vertically down sections at all. At phase densities below 40, and this includes all dilute phase (suspension flow) systems, there will be a pressure loss. The equivalent length of straight horizontal pipeline will generally be less than that of the vertical fall, although for materials conveyed at phase densities below about 5 there will be little difference.

For materials conveyed in dense phase (non-suspension flow) at a phase density above 40 there will be a pressure recovery and it will be possible to allow for this by reducing the equivalent length of straight horizontal pipeline. For materials conveyed at a phase density of about 100 the reduction will amount approximately to the length of the vertically downward section.

1.3.4.4.4. Pipeline Bends.   The pressure drop associated with pipeline bends is complex and no simple correlation applies. However, the equivalent length of bends correlates reasonably well with the conveying line inlet air velocity. This means that the pressure loss will be approximately the same for each bend in a pipeline. The total pressure drop will simply be equal to the equivalent length, corresponding to the conveying line inlet air velocity, multiplied by the total

number of bends in the pipeline.

A relationship between the equivalent length of bends and the conveying line inlet air velocity is shown in Figure 7. This shows that the equivalent length for each bend varies from about 2 m in the low velocity dense phase conveying region to more than 20 m in high velocity dilute phase flow. These equivalent lengths are for 90 degree bends having a bend diameter to pipe bore (D/d) ratio of 24:1. The relationship can be described approximately by the following equation:

$$b = 0.17C_i^{1.7} \text{ m} \tag{8}$$

where b = equivalent length of a bend   m
      C_i = conveying line inlet air velocity m s^{-1}

The relationship shown in Figure 7 and Equation (8) is not significantly different for bends having a shorter radius down to a radius to bore (D/d) ratio of about 6:1. Below this, however, the equivalent length increases significantly. The pressure drop across short radius bends, elbows and blind tees is very much greater than the pressure drop across long radius bends, with the loss for blind tees 40 to 50 per cent higher. Unless these bends are specifically needed because of space limitations, or for reasons of erosive wear, their use cannot be recommended in pneumatic conveying system pipelines [see Section 9.3.8.].

1.3.4.4.5. The Scaling Model.   The recommended model for scaling materials flow rate in terms of conveying distance, pipeline orientation and geometry is as follows:

$$\dot{m}_p L_e = \text{constant} \tag{9}$$

where $\dot{m}_p$ = material mass flow rate t h^{-1}
      L_e = equivalent length of pipeline   m

The working form of this model is:

$$\dot{m}_{p_1} L_{e_1} = \dot{m}_{p_2} L_{e_2} \tag{10}$$

where subscripts 1 and 2 refer to different pipelines of the same bore. [These models are discussed in Chapter 9, Design of the Conveying Line Layout, Sections 9.3.2.4. to 9.3.4.]

The equivalent lengths for the test and plant pipelines are obtained as follows:

$$L_e = (h + 2v + nb) \text{ m} \tag{11}$$

where h = total length of horizontal pipeline m
      v = total length of vertical lift   m
      n = total number of bends
      b = equivalent length of bends   m

1.3.4.4.6. Scaling Requirements.   There are two requirements to be met in scaling.

a) The conveying line inlet and exit air velocities should be the same for the test line and the plant line, meaning that the air flow rates and the conveying line pressure drop should be identical.

b) The pressure drop due to the material in the pipeline should be the same for the test and plant pipelines.

(It is necessary to make an allowance for the difference in empty line pressure drop values between the test and plant pipelines having the same bore.)

1.3.4.4.7. Empty Line (Air Only) Pressure Drop Datum (Single-Phase Flow). If there is a difference in length between the test and plant pipelines, there will be a corresponding difference between the air only pressure drop values for the two pipelines [see Sections 9.2.3.1.2. and 14.2.4.4., and Figure 235]. For the same air supply pressure and air flow rate, the pressure drop available for conveying material through the longer line will be less than that through the shorter line. The model is based on equality of pressure drop for conveying the material (see Section 1.3.4.4.6.). Thus an allowance must be made for the difference in empty line pressure drop values.

1.3.4.4.8. Results of Scaling. A change of conveying distance can have a very significant influence on the conveying capabilities of a material. From the reciprocal law model in Equation (9) (Section 1.3.4.4.5.) it can be seen that if the distance is doubled, the material mass flow rate will be halved for the same conveying line pressure drop. The material mass flow rate will, in fact, be less than half. The reason for this is that the air only pressure drop value for the longer line will be much greater, and so the pressure drop available for conveying the material through the longer pipeline will be less. The situation can be restored if the air supply pressure is increased to maintain the same pressure gradient in the pipeline. However, there is not usually scope for increasing the air supply pressure.

If the material mass flow rate is halved, the phase density at which the material is conveyed will also be halved, if there is no change in air flow rate. For materials capable of being conveyed in dense phase, a change in the phase density at which the material is conveyed will result in a change in the minimum conveying air velocity. This is illustrated in Figure 2 and Equation (6) (Section 1.3.4.3.1.). If an increase in minimum conveying air velocity is necessary, then more air will be required resulting in a lower phase density. It is an iterative process and is slow to converge. For this reason, relatively small changes in conveying distance can have very significant effects on material flow rates, phase densities, and air requirements for materials which can be conveyed in dense phase. [See also Section 7.5.5.]

1.3.4.4.9. Conveying Limit Changes. To illustrate the effects of scaling, and the influence of material type, the results of scaling the data [see Chapter 9, Design of the Conveying Line Layout, and Chapter 14, Case Study, Section 14.3.4.] for the two materials in Figure 3, sodium sulphate, a material having very poor air retention properties, a material type B [see Chapter 4], and Figure 4, dicalcium phosphate, a material having very good air retention properties, a material type A [see Chapter 4], are presented. The results of scaling to a distance of 300 m (990 ft) are given in Figures 8 and 9. If these are compared with Figures 3 and 4 it can be seen that for the sodium sulphate the material flow rate and phase density have both fallen to about 28 per cent of their values over 100 m (330 ft). The reason for these values being less than a third is that the empty line pressure drop value has increased by a factor of about three.

A comparison of Figures 4 and 8 for the dicalcium phosphate shows that the maximum material flow rate has fallen to about 25 per cent, and the phase

density to 13 per cent of the 100 m long pipeline value. The resulting influence on the change in air requirements can be clearly seen. To illustrate this point further the change in conveying limits with respect to a range of conveying distances is shown in Figure 10. Approximate values of conveying line pressure drop, and lines of constant conveying line inlet air velocity, are superimposed to illustrate the nature of the changes[1].

If the scaling were to be extended to 500 m (1650 ft), the conveying limit would correspond with the $12 \, \mathrm{m \, s^{-1}}$ ($40 \, \mathrm{ft \, s^{-1}}$) conveying line inlet air velocity value (see Section 1.3.4.3.1.), because over this distance it is possible to convey the material only in dilute phase, even with a conveying line pressure drop of 3 bar ($300 \, \mathrm{kN \, m^{-2}}$). The change in air requirements with respect to conveying distance is illustrated in Figure 11. The difference in air requirements for the two materials is considerable for short distances, when the dicalcium phosphate can be conveyed in dense phase, but is identical for long distances when it can be conveyed only in dilute phase.

1.3.4.5. Can Material Mass Flow Rate be Achieved?

If the required material mass flow rate can be achieved in the given pipeline bore, the corresponding conveying line pressure drop value has to be noted. This value will correspond to a continuously operating system. If alternative batch operating systems are to be considered, then correspondingly higher values of material mass flow rate will have to be met (see Section 1.3.4.1.1.).

From the conveying characteristics produced, a horizontal line should be drawn through each material mass flow rate which is to be considered. Design points should then be located within the body of the conveying characteristics. These are points where the air mass flow rate is 20 per cent greater than the minimum value necessary to convey the material at the given flow rate. The air flow rate and the conveying line pressure drop corresponding to these points represent the data which is necessary for the design of the system.

If the required material flow rate cannot be achieved, within some given upper limit of conveying line pressure drop value, it will be necessary to advance to Section 1.3.4.7., Scale to Different Pipeline Bore, and consider a larger bore pipeline for the duty.

1.3.4.6. Calculate Power Requirements of Air Mover

Having evaluated all the parameters necessary for the system, it is now possible to determine the power required by the air mover, and hence the approximate cost of operating the system. For an accurate assessment of the power required, it is necessary to consult manufacturers' literature to compare different air movers capable of meeting the conveying duty. For a quick approximate assessment, allowing comparison of different variables in the design, a simple model based on isothermal compression can be used [see Section 5.2.2.13.]. The influence of conveying distance, pipeline bore and material type on power requirements is:

$$\text{Power} = 165\dot{m}_a \ln\left(\frac{p_1}{p_2}\right) \text{kW} \tag{12}$$

where $\dot{m}_a$ = air mass flow rate $\mathrm{kg \, s^{-1}}$
       p_1 = conveying line inlet air pressure   bar abs
       p_2 = conveying line outlet air pressure   bar abs

This gives the approximate power required to drive the air mover. From this running costs can be calculated [see Section 6.8., Power Costs].

In an economic assessment of alternative systems [see Chapter 14, Case Study], this operating cost should be considered alongside the capital cost of the plant and the maintenance costs.

1.3.4.7. Scale to Different Pipeline Bore

If the required material mass flow rate cannot be achieved with a given pipeline bore, or if the power requirement for a certain pipeline bore is not acceptable, the conveying characteristics should be scaled to a different pipeline bore [see Chapter 9, Design of the Conveying Line Layout, Section 9.3., Material Conveying – Pipeline Scaling Parameters: Sub-sections 9.3.6. to 9.3.6.1.] and the process repeated. As part of a comprehensive study it may be necessary to investigate the influence of a range of pipeline bores [see Chapter 14, Case Study, Sections 14.2.5. and 14.3.6.].

A wide range of combinations of pipeline bore and conveying line pressure drop can be used to meet the required duty [see Chapter 5 and Chapter 14]. The power requirement will probably vary from one combination to another. In addition, material type has a significant influence on the relationship between power requirements and pipeline bore/pressure drop combinations.

1.3.4.7.1. The Scaling Model.

The model recommended for scaling material mass flow rate in terms of pipeline bore is as follows:

$$\dot{m}_p \propto A \propto d^2 \tag{13}$$

where $\dot{m}_p$ = material mass flow rate $t\,h^{-1}$
         A = pipe section area m^2
         d = pipeline bore m

The usual working form of this model is:

$$\dot{m}_{p_2} = \dot{m}_{p_1} \times \left(\frac{d_2}{d_1}\right)^2 \tag{14}$$

where subscripts 1 and 2 refer to appropriate pipelines of different bores [see Section 9.3.6.].

This model applies for the scaling, in terms of pipeline bore, of pipelines having the same length, geometry and orientation. This scaling is carried out in Section 1.3.4.4. in the pipeline design procedure and so these requirements are met automatically.

1.3.4.7.2. Scaling Requirements.

There are two requirements to be met in this scaling.

a) The conveying line inlet and exit air velocities should be the same for the test line and plant line. This requires that the air flow rates should be scaled in proportion to the pipe cross-sectional areas, and that the conveying line pressure drops should be identical.

b) The pressure drop due to the material in the pipeline should be the same for the test and plant pipelines. For this it is necessary to make an allowance for the difference in empty line pressure drop values between the test and plant pipelines, having the same length and number and geometry of bends.

1.3.4.7.3. Empty Line (Air Only) Pressure Drop Datum (Single-phase Flow).
With a difference in bore between test and plant pipelines, there will be a corresponding difference between the air only pressure drop values for the two pipelines [see Sections 9.2.3.1.3. and 14.3.5.1., and Figure 236]. For the same air supply pressure and conveying air velocities, the pressure drop available for the conveying of material through a large bore line will be greater than that through a small bore pipeline. The model is based on equality of pressure drop for conveying the material (see Section 1.3.4.7.2.). Thus an allowance must be made for the difference in empty line pressure drop values.

1.3.4.7.4. Results of Scaling.   A change of pipeline bore will have little influence on the conveying capabilities of a material. The reason for this is that with a larger bore pipeline the air flow rate must be increased in proportion to the pipe cross-sectional area to maintain the same values of conveying air velocity. Since material mass flow rate is also increased in proportion to pipe cross-sectional area, there is essentially no change in the phase density at which the material is conveyed.
This means that there will be no change in minimum conveying air velocity to take into account. The only differences result from the change in air only pressure drop datum. Conveying characteristics for different pipelines will be geometrically similar [see Sections 9.3.6. and 9.3.6.1.] since both material and air flow rate axes are changed by the same factor [see Sections 14.3.5.2. and 14.3.5.3.].

1.3.4.7.5. Conveying Parameters.   Having derived a further set of conveying characteristics for the material over the required distance (see Section 1.3.4.4.), it is necessary to determine the air requirements, in terms of mass flow rate and conveying line pressure drop. At this point, therefore, it is necessary to return to Stage 1.3.4.7., Scale to Different Pipeline Bore, for it is here that these parameters are noted for the various continuous and batch conveying systems which are to be considered.

1.3.4.7.6. Cautionary Note.   Checks have been carried out on the validity of the scaling model given in Equation (14). Although in many instances very close agreement was obtained, in a few cases the increase in material mass flow rate was only about half of that predicted by the model. In no instance was the material mass flow rate greater than that predicted by the model. It is recommended, therefore, that the model should be used with caution, and that it would be wise to add a constant of 0.75 to the models in Equation (14) when scaling between any two pipelines of different bore. [See Section 9.3.6.1.]

1.3.4.7.7. First Estimate of Pipeline Bore.   In cases where an approximate value of the phase density, ϕ, is known, this can be used, together with the required material mass flow rate, $\dot{m}_p$, to obtain a first estimate of the pipeline bore, d. By combining:

$$\dot{m}_p = 3.6\phi\dot{m}_a \tag{15}$$

$$pV = \dot{m}_a RT \tag{16}$$

$$V = 0.25\pi d^2 C \tag{17}$$

Eliminating V and $\dot{m}_a$ from these equations, substituting $R = 0.287 \text{ kJ kg}^{-1}\text{K}^{-1}$ for air, and making the pipe bore the subject of the equation, gives:

$$d = 31.8\left(\frac{\dot{m}_p(t + 273)}{\phi pC}\right) \tag{18}$$

where d is in cm.

1.3.4.8. Specify Pipeline Bore
The final requirement in the design process is to specify the pipeline bore required and the necessary rating of the air mover. If the full analysis has been carried out, as specified in the logic diagram, Figure 6, then the most suitable pipeline bore should result.

1.3.4.8.1. Stepped Pipelines.
If a system is selected which requires the conveying line inlet air pressure to be greater than about one bar gauge (201.3 kN m^{-2}), the possibility of stepping the pipeline to a larger bore part way along its length should be considered [see Chapter 6, Theory and Use of Compressed Air in Pneumatic Conveying, Section 6.2.6., Stepped Pipeline Systems, and Section 9.3.4.3., Stepped Pipelines]. Air is compressible, therefore high conveying air velocities will occur in a single-bore pipeline if a high air supply pressure is used. High air velocities will add significantly to problems of erosion with abrasive materials and particle degradation with friable materials.

1.3.4.9. Specify Air Requirements
Air requirements are specified in terms of volumetric flow rate under 'free air' conditions and the delivery or exhaust pressure.

1.3.4.9.1. Volumetric Flow Rate.
The air mass flow rate is evaluated in Section 1.3.4.5. The relationship between mass and volumetric flow rates is given by [see Section 7.2.2.]:

$V = 49\dot{m}_a \text{ m}^3\text{min}^{-1}$

$V = 816\dot{m}_a \text{ litres s}^{-1}$

1.3.4.9.2. Air Leakage/Ingress Across Feeding Device Allowance.
In positive pressure systems an allowance in volumetric flow rate (see Section 1.3.4.9.1.) has to be made for air leakage across the feeding device. This is not necessary for blow tanks, but for rotary valves it is very important [see Section 3.2.3.1. and Figure 17]. The air leakage rate generally has to be obtained from the manufacturers of the feeding device. For a negative pressure system an allowance has to be made for air ingress into the system, should this be a possibility.

1.3.4.9.3. Specification for Air Mover (Flow Rate).
The volumetric flow rate to be specified for the air mover is that required for conveying the material through the pipeline, plus an allowance for that which is either lost via leakage across the feeding device in positive pressure systems, or which is gained by ingress in negative pressure systems (see Section 1.3.4.9.2.).

1.3.4.10. Delivery Pressure
The delivery pressure to be specified for the air mover is equal to the sum of the

pressure drops across the various plant components. The main items to take into account are:

a) The air supply or extraction lines between the air mover and the system.
b) The material feeding device.
c) The conveying line.
d) The gas–solid separation device.

1.3.4.10.1. Pressure Drop in Air Lines.   Whether this has to be considered depends on the distance of the air mover from the conveying system [see Section 10.2.6.1.1.].

1.3.4.10.2. Pressure Drop Across Feeding Device.   The pressure drop across the feeding device depends upon the type of feeder used. For rotary valves [Sections 2.3.2., 3.2.3. and 10.2.5.2.1.] and gate lock valves [Sections 3.2.6. and 10.2.5.2.4.] it can generally be neglected. A pressure drop is required across a blow tank [Sections 2.3.7., 3.2.7. and 10.2.5.2.5.] to discharge the material into the conveying line. The pressure drop depends very much upon the blow tank type and configuration. Screw feeders [Sections 2.3.2., 3.2.4. and 10.2.5.2.2.] generally require the air to be at a pressure of about 0.5 bar (50 $kN\,m^{-2}$) above the conveying line inlet air pressure for the air nozzles. Venturi feeders [Sections 2.3.2., 3.2.5. and 10.2.5.2.3.] also require the air supply to be at a higher pressure. [See also Section 10.2.5.1.3.]

1.3.4.10.3. Pressure Drop in the Conveying Line.   In most cases the greatest pressure drop occurs from conveying the material through the pipeline. In some cases, such as rotary valve systems [Sections 2.3.2., 3.2.3. and 10.2.5.2.1.], it can be taken as the air supply pressure itself, as all other pressure drops are negligible in comparison.

1.3.4.10.4. Pressure Drop Across Gas–Solid Separation Device.   In general the pressure drop across the gas–solid separation system can be neglected [Sections 3.3.3.3. to 3.3.3.4. and 10.2.7.1. to 10.2.7.1.4.]. It should be taken into account with low pressure fan systems where the total pressure drop available is very low.

1.3.4.10.5. Specification for Air Mover (Air Supply Pressure).   The delivery pressure to be specified for the air mover, equivalent to the air supply pressure required, is equal to the conveying line pressure drop plus any allowances that might need to be made for the air lines, feeding device and gas–solid separation systems.

It is wise to add a small margin to allow for feed surges. A maximum value of 20 per cent should be adequate. A surge in material feed rate will demand a small increase in supply pressure for a short time to clear the material through the pipeline. If this margin is available it will prevent the possibility of material surges either blocking the pipeline or causing the system to shut down [see Section 11.5.].

1.3.5. Choice of Air Mover

For negative pressure conveying systems the choice is essentially between Roots-type exhausters [Section 6.6.4.] and liquid ring vacuum pumps [Section 6.6.5.].

Liquid ring vacuum pumps, however, are capable of creating much lower pressures. For positive pressure systems below about one bar gauge ($201.3 \, kN \, m^{-2}$) Roots-type blowers are used extensively. From one to four bar gauge (201.3 to $501.3 \, kN \, m^{-2}$), the choice is generally between sliding vane rotary compressors [Section 6.6.3.], rotary screw compressors [Section 6.6.6.] and reciprocating compressors [Section 6.6.7.]. These are considered further in Section 1.4., Specification of Components: Sub-section 1.4.5. Approximate ranges of operation of various types of air mover are shown in Figure 13.

1.3.5.1. Power Requirements

The power required depends upon the type of air mover selected. The model presented in Equation (12), Section 1.3.4.6., gives an approximate value of the drive power required. Provided that the machine is capable of delivering the volumetric flow rate of air at the delivery pressure required it is unlikely that any further margins need to be taken into account.

A margin of 20 per cent on volumetric flow rate is recommended to ensure that the conveying line inlet air velocity is above the minimum conveying air velocity (see Sections 1.3.2.1. and 1.3.4.5.). A margin of 20 per cent on pressure is recommended to cater for possible surges in material flow rate (see Section 1.3.4.10.5.). A larger drive motor would only be necessary should there be a requirement to uprate the system at a later date.

1.3.6. Other Considerations

Having designed the pipeline and specified the air requirements, for the conveying of the given material over the distance required and at the flow rate required, consideration should be given to possible changes or alternative requirements. If there is an extension to the plant it may be necessary to convey the material over a longer (or shorter) distance. It may also be necessary to convey an alternative material at some future date. A change of material or distance is likely to result in a change in conveying potential. Any of these changes could result in the need for totally different air requirements. It would be worthwhile considering the possibility of any such future change before finalising the design.

1.3.6.1. System Uprating

If there is likely to be a possible future need for the system to be uprated, the conveying characteristics produced for the design study could be checked to determine the range of pipeline bore and air supply pressure combinations which would meet the future need. A comparison of the two sets of design data would show what changes would be required. Consideration would have to be given to the capability of the feeding device, the diameter of the pipeline, the filtration unit and the air mover in terms of volumetric flow rate, delivery pressure and motor power.

With a careful choice of parameters the smallest number of changes and minimum cost would be incurred at the original design stage. It is possible that a feeding device could meet both duties, for example. If the same pipeline bore is used and the uprating achieved by means of an increase in pressure, the filtration unit is likely to meet both duties. If the air supply pressure is kept approximately constant and uprating is achieved by means of an increase in

pipeline bore, it is possible that the same air mover could be used, provided that a drive motor with sufficient power is installed. A larger filtration plant would be needed. This could either be installed with the plant as a single unit, or it could be uprated later with an additional unit as necessary. [Optimising and Uprating Existing Systems is discussed in Chapter 11.]

1.3.6.2. Alternative Conveying Distances
If there is a need to convey the material over more than a single fixed distance, it is advised to carry out the design procedure for both the longest and shortest distance. If the design is based on a given flow rate over one specified distance, the material flow rate will be different over any other distance. The influence of conveying distance on material flow rate is shown in Figures 3 and 8 for dicalcium phosphate and in Figures 4 and 9 for sodium sulphate. For a material capable of being conveyed in dense phase, there may also be a change in air requirements with respect to conveying distance, as shown in Figure 11. [See Chapter 5, Pneumatic Conveying System Design Procedures.]

A change in conveying distance will result in a change in material flow rate. Therefore it is advisable to have a feeding device which is capable of adjustment or is automatically controlled. If a high feed rate is set for the short distance and no change is made for the long distance, the pipeline is likely to block as a result of over-feeding. However, if a low feed rate is set for the long distance and no change is made for the short distance, the pipeline will be under-utilised for the short distance. Similar problems will be experienced with regard to the air flow control if the change in distance results in a significant change in air requirements.

If, for the chosen design, the conveying characteristics are scaled to the other distances over which it is required to convey the material the necessary data on material flow rate and air requirements will be obtained so that all these influences can be taken into account.

1.3.6.3. Alternative Materials
If there is a need to convey more than one material through the pipeline it is essential to carry out the design procedure for each material. Different materials can vary significantly in their conveying potential and air requirements, Figures 3 and 4. [Chapter 5, Pneumatic Conveying System Design Procedures.]

If the same air mover, feeding device and filtration unit are to be used for each material, careful consideration has to be given to their specification. The material flow rate achieved with each material is likely to be different and so the feeding device must be capable of adjustment or be automatically controlled. The air requirements are also likely to differ and so due consideration should be given to this. The filtration unit needs to be sized to accommodate the highest volumetric air flow rate.

1.4. Specification of Components

1.4.1. General

Having completed the design of the pipeline, the mode of operation and the main plant components can be specified. To a certain extent many of the basic parameters may already have been decided in the detailed design work

associated with the pipeline. Air supply pressure, for example, once specified, will limit the choice available on both a suitable feeding device and the type of air mover.

1.4.2. Economic Considerations

The logic diagram presented in Figure 6, for the design procedure for the pipeline based on available conveying characteristics, is directed essentially at optimising the pipeline and conveying conditions in terms of achieving the minimum power requirements, and hence operating cost, for the conveying of the material through the pipeline. This, however, will not necessarily result in a system having the lowest capital cost. In terms of system selection, capital cost is just as important as operating cost, therefore a number of possible systems should be investigated.

The best approach to this is to consider a range of pipeline bores in the design procedure for the pipeline. This would automatically cover a range of air supply pressures. A limit of the study could be imposed by means of an upper and lower limit on air supply pressure.

From the pipeline design study all the necessary operating parameters are evaluated at each pipeline bore to enable the plant components to be specified. This allows the various plant components to be costed in order that the capital cost of the alternative systems can be determined. The final selection of the best system can then be made by comparing both capital costs and operating costs. [Such a comparison of pneumatic conveying systems is given in Chapter 14, Case Study, Section 14.6.]

1.4.3. Mode of Operation

A classification of conveying systems is based on the mode of operation, see Figure 1. Conveying can either be carried out on a continuous basis or in a continuous sequence of isolated batches. It should be noted that there is essentially no difference in the nature of the gas–solid (two-phase) flow in the pipeline with respect to the mode of conveying at any given value of phase density.

Although a batch conveying system may be chosen for a specific process need, the mode of conveying is, to a large extent, dictated by the choice of feeding device. The majority of batch conveying systems are based on blow tanks [see Sections 2.3.7., 3.2.7. and 10.2.5.2.5.]. Blow tanks are selected either because of their high pressure conveying capability or because of the nature of the material feed into the pipeline.

A particular problem with batch type systems is, as conveying is not continuous, the instantaneous values of flow rate during conveying have to be higher to achieve the equivalent material mass flow rate of a continuous system.

1.4.4. Material Feeding Devices

Devices available for feeding a conveying pipeline include venturis, screws, gate lock valves, suction nozzles, and a variety of rotary valve types and blow tank configurations [see Chapter 3, Feeding and Discharging the Conveying Line].

The approximate operating pressure ranges for feeding devices are shown in

Figure 12. Rotary valves and gate lock valves can be used in positive and negative pressure systems but are limited to low pressure differentials. The screw feeder can cope with higher pressures as well as negative pressure systems. Devices like suction nozzles are applicable only to negative pressure systems. Blow tanks are commonly employed in high pressure systems operating batch-wise, although they can be adapted for continuous conveying.

1.4.4.1. Selection Considerations

The capability of the feeding device in terms of pressure rating must be considered. It is possible that several devices will be satisfactory but the performance of the feeder in terms of air leakage, pressure drop and flow control also needs to be taken into account, as well as its suitability for the material to be handled [see Section 10.2.5.1., Selection Considerations: Sub-sections 10.2.5.1.1. to 10.2.5.1.4.].

1.4.4.2. Types of Feeding Device

1.4.4.2.1. Rotary Valves [See Sections 2.3.2. and 3.2.3.]. Rotary valves are ideally suited to positive and negative pressure systems but a single valve unit is generally limited to a maximum operating pressure of about one bar gauge $(201.3 \, kN \, m^{-2})$. A wide variety of designs are available for different situations. For pellet feeding, where shearing of the material should be avoided, a rotary valve with an off-set inlet should be used [Figure 16(a)]. Cohesive materials may not be discharged satisfactorily from a drop-through valve [Figure 15] and a blow-through valve [Figure 16(b)] should be used. Rotary valves are not recommended for the handling of abrasive materials.

Air leakage is a major problem with rotary valves [see Section 3.2.3.1. and Figure 17] and, apart from the energy loss, material flow into the valve may be severely affected. Large granular materials and pellets may not be affected by air leakage but for fine materials and light fluffy materials air venting may be necessary. [See also Sections 3.2.3.3., Entrainment Devices; 3.2.3.4., Rotor Design; 3.2.3.5., Feed Rate.]

1.4.4.2.2. Screw Feeders [See Sections 2.3.2. and 3.2.4.]. Screw feeders are suited to both positive and negative pressure systems. They can feed into conveying lines at pressures of up to 2.5 bar gauge $(351.3 \, kN \, m^{-2})$. They are widely used in the cement industry and for handling pulverised fuel ash (p.f. ash). They are used in positive pressure closed loop systems because they can cope with high pressure differentials.

Air leakage represents a major problem with the simple screw [Figure 22] and this design is generally limited to negative pressure systems where operating pressure differentials are negligible. With a decreasing pitch screw [Figure 23], fine cohesive materials form a compact plug and act as an air seal. The decreasing pitch screw requires more power than the constant pitch type for a given flow rate. Power requirements are significantly greater than for rotary valves.

1.4.4.2.3. Venturi Feeders [See Sections 2.3.2. and 3.2.5. and Figures 24 and 25]. Venturi fed systems are very limited in terms of conveying capability as the maximum operating conveying line pressure drop which can be achieved is

only about 0.3 bar (30 kN m^{-2}). A venturi feeder can be relatively inexpensive. Since there are no moving parts, venturi feeders are suitable for abrasive and friable materials. They are best suited to the handling of free–flowing materials. It is normally advisable to control the flow of material.

1.4.4.2.4. Gate Lock Valves [See Section 3.2.6. and Figures 26 and 27].   Gate lock valves are suitable for positive and negative pressure systems but in positive pressure systems account must be taken of the loss of air from the bottom gate. They are limited to dilute phase conveying because of the intermittent nature of the material feeding. High conveying line inlet air velocities must be maintained to ensure successful conveying. Gate lock valves can be relatively cheap items and as there are few moving parts these feeders are suitable for handling abarasive and friable materials.

1.4.4.2.5. Blow Tanks [See Sections 2.3.7. and 3.2.7.1.].   A major feature of blow tanks is that a high pressure air supply can be used. This means that it is possible to convey materials in dense phase and convey materials over long distances. Blow tanks are generally used to convey batches but it is possible, with two blow tanks in parallel [see Sections 3.2.7.7. and 3.2.7.11.], to achieve continuous conveying. Blow tanks require more headroom than other feeding devices, particularly blow tanks arranged for continuous conveying.

Blow tank systems are not synonymous with high pressure systems. They can be used equally well in low pressure applications. At low pressures the blow tank does not need to be a coded vessel [see Section 14.5.2.1.], therefore it can be cheaper to construct. Since there are no moving parts, blow tanks are particularly suitable for handling friable and abrasive materials.

It is not necessary to have a discharge valve on the blow tank. In terms of simplicity of plant operation, and minimum maintenance requirements, a system based on a blow tank without a discharge valve [see Section 3.2.7.3.] would probably be one of the most suitable.

An advantage of blow tank systems is that the blow tank acts as the feeder and the problems associated with feeding against an adverse pressure gradient do not arise. With single blow tank systems there is usually an air surge at the end of the conveying cycle. The gas–solid separation device has to be large enough to cater for the increase in air flow rate. This point is considered in Section 1.4.6., Gas–Solid Separation System.

With most blow tanks there is a pressure drop across the discharge section to feed the material into the conveying line. In bottom discharge blow tanks this pressure drop will generally be less than 0.1 bar (10 kN m^{-2}) since the conveying air can be introduced very close to the discharge point. In top discharge blow tanks this pressure drop may be greater than 0.1 bar if the material has to be conveyed through a long section of discharge line within the blow tank. In very large blow tanks it is often necessary to take the discharge line out through the side of the blow tank to reduce the length. In addition there is a further pressure drop across the fluidising membrane in many top discharge blow tanks. This is typically 0.05 bar (5 kN m^{-2}) but depends on the air flow rate and size of membrane.

A problem with both single and twin blow tank arrangements conveying batch-wise is in making a reasonable assessment of the value of the ratio of the time averaged mean material flow rate to the maximum, or steady conveying

rate achieved during the conveying cycle. Such a value is necessary to determine the correct pipeline bore and air requirements for a given duty (see Sections 1.3.4.8. and 1.3.4.9.).

1.4.5. Air Mover

The air requirements are determined at the pipeline design stage (see Section 1.1.3.). For the final specification it is necessary only to make allowances for air losses and any additional pressure required. The most appropriate choice of air mover can then be made from the various types which are capable of meeting the required duty [see Chapter 6, Theory and Use of Compressed Air in Pneumatic Conveying, Section 6.6., Types of Air Mover].

1.4.5.1. Specification of Air Requirements
Air requirements are specified in terms of a volumetric flow rate, which is usually expressed in terms of 'free air' delivered, and a delivery or exhaust pressure. These are considered in detail in Section 1.3.4.9.

1.4.5.2. Choice of Air Mover
It is possible that a number of different air movers may be suitable for a given duty. The choice then has to be made in terms of reliability, cost, control, power required for the duty, and the availability of a suitable model for the duty.

1.4.5.3. Control Requirements
A particularly important point to consider when selecting an air mover is the degree of control which can be achieved over the air supply. This will depend to a large extent upon the requirements of the conveying system. For example, if it is necessary to operate the plant with a reduced throughput, approximately the same volumetric flow rate will be required at a lower pressure. Ideally the air mover should be capable of being controlled to provide air at reduced pressure and with a corresponding lower energy demand.

1.4.5.4. Use of Plant Air
In some plants a plant air supply may be available. If plant air is used the capital cost of the system will be reduced but careful consideration has to be given to the operating cost of this arrangement. If plant air is available at 6 or 7 bar gauge (701.3 or 801.3 kN m^{-2}) and the system requires air at only 1 bar gauge (201.3 kN m^{-2}), the cost of using plant air will be significantly higher than that from an air mover dedicated to the conveying system. It may be more economical to provide the system with its own air mover.

If there is a requirement to use available plant air it would be advisable to design the system with this in view and to design the pipeline and select the feeding device appropriately. If the plant air is at a high pressure this will probably dictate a blow tank system [see Section 3.2.7.] and a stepped pipeline [see Sections 6.2.6. and 9.3.4.3.].

1.4.5.5. Positive Pressure Systems
The approximate operating ranges of a number of air movers for positive pressure systems [see Section 2.3.1.] are presented in Figure 13.

1.4.5.6. Negative Pressure (Vacuum) Systems

For low negative pressure systems [see Section 2.3.5.] fans can be used. Roots-type blowers [see Section 6.6.4.] are often used as exhausters and are typically capable of holding a continuous vacuum of about 400 mm of mercury (360 mm mercury absolute, 0.48 bar). Liquid ring vacuum pumps [see Section 6.6.5.] can reach a vacuum of 600 mm of mercury (160 mm mercury absolute, 0.23 bar) in a single stage and over 700 mm of mercury (60 mm mercury absolute, 0.08 bar) in two stages. Sliding vane machines [see Section 6.6.3.] can also be used as exhausters. A source of high pressure air can also be used to produce high vacuum levels by means of multi ejectors.

1.4.5.7. Combined Negative and Positive Pressure Systems

Fans can be used on combined negative and positive systems [see Section 2.3.6.] where, with light or fluffy materials, it is sometimes possible to convey the material through the fan itself. Roots-type blowers [see Section 6.6.4.] are widely used for combined systems but efficient filtration must be provided; on no account must the material be allowed to pass through the machine. The available power for the system has to be shared between the two sections.

1.4.6. Gas–Solid Separation System

Gas–solid separation devices associated with pneumatic conveying systems [see Chapter 3, Feeding and Discharging the Conveying Line] have two functions. The first is to recover as much as possible of the conveyed material. The second is to minimise pollution of the environment by the material. Where the conveyed material is potentially hazardous (e.g. toxic or explosive) particular care must be taken to ensure its containment within the handling plant.

1.4.6.1. Choice of Gas–Solid Separation System

The choice of gas–solid separation system to be used on any given application is influenced by a number of factors, notably the amount of bulk solid involved, the particle size range, the collecting efficiency required, and the capital and running costs. In general, the finer the particles to be collected, the higher will be the cost of a disengaging system.

1.4.6.2. Gravity Settling Chambers

Where a bulk material consists of relatively large (and heavy) particles, with no fine dust, it may be sufficient to collect it in a simple bin, the solid material falling under gravity to the bottom of the bin, the gas being taken off through a suitable vent. To improve the efficiency of the basic gravity settling chamber when working with materials of low density, or of a fibrous nature, a mesh separating screen may be fitted. [See Section 3.3.3.1.]

1.4.6.3. Cyclone Separators

With a material of a smaller particle size than described in Section 1.4.6.2. it is often necessary to enhance the gravitational effect. The most common method of achieving this is to impart a spin to the gas–solid stream so that the particles are thrown outwards, while the gas is drawn off from the centre of the vortex. This is the principle on which the cyclone separator operates [see Section

3.3.3.2. and Figures 51 to 54]. For dusty materials a fabric filter [see Section 3.3.3.3.] (see Section 1.4.6.4.) unit may be combined with a cyclone separator.

1.4.6.4. Fabric Filters

Separation of fine particles in a cyclone separator, especially if they are of low density, is not fully effective. In pneumatic conveying systems handling fine or dusty material, the method of separation almost universally adopted is the fabric filter [see Section 3.3.3.3. and Figures 55 and 56], used either on its own or as a back-up to cyclone separators. In situations where all the solid material to be collected is blown into a hopper, the clean air is vented off at the top through a fabric filter unit, whilst the collected solids are discharged from the base of the hopper through an airlock.

Many different types of fabric filter are now in use and selection depends mainly upon the nature of the solid particles being collected, the air flow rates involved and the temperature of the conveying gas and material [see Section 3.3.3.3.1. and Table 3.7.].

1.4.6.5. System Considerations

The importance of the gas–solid separator is often overlooked. Incorrect design and specification can cause considerable problems with the conveying system.

1.4.6.5.1. Continuously Operating Systems.

Any of the separation systems discussed in Sections 1.4.6.2. to 1.4.6.4. can be used with continuously operating systems. Pulse jet cleaning of fabric filters [see Section 3.3.3.3.2.] is a commonly used form of cleaning. Separation devices for positive pressure systems normally operate at atmospheric pressure. In negative pressure conveying systems, the separation process takes place under vacuum and this must be considered when sizing the filter.

In negative pressure systems, the clean air at the outlet from the separator is drawn through an exhauster. Failure of the separator will allow conveyed material to be carried over to the exhauster. Air movers such as Roots-type blowers must be protected from the ingress of dusty air. A cyclone is often used for this purpose and although its efficiency with respect to fine particles is rather low, it will allow time for the system to be shut down before serious damage occurs to the air mover.

1.4.6.5.2. Batch Conveying Systems.

Any of the separation systems discussed in Sections 1.4.6.2. to 1.4.6.4. are suitable for batch conveying systems. Fabric filters can be cleaned by mechanical shaking provided the batch size is not too large and the mean particle size too small. Mechanical shaking of the filter at the end of each conveying cycle, when the air supply is isolated, is generally satisfactory.

With single blow tank systems there is usually an air surge at the end of the conveying cycle, particularly if high air pressure and a large blow tank are used. The gas–solid separation device must be large enough to accept the increase in air flow rate. The magnitude of the surge can be reduced if the blow tank is isolated from the pipeline at the end of the conveying cycle.

Appendix

A.1. Reference

1. Mills, D and Mason, J S (1985) The influence of conveying distance on the performance and air requirements of pneumatic conveying system pipelines. *International Symposium on the Reliable Flow of Particulate Solids, Chr. Michelson Institute* (Bergen, August 1985)

A.2. Nomenclature

A.2.1. Symbols

A	pipe cross-sectional area	m^2
b	equivalent length of bends	m
C	conveying air or gas velocity	$m\,s^{-1}$
C	permeability factor	$m^3\,s\,kg^{-1}, m^2\,N^{-1}\,s^{-1}$
C_i	conveying line inlet air velocity	$m\,s^{-1}$
C_{min}	minimum conveying air velocity	$m\,s^{-1}$
C_p	specific heat at constant pressure 1000 for air	$kJ\,kg^{-1}\,K^{-1}$
C_v	specific heat at constant volume 714.3 for air	$kJ\,kg^{-1}\,K^{-1}$
D	pipeline bend diameter	m
d	pipeline diameter, bore, size	m
d_p	particle diameter	m
f	friction coefficient	dimensionless
h	total length of horizontal pipeline	m
H	hardness (Vickers)	$kg\,mm^{-2}$
k	constant in 'head' loss terms	dimensionless
k'	de-aeration constant	$m\,s^{-1}$
k'_v	vibrated de-aerated constant	$m\,s^{-1}$
L	pipeline length, distance	m
L	bed height	m
L	length of plug	m
L_e	equivalent length of pipeline	m
M	molecular weight	dimensionless
m	mass	kg

$\dot{m}$	mass flow rate	$kg\,s^{-1}$
$\dot{m}_a$	air mass flow rate	$kg\,s^{-1}$
$\dot{m}_p$	material mass flow rate	$t\,h^{-1}$
$\bar{\dot{m}}_p$	time averaged mean value of material flow rate	$t\,h^{-1}$
$\dot{m}_p$	mean material flow rate	$t\,h^{-1}$
$\dot{m}_p$	steady state value of material flow rate	$t\,h^{-1}$
$\hat{\dot{m}}_p$	material flow rate to be achieved to reach time averaged duty of batch conveying	$t\,h^{-1}$
$\hat{\dot{m}}_p$	maximum material flow rate	$t\,h^{-1}$
m_v	mass of water vapour	kg
mol	gram molecular weight	g, (kg)
	number of mols $= m$(mass)$/M$(molecular weight)	
n	total number of bends	dimensionless
p	conveying air pressure	bar, $kN\,m^{-2}$
p	absolute pressure of air/gas	bar, $kN\,m^{-2}$
p_a	partial pressure of air	bar, $kN\,m^{-2}$
p_i	conveying line inlet air pressure	bar, $kN\,m^{-2}$
p_v	partial pressure water vapour	bar, $kN\,m^{-2}$
$p_{v_{sat}}$	partial pressure of water vapour when saturated	bar, $kN\,m^{-2}$
Δp	conveying line pressure drop	bar, $kN\,m^{-2}$
Δp	pressure drop	bar, $kN\,m^{-2}$
Δp_a	conveying line pressure drop due to air only (empty line pressure drop, single-phase flow)	bar, $kN\,m^{-2}$
q	air flow rate	$m^3\,s^{-1}$
q	rate of flow of an incompressible fluid through a bed of powder	$m^3\,s^{-1}$
R	characteristic gas constant (R_0/M) 0.287 for air, 0.297 for nitrogen	$J\,kg^{-1}\,K^{-1}$
R_0	universal gas constant, 8.31434	$J\,mol^{-1}\,K^{-1}$
S	particle surface area	m^2
S_v	specific surface	$m^2\,m^{-3}$
S_w	specific surface	$m^2\,kg^{-1}$
t	temperature	°C
T	absolute temperature $(= t + 273)$	K
U	superficial air velocity	$m\,s^{-1}$
U_{mf}	minimum fluidising velocity	$m\,s^{-1}$
V	volume	m^3
V	particle volume	m^3
$\dot{V}$	volumetric air flow rate	$m^3\,s^{-1}$
v	total length of vertical lift	m
w	specific humidity	dimensionless
α	particle impact angle	degrees
γ	ratio of specific heats $(= C_p/C_v)$ 1.4 for air	dimensionless
ε	surface roughness	m
ε	voidage	dimensionless
η	efficiency	per cent
η	isentropic efficiency	per cent
θ	angle	degrees
μ	viscosity	$kg\,m^{-1}\,s^{-1}$

ρ	density	$kg\,m^{-3}$
ρ	gas density	$kg\,m^{-3}$
ρ_b	bulk density	$kg\,m^{-3}$
τ	time	s
ϕ	phase density	dimensionless
ϕ	sphericity	dimensionless
χ	relative humidity	per cent
χ	ratio of mean to maximum values of material flow rate	dimensionless

A.2.2. Prefixes

Δ difference in value

A.2.3. Subscripts

a	conveying air
b	bulk (solids)
e	equivalent value
i	inlet conditions
i	isentropic conditions
m	surface material
p	material conveyed
s	suspension
t	throat
v	water vapour
0	free air conditions
0	reference conditions $(p = 101.3\ kN\,m^{-2},\ t = 15°C,\ T = 288\,K)$
1,2	actual conditions
∞	value after infinite time interval

A.2.4. Non-dimensional Groups

R_e Reynolds number $= \dfrac{\rho C d}{\mu} = \dfrac{4\dot{m}_a}{\pi d \mu}$

A.3. Conversion Factors

1 bar abs = 1 atm = 101.3 kN m^{-2} = 760 mm mercury = 14.7 lbf in^{-2}
1 bar = 100 kN m^{-2} = 10^5 N m^{-2}
100 mm Hg = 0.133 bar = 13.3 kN m^{-2}
1 N = 1 kg m s^{-2}
1 J = 1 N m
1 kW = 1 kJ s^{-1}

1 h.p. = 0.7457 kW	1 kW = 1.341 h.p.
1 inch = 2.54 cm ($\sim$ 2.5 cm)	1 cm = 0.3937 in ($\sim$ 0.4 in)
1 foot = 0.3048 m ($\sim$ 30 cm)	1 m = 3.281 ft ($\sim$ 3.3 ft)
1 oz = 28.35 g	1 g = 0.035 oz

1 lb = 0.4536 kg (~ 0.454 kg)   1 kg = 2.2 lb
1 ton = 1.016 tonnes   1 t = 0.984 tons ~ 1000 kg
1 in^2 = 6.452 × 10^{-4} m^2
1 in^3 = 1.639 × 10^{-5} m^3
1 ft^2 = 0.0929 m^2 1 m^2 = 1.196 yards^2 = 10.76 ft^2
1 ft^3 = 0.0283 m^3 1 m^3 = 1.316 yards^3 = 35.35 ft^3
1 ft s^{-1} = 0.3048 m s^{-1} 1 m s^{-1} = 3.281 (= 3.3) ft s^{-1}
1 lb in^{-3} = 2.768 × 10^4 kg m^{-3}
1 lb ft^{-3} = 16.0185 kg m^{-3} 1 kg m^{-3} = 0.0624 lb ft^{-3}
1 lbf = 4.448 N
1 lbf in^{-2} = 6894.76 N m^{-2}
Multiply m^{-3} s^{-1} by   60   to obtain m^{3}min^{-1}
                              1000   litres s^{-1}
                              1.205*   kg s^{-1}
                              72.3   kg min^{-1}
                              35.31   ft^3 s^{-1}
                              2119*   ft^3 min^{-1} (cfm)
                              2.66*   lb s^{-1}
                              159.4   lb min^{-1}
* Where a conversion is from a volume to a mass, the conversion is based on free air conditions of temperature and pressure and is for air only.

A.4. Formulae

cross-sectional area of a pipe, $A = \dfrac{\pi d^2}{4}$ m^2 [5]

density of gas, $\rho = \dfrac{p}{RT}$ kg m^{-3} [14]

Ideal Gas Law, $pV = m_a RT$ [16], [17], [21], [49], [50]

volumetric flow rate, $\dot{V} = C \times A$ m^{3}s^{-1} [19]

$\dot{V} = 0.816\dot{m}_a$ m^{3}s^{-1} at free air conditions   [25]

$\dot{V} = 816\dot{m}_a$ litres s^{-1}

$\dot{V} = 49\dot{m}_a$ m^{3}min^{-1}

power $= 165\dot{m}_a\ln\left(\dfrac{p_2}{p_1}\right)$ kW   [12], [24]

material mass flow rate, $\dot{m}_p = 3.6\dot{m}_a\left(\dfrac{\Delta p}{\Delta p_a} - 1\right)$ t h^{-1} [27]

Darcy equation for pressure drop, $\Delta p = \dfrac{4fL\rho C^2}{2d}$ N m^{-2} [55]

conveying air velocity, $C = 0.365\dot{m}_a \times \dfrac{T}{pd^2}$ m s^{-1} [56]

superficial air velocity, $U = V/A = \dfrac{C\Delta p}{L}$ m s^{-1} [87]

surface area of a sphere $= 4\pi r^2$ m^2

volume of a sphere $= \frac{4}{3}\pi r^3$ m^3

A.5. Illustrations

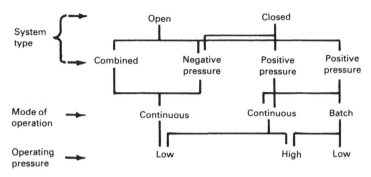

Figure 1 Diagram to illustrate the wide range of pneumatic conveying systems available. For conventional systems operating with a single air source

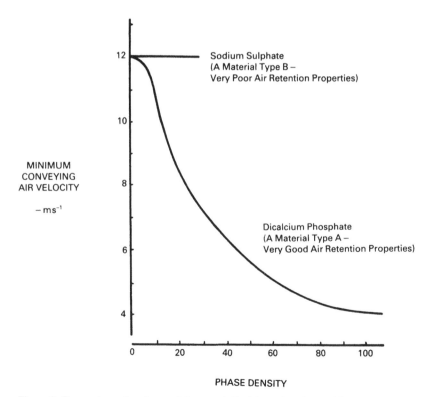

Figure 2 Comparison of sodium sulphate and dicalcium phosphate with respect to minimum conveying air velocity and phase density at which material is conveyed

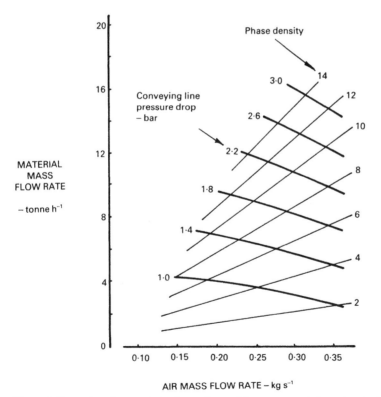

Figure 3 Conveying characteristics for sodium sulphate conveyed through a horizontal pipeline 100 m long, 81 mm bore, having eight bends at 90°

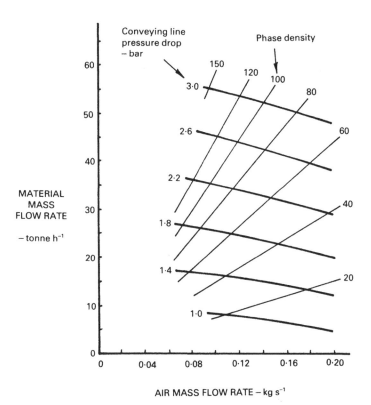

Figure 4 Conveying characteristics for dicalcium phosphate conveyed through a horizontal pipeline 100 m long, 81 mm bore, having eight bends at 90°

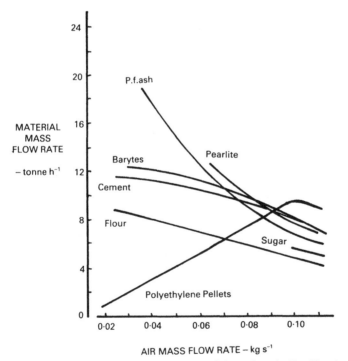

Figure 5 A comparison of materials conveyed through a pipeline 50 m long, 50 mm bore, having nine bends at 90° ($D/d = 24$). [Pipeline No.1 shown in Figure 173.] Conveying line pressure drop 1.5 bar

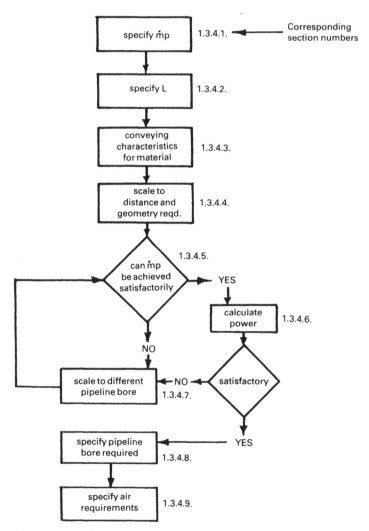

Figure 6 Logic diagram for pneumatic conveying system design based on the use of available conveying characteristics for material

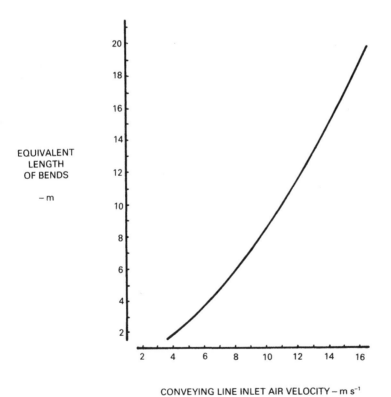

Figure 7 The influence of a bend at $90°$ ($D/d = 24$) expressed as the equivalent length of a straight horizontal pipeline

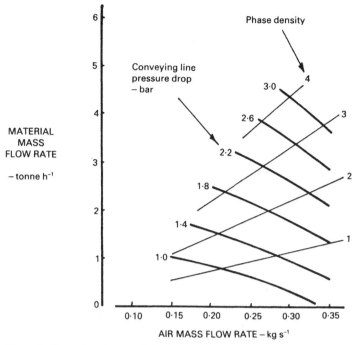

Figure 8 Conveying characteristics for sodium sulphate conveyed through a pipeline 300 m long. (Scaling of the conveying characteristics shown in Figure 3)

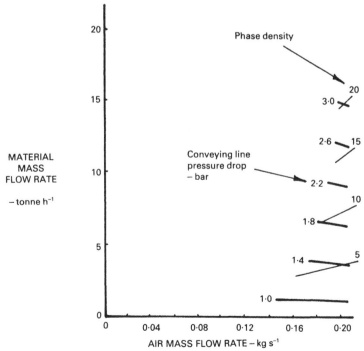

Figure 9 Conveying characteristics for dicalcium phosphate conveyed through a pipeline 300 m long. (Scaling of the conveying characteristics shown in Figure 4)

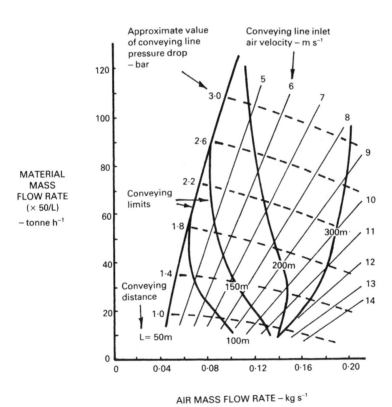

Figure 10 Influence of conveying distance on conveying line inlet air velocity for dicalcium phosphate

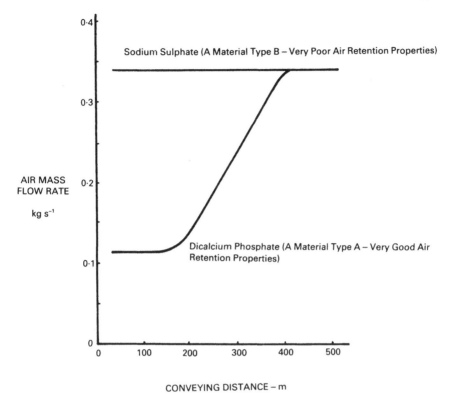

Figure 11 Influence of conveying distance on air required for successful conveying of sodium sulphate and dicalcium phosphate. Pipeline bore 81 mm, conveying line pressure drop 3 bar

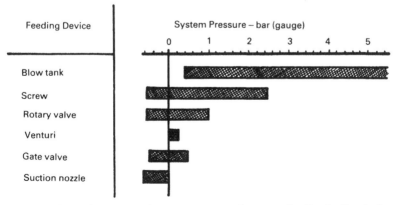

Figure 12 Approximate operating pressure ranges for conveying line feeding devices

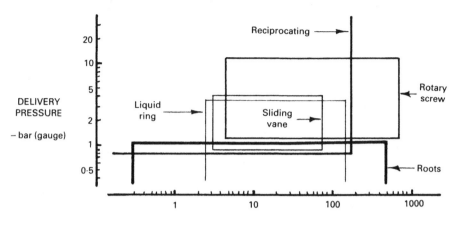

VOLUMETRIC FLOW RATE – free air delivered – m³ min⁻¹

Figure 13 Approximate ranges of operation of various types of air mover for pneumatic conveying applications

Index

Pneumatic Conveying Design Guide

Main entries and definitions are given in bold type. The numbers refer to sections in the text.

Abrasion, abrasive wear, *see* Erosion
Abrasive materials, particles, (*see also* Particle hardness; Erosion) 2.3.2, 2.4.5., 2.5.1., 2.5.5., 3.2.2., 3.2.3., 3.2.3.4., 3.2.5., 3.2.6., 3.2.7.1., 4.5.2., 6.1.3., 9.3.8., 10.2.2.7., 10.2.5.2.1., 10.2.5.2.3., 10.2.5.2.4., 10.2.5.2.5., 12.1., 12.3.1., 12.3.7.1., 12.3.7.2., 13.2.2.8.1., 13.3.3.2., 13.3.5.1., 13.4.4.6., 14.1.4., 14.7.
Absorber 15.2.2.3.3.
Aeration, (*see also* Air retention properties; Fluidisation; Material type A; Material type B; Permeability)
air leakage 13.2.2.7.1.
bulk solid 5.2.2.3., 8.4.: 8.4.1. to 8.4.5., 8.5.: 8.5.1 to 8.5.4.1.4., 15.3.1., 15.3.3.1.3., **15.4.3.1.3., 15.: 15.5.1. to 15.5.8.3.**
characteristics 8.3.1., 8.3.3., 8.5.4.1.
Aerodynamic compressors, (*see also* Air mover) **6.6.2.**, Figure 73
Air, (*see also* Conveying air; Gas; Inert gas; Nitrogen)
single-phase flow
blow off to atmosphere 11.3.2.
insulator 12.5.1.
Air-assisted gravity conveyor 1.4.2.,**2.2.5.**, **6.5.**, 8.4.5., 15.5.2., 15.5.2.2., Figure 48
air requirements **6.5.**
costs, *see* Costs
fluidising membrane 2.5.5., 6.5.
fliudising velocity 6.5.
slope 2.5.5., 6.5.
Air comparison pycnometer 15.3.2.2.2., 15.3.5.
Air (gas) compression, *see* Compression
compressibility 1.4.6., 2.2.2., 2.2.4., 6.1.2., 6.2.2., 7.2.2., 9.2.3., 9.2.3.1., 12.3.7.3.
Air (gas) density, *see* Density
Air drying **6.4.3.**, 6.4.4., **6.4.5.: 6.4.5.1.**, **6.4.5.2.**, 10.2.2.7., 10.4.8., 13.2.2.3.1., 13.4.3.2., 13.5.3.
equipment **6.4.4.**, **6.4.5.: 6.4.5.1.**, **6.4.5.2.**, 10.2.2.7., 10.4.8., 13.4.3.2.

Air drying (*continued*)
equipment (*continued*)
dessicant driers **6.4.5.2.**, 13.4.3.2.
dew point 6.4.5.1., 6.4.5.2.
filter 6.4.5.2.
heat exchange 6.4.5.1.
refrigerant driers 6.4.4., **6.4.5.1.**, 13.4.3.2.
Air extraction lines 13.2.2.2.2., 13.2.2.3.3., 13.2.2.8.1., 13.2.2.8.2., 13.4.5.2., Figure 10
Air flow rate, (*see also* Air mass flow rate; Conveying air velocity; Conveying line inlet air velocity; Single-phase flow; Superficial air velocity; Volumetric flow rate) 1.4.7., 2.2.1., 2.3.7., 2.4.7., 3.2.6., 3.2.7.4., 3.2.7.8., 3.3.2.1., 3.3.3., 3.3.3.3., 4.3.2.3., 4.3.4.1., 4.4., 4.6.1., 4.6.2., 4.6.3.1., 5.2.2.6., 5.3.3.1., 5.3.3.5., 5.3.6., 5.4.2., 5.4.3., 5.4.4., 5.4.6., 6.1.3., 6.6.2., 6.8., 7.3.3., 7.3.4., 7.3.5., 7.4.2., 7.4.3., 7.4.5., 7.4.7., 7.5.1., 7.5.2., 7.5.3., 7.5.5., 7.5.6., 8.1., 8.2.2., 8.2.4., 8.3.2., **9.2.3.1.1.**, 9.2.4., 9.3.4.1., 9.3.7., 9.3.8., 10.2.5.2.5., 10.2.7.1.3., 10.2.7.2.2., 10.3.5., 10.5.2.1.1., 11.1.2., 11.1.3., 11.1.4., 11.2.1., **11.2.2.: 11.2.2.1.**, **11.2.2.2.**, 11.2.4., 11.3.1., 11.3.2., 11.4., 11.5., 13.1., 13.2.2.2.1., 13.2.2.4., 13.2.2.6., **13.2.2.7.3.**, 13.2.2.8.1., 13.2.2.9.1., 13.3.3.1., 13.4.5.3., 13.4.5.4., 14.2.1., 14.3.4.4., 14.3.5.2., 14.3.5.3., 14.4.1., 14.5.3.1., 14.5.3.1.2., 14.5.3.2.1., 14.5.5., Tables 14.8. to 14.10., Figures 329 to 331
changing 7.4.3., **11.2.2.: 11.2.2.1.**, **11.2.2.2.**
control, *see* Air supply
high 2.4.7., 8.2.2.
low 8.3.2., 9.3.4.1.
maximum 3.3.3.3.
minimum 4.3.2.3., **5.2.2.6.**, 5.4.2., 5.4.5., 5.4.6., 7.3.4., 7.4.5., 7.5.1., 7.5.2., 7.5.3., 7.5.5., 7.5.6., 8.2.2., 8.3.2., 11.1.2., 14.4.1., 14.5.3.1.
optimum 11.3.2., 11.4.

Air, fluidising, *see* Fluidising air
Air, free, *see* Free air
Air ingress, *see* Ingress of air
Air knife 2.5.3., 3.2.9.
Air leakage (losses) 1.4.10., 10.2.6.
  feeding devices 2.3.2., 3.1., 3.2.2., 5.2.2.16.,
    5.3.2.9., 10.2.5.1., **10.2.5.1.2.**,
    10.2.5.2.1., 10.2.5.2.2., 10.2.5.2.4.,
    10.2.6.1.1., 10.2.6.1.2., 10.3.1., 11.1.4.,
    12.3.7.2., 13.2.2.2.1., 13.2.2.4., 13.2.2.5.,
    13.2.2.7.1., 13.2.2.8.1., 13.3.1.1.,
    13.3.3.1., 14.4.2.1.
  energy loss 13.3.1.1.
  gate lock valves 3.2.6., 5.2.2.16., 5.3.2.9.,
    10.2.5.2.4., 10.2.6.1.2., 13.2.2.4.
  rotary valves 2.3.2., 2.3.4., **3.2.3.1.**,
    3.2.3.2., 3.2.3.3., 3.2.3.5., 5.2.2.16.,
    5.3.2.9., 7.3.6., 10.2.2.3., 10.2.2.5.,
    10.2.5.2.1., 10.2.6.1.2., 10.3.1., 11.1.4.,
    12.3.7.2., 13.2.2.4., 13.2.2.7.1.,
    13.2.2.8.1., 13.4.4.1., **13.4.4.4.**,
    13.4.4.6., 14.4.2.2.3., 14.5.1., **14.5.2.3.**,
    Table 14.7., **Figure 17**
  energy loss 13.4.4.4.
  screw feeders 13.2.2.8.1., 14.5.1., 14.5.3.1.
  constant pitch (simple) 3.2.4., 10.2.5.2.2.
  decreasing pitch 3.2.4., 10.2.5.2.2.
Air line, *see* Air supply line
Air losses, *see* Air leakage
Air mass flow rate, (*see also* Air flow rate; Air
  requirements; Single-phase flow) 1.6.1.1.,
  2.2.2., 2.2.3., 3.2.7.8., 3.2.7.9., 4.3.2.2.,
  4.3.3., 5.2.2.6., **5.2.2.7.**, 5.2.2.8., 5.2.2.13.,
  5.2.2.16., **5.2.3.6.**, 5.2.4., 5.3.2.6., 5.3.3.4.,
  5.3.5., 5.4.2., 5.4.5., 6.1.3., 6.2., 6.2.1.,
  6.3.3., 7.2., **7.2.2.**, 7.3.1., 7.3.3., 7.3.4.,
  7.3.5., 7.3.6., 7.4.4., 7.5.1., 7.5.5., 7.5.6.,
  8.2.2., 8.2.4., 8.5.2., 8.5.3., 8.5.4.,
  9.2.3.1.1., 9.2.3.1.2., 9.2.3.1.3., 9.3.2.2.,
  9.3.2.3., 9.3.4., 9.3.4.2., 9.3.6., 9.3.7.,
  10.2.6.1.2., 10.5.2.1.1., 10.5.2.6.1., 11.1.2.,
  11.2.1., 11.2.2., 11.2.2.1., 11.2.2.2., 11.2.5.,
  11.3.2., 11.4., 11.5., 14.3.4.5., 14.3.5.1.,
  14.4.2., 14.4.2.1., 14.5.3.1., Table 14.2.,
  Figures 136, 137, 142, 167 to 170, 229, 230,
  235, 236, 257, 258, 299
  changing **11.2.2.: 11.2.2.1., 11.2.2.2.**
  control, *see* Air supply
  conveying characteristics, *see* Conveying char-
    acteristics
  high 8.2.2.
  lines of constant 14.3.5.2.
  low 9.3.4.1.
  mathematical model, *see* Mathematical models
  minimum 4.3.2.3., **5.2.2.6.**, 5.4.2., 5.4.5.,
    5.4.6., 7.3.4., 7.4.5., 7.5.1., 7.5.2., 7.5.3.,
    7.5.5., 7.5.6., 8.2.2., 8.3.2., 11.1.2.,
    14.4.1., 14.5.3.1.
  optimum 11.3.2., 11.4
  ratio with material mass flow rate Figures 257
    and 258

Air mover (blower, compressor), (*see also*
  Aerodynamic compressor; Blow tanks; Centrifugal compressor; Fans; Reciprocating
  compressor; Rotary screw compressor;
  Roots type blower; Sliding vane rotary compressor; Exhauster) 1.4.6., 1.5.1., 1.6.1.7.,
  2.3.: 2.3.1. to 2.3.8., 3.2.2., 4.2.2.1., 4.6.1.,
  4.7.2., **5.2.3.8.**, 5.2.3.14., 5.3.3.1., 5.3.3.4.,
  5.4.3., **Chapter 6**, 7.4.5., 10.1., 10.2.5.1.3.,
  10.2.6.: 10.2.6.1. to 10.2.6.2.5., 10.2.7.2.1.,
  10.6.3.1., 11.2.2., 11.2.2.1., 11.2.2.2.,
  11.2.5., 11.2.6., 11.3.2., 13.2.2.2.3., **13.4.2.**,
  13.4.4.4., **14.5.3.: 14.5.3.1. to 14.5.3.2.3.**,
  14.6.2.1., 14.6.3.1., Table 13.1., Tables
  14.17. to 14.20., Figures 71, 73, 329 to 331.
  air cooling 6.3.2., 6.3.3., 6.4.3., 6.4.5.1.,
    6.6.1., 14.5.3.2.2.
  air filter 11.3.2.
  air supply pressure, *see* Air supply pressure
  capability 5.2.3.14., **5.2.3.8.**, 5.2.3.14.,
    5.3.3.4., 5.3.3.5., 5.4.3., 10.2.6.,
    13.2.2.7., 13.3.3.
  capacity 11.1.2., 11.5.
  spare 7.4.5., 11.1.2., 11.1.4., 11.5.
  characteristics 5.3.3.4., 5.4.3., 11.1.4., 11.1.5.,
    11.2.: 11.2.1. to 11.2.6., 13.2.2.4., 13.4.2.
  case study 11.2: 11.2.1. to 11.2.6.
  control 5.4.3., 10.2.6.2.1., 10.2.6.2.3., 11.3.2.,
    13.2.2.3.2.
  control valve 13.2.2.3.2.
  cooling 6.3.2., 6.3.3., 6.6.1., 6.6.3., 6.6.5.,
    6.6.6.
  cost, *see* Costs
  delivery pressure, *see* Air supply pressure; *see
    also* Air mover, free air delivery
  differential pressure switch 13.2.2.2.3.
  distance from conveying system 10.2.6.1.1.
  drive motor 14.6.2.1.
    power 4.6.1., 14.4.2.1.
    speed 11.1.1., 11.1.4., 11.2.2., 11.2.2.1.,
      11.2.2.2., 11.2.5., 11.3.2., 13.1.
  dual negative and positive conveying system
    10.2.2.6.
  duty 14.5.3.2.1., 14.5.3.2.2., 14.5.3.2.3.,
    Tables 14.11 to 14.13
  efficiency value 14.4.2.1.
  filter
    inlet 13.4.2.
    exit 6.4.3., 6.6.6.
  free air delivery, (*see also* Air supply press-
    ure; Volumetric flow rate) 6.1.2., 6.1.7.,
    6.2.4., 6.2.5. 6.6.1., 6.6.2., 6.6.3., 6.6.4.,
    6.7., 10.2.6., 13.2.2.4., Figure 72
  ingress of material, *see* Ingress of material
  mathematical model, *see* Mathematical models
  multi-stage 6.3.2., 6.6.2., 6.6.7.
  non-return valves 13.4.2.
  oil-free air 6.6.5., 14.5.3.2.1., 14.5.3.2.2.,
    Tables 14.11. and 14.12.
  operating pressure 10.2.6., 10.2.6.2.3.,
    10.2.6.2.4., 10.2.6.2.5., 13.3.3., 14.5.3.2.,

Air mover (*continued*)
  operating pressure (*continued*)
    Tables 14.11. to 14.13., Figure 72
  performance 5.4.3., 13.2.2.4., 13.2.2.8.1.,
    13.4.2.
  positive displacement 6.6.4., 13.2.2.4.
  power requirements, *see* Power requirements
  pressure ratio 13.3.3.
  pulsation **1.6.1.20.**, 6.6.4., 6.6.6., 6.6.7.
  rating 1.4.6., 3.3.2.1., 5.2.2.15., 5.2.3.4.,
    5.3.3.4., 6.1.2., 6.1.3., 6.1.7., 6.2., 6.6.1.,
    6.6.2., 6.6.3., 6.7., 7.3.5., 7.3.6., 8.2.3.,
    10.2.3., 11.1.4., 11.3.2., 11.5.,
    13.2.2.2.1., 13.2.2.7.4., 14.2.1., Figure 80
  overrating 11.1.2., 11.2.2., 11.3.2.,
    13.2.2.2.1., 13.3.2.2.
  replacing **11.1.4.**
  selection 1.4.10., 1.5.1., 5.2.2.16., 7.4.5.,
    10.1., 10.2.5.1.3., **10.2.6.: 10.2.6.1.** to
    10.2.6.2.5., **14.5.3.2.: 14.5.3.2.1.** to
    14.5.3.2.3., 14.6.3.2., 14.7.
  self lubricating 14.5.3.2.2.
  single-stage **6.6.1.**, 6.6.3., 6.6.5., 6.6.6., 6.6.7.
  specification 1.4.10, 1.5.1., 1.5.2., 1.6.1.7.,
    5.2.3.3., 5.2.3.8., 6.1.3., 6.1.5., 7.4.5.,
    8.2.3., 10.2.5.1.2., 10.2.5.1.3., 10.2.6.1.:
    10.2.6.1.1. to 10.2.6.1.2., 10.3.4.,
    13.2.2.2.1., 13.2.2.2., 13.2.2.4., 13.3.2.2.,
    13.5.2., Table 13.1.
  incorrect **13.2.2.2.1.**
  supply pressure, *see* Air supply pressure
  thermodynamic efficiency 6.6.4., 6.6.7.
  two-stage **6.6.1.**, 6.6.3., 6.6.5., 6.6.6.,
  types **6.6.: 6.6.1.** to **6.6.7.**, 10.1.
  volumetric flow rate, *see* Volumetric flow rate
  wear 13.2.2.8.1., 13.4.2.
Air pressure, *see* Pressure,
  atmospheric, *see* Pressure
  conveying, *see* Conveying air pressure
  conveying line exit, *see* Conveying line exit air
    pressure
  conveying line inlet, *see* Conveying line inlet
    air pressure
  partial pressure, *see* Pressure
  supply, *see* Air supply pressure
Air purge, *see* Purge
Air quality
  control **2.4.8.**
Air requirements, (*see also* Air velocity; Air
  flow rate; Air mass flow rate; Air supply
  pressure; Exhaust pressure; Pressure drop;
  Volumetric flow rate) 1.4.10., 1.5.1., 4.3.3.,
  4.3.2.2., 5.1., 5.2.2.6., 5.2.2.15., 5.2.2.16.,
  5.2.3., **5.2.3.14.**, 5.3.1., 5.3.2.4., **5.3.2.9.**,
  5.3.3.4., 5.3.3.5., 5.3.5., 5.3.6., 6.1.5., 6.8.,
  7.4.5., 7.5.5., 9.3.2.4., 10.1., 10.2.2.3.,
  10.2.2.7., 10.2.4., 10.2.5.1.3., 10.2.5.2.5.,
  10.2.6., **10.2.6.1.: 10.2.6.1.1. to 10.2.6.1.2.**,
  10.2.6.2.1., 10.3.4., 10.3.5., 10.4.4., 10.5.1.,
  11.1.1., 11.1.2., 13.2.2.2.1., 13.4.4.4.,
  13.2.2.9.1., 14.1.1., 14.4.2., 14.4.2.1.,

Air requirements (*continued*)
  14.5.1., **14.5.3.1.: 14.5.3.1.1. to 14.5.3.1.2.**,
  14.6.1., Tables 14.2., 14.10 to 14.13., Figures 329 to 331, 167 to 170
Air retention properties, (*see also* Aeration;
  Fluidisation; Geldart's classification of
  fluidisation behaviour; Material type A;
  Material type B; Permeability) 4.2.1.,
  4.3.2.1., 5.2.2.1., 8.4.1., 8.5.3., 8.5.4.1.,
  15.5.5.: 15.5.5.1. to 15.5.5.2
  good 1.4.8., 4.2.1., 4.3.2.1., 4.3.2.3., 4.3.4.1.,
    4.5.2., 4.6.2., 4.6.2.1., **4.6.3.1.**, 4.6.3.2.,
    4.7.1., 4.7.2., 5.2.2.6., 5.3.5., 5.3.6.,
    5.3.7., 5.4.5., 8.4.1., 8.4.4., 9.3.1.,
    9.3.4.2., 15.5.1., 15.5.4.4., 15.5.5.,
    Figures 64, 101, 103, 105, 108, 110, 112,
    114, 116, 117, 119, 120 to 123, 126, 127,
    130, 139, 150 to 153, 155, 157, 159, 161,
    163, 165, 167 to 170
  poor 1.4.4., 4.3.2.1., 4.3.5., 4.6.2., 4.6.2.1.,
    4.6.3.2., 4.7.2., 5.1., 5.2.2.6., 5.3.5.,
    5.3.6., 5.3.7., 5.4.5., 8.4.1., 9.3.1.,
    9.3.4.2., 13.4.3.4., 15.5.1., 15.5.4.4.,
    Figures 64, 102, 104, 106, 109, 111, 113,
    115, 116, 118, 119 to 121, 124, 125, 128,
    129, 132, 133, 139, 150 to 152, 154, 156,
    158, 160, 162, 164, 166, 167 to 170
Air–solid flow, *see* Two-phase flow
Air–solid interaction 15.1.1.
Air supply, (*see also* Air flow rate; Air mass
  flow rate; Air requirements; Air supply
  pressure; Conveying air velocity; Conveying
  line inlet air velocity; Single-phase flow;
  Superficial air velocity; Volumetric flow
  rate) 3.2.7.9., 3.3.2.1., 5.4.2., 5.4.6., 6.8.,
  7.3.2., 7.5.5., 10.2.6.2.2., 11.3.2., 12.3.7.2.,
  13.2.2.2.1., 13.2.2.7., 13.2.2.7.1.,
  13.2.2.7.3., 13.4.2., 14.4.1., Figures 10, 11
  air mover, *see* Air mover
  control 5.4., 5.4.2., **5.4.3.**, 5.4.4., 5.4.6.,
    10.2.6.1.1., **10.2.6.2.1.**, 10.3.4., **11.3.2.**,
    13.2.2.3.2.
  limits 7.4.2.
  overrated 13.2.2.7.3.
  plant **10.2.6.2.2.**
  proportioning, *see* Blow tank control
  rating 7.1.
  supplementary **3.2.7.1.**, 3.2.7.3., 3.2.7.4.,
    3.2.7.6., 3.2.7.8., 3.2.7.10., 10.2.5.1.4.,
    10.5.2.6., 10.5.2.6.1., 10.5.3.1., 10.5.3.2.,
    10.5.4.
  conveying system, negative pressure 3.2.8.
  total 3.2.7.8.
Air supply line 13.2.2.2.2., 13.2.2.3.2.,
  13.2.2.3.3., 13.2.2.8.1., 13.2.2.8.2., 13.3.5.,
  13.4.2., 13.4.3., 13.4.5.2., 14.5.4.3., Table
  13.1., Figure 11
  boosters **2.5.4.2.**, 3.2.7.5.
  bypass **2.5.4.1.**, 13.2.2.3.2.
  filter 6.4.3.
  pressure drop, *see* Pressure drop

Air supply line (*continued*)
  seeding 7.3.1.
  supplementary 10.5.3.1., 10.5.3.2., 13.4.3.1.,
    13.4.3.3.
  valves 10.5.3.2.
  tracelines 3.2.7.5.
Air supply (delivery, exhaust) pressure, (*see also*
  Air mover free air delivery; Air requirements; Conveying line inlet air pressure;
  Exhaust pressure; Volumetric flow rate)
  1.2., 1.4.3., 1.4.6., 1.4.14., 1.6.1.4.,
  1.6.1.5., 1.6.1.6., 1.6.1.8., 2.2.5., 2.3.2.,
  2.4.3., 3.2.2., 3.2.5., 3.2.6., 3.2.7.9., 4.6.1.,
  4.6.3.1., 4.6.3.2., 5.2.2.6., 5.2.2.13.,
  5.2.2.16., 5.2.3.8., 5.3.2.1., 5.3.3.5., 5.4.3.,
  5.4.6., 6.1., **6.1.1.**, 6.1.3., 6.1.6., 6.2.4.,
  6.2.6., 6.3.2., 6.6.1. to 6.6.7., 7.2.2., 7.3.2.,
  7.3.5., 7.3.6., 7.5.3., 7.5.5., 9.1., 9.2.3.1.3.,
  9.3.5.2., 10.1., 10.2.3., 10.2.5., 10.2.5.1.2.,
  10.2.5.1.3., 10.2.6., 10.2.6.1., **10.2.6.1.1.**,
  11.1.1., 11.1.3., 11.1.4., 11.2.1., 11.2.2.1.,
  11.2.2.2., 11.2.3., 11.2.5., 11.3.2., 11.5.,
  12.3.7.3., 13.2.2.2.1., 13.2.2.2.2., 13.2.2.4.,
  13.3.3., 13.4.5.1., **14.1.3.**, 14.2.1., 14.3.5.,
  14.3.6., 14.4.2.1., 14.4.2.2.2., 14.5.2.2.,
  14.6.3.2., Tables 14.11 to 14.13., Figures
  96, 99, 100, 329 to 331
Air surge, *see* Surge
  blow tank, *see* Blow tank
Air velocity 1.6.1.8., 3.2.7.4., 6.1.3., 9.2.1.,
  9.2.3.1., 10.5.3.2., 11.1.3., 13.3.5.1.
  conveying, *see* Conveying air velocity, *see also*
    Conveying velocity
  conveying line exit (outlet), *see* Conveying
    line exit air velocity
  conveying line inlet, *see* Conveying line inlet
    air velocity
  fluidising, *see* Fluidising air
  free, *see* Free air velocity
  interstitial 15.5.4.2.
  open duct 1.6.1.8.
  permeameter 15.5.3.1.
  superficial, *see* Superficial air velocity
Airborne particulate material Figure 284
Alumina 2.1., 2.4.2., 8.2.3., 12.3.5., Figures
  140, 228, 230
  impurity 12.3.6.1., 13.5.5.
Altitude 6.6.1., **13.5.2.**, 13.4.5.3.
Ambient conditions 6.1.7., 6.2.5.1., 6.3.3.,
  13.5.1., 13.5.2.
Ammonium chloride Figure 81
Angel hairs, *see* Extrusion hairs
Angle of repose 15.4.3., **15.4.3.1.**, 15.4.3.2.
  drained **15.4.3.1.2.**
  fluidised **15.4.3.1.3.**, **15.5.2.1.**
  poured **15.4.3.1.1.**, 15.4.4., 15.5.2.1., Table
    15.3.
Angular particles 12.3.6.1.
Anti-static clothing 12.5.2.
Anti-vibration devices 12.5.2.

Area, cross sectional of pipe, see Pipeline, cross
  sectional area
Arnell, Carmen and, equation **15.5.6.1.**,
  15.5.8.1.
Atmospheric pressure, *see* Pressure
Atmospheric standard conditions, *see* Free air
  conditions
Axial flow compressor, *see* Aerodynamic compressor

Backflushing of materials 13.4.2.
Barytes 2.4.2., 2.4.3., 4.3.2.1., 5.3.8., 8.1.,
  8.2.2., 8.2.3., 8.2.4., 8.3.1., 8.3.3., 8.4.1.,
  8.4.4., 8.4.4.1., 8.5., 9.3.1., 9.3.2.1.,
  9.3.2.4., 9.3.3., 9.3.4.1., 9.3.5.1., 9.3.5.2.,
  9.3.6.1., 9.3.7., 10.5.2.1.1., 10.5.2.2.,
  10.5.2.2.1., 10.5.2.4., 10.5.2.5., 12.3.6.1.,
  13.5.5., 14.3.4.1., 15.1.1., 15.2.2.4., 15.2.3.,
  15.3.5., 15.4.4., 15.5.8., 15.5.8.1., 15.5.8.2.,
  15.5.8.3., Tables 8.1., 15.1. to 15.4.,
  Figures 40, 41, 81, 82, 140, 225, 227, 229,
  246, 247, 249, 252, 253, 254, 256, 258, 260,
  275 to 281, 283
  conveying characteristics Figures 187 to 196
Batch conveying, *see* Conveying system, batch
Batch size 10.2.7.2.2., 10.5.2.1., **10.5.2.2.**,
  10.5.2.2.1., **10.5.3.3.**, **10.5.4.**, 14.3.1.,
  14.3.2., 14.3.3., 14.4.4., 14.5.2.1.,
  14.5.3.1.2., 14.5.3.2., 14.6.1., 14.6.3.,
  Tables 14.5 and 14.6., Figures 40, 41, 58,
  60, 61
Bed
  bulk solid, *see* Bulk solid
  compacted
    pores
      number 15.5.6.3.
      size 15.5.6.1., 15.5.6.3.
  permeameter, *see* Permeameter
  pressure drop, *see* Pressure drop
Belt feeders 3.2.5.
Bench scale tests, (*see also* Correlation studies;
  Test data) 1.4.15, **5.3.8.**, Chapter 8, **Chapter 15**
  correlations 1.4.5., 1.4.8., 1.4.15., 5.1., 1.3.1.,
    5.3.8.,
Bend diameter, *see also* Bends, radius
  ratio to pipeline bore (D/d) **4.2.3.3.**, 5.2.2.3.,
    9.2.3.1.4., 9.3.6.1., 9.3.8., 12.3.4.,
    12.3.8.2., 14.5.4.2., Figures 238, 264, 265
Bends 1.3., 1.4.9., 2.4.4., 2.4.5., 2.4.7.,
  4.2.3.3., 5.3.2.4., 7.4.2., 9.2.1., 9.3.2.4.,
  9.3.3., 9.3.5., 10.4.5., 10.4.6., 11.3.3.,
  12.1., 12.2.2.4., **12.3.: 12.3.1. to 12.3.9.**,
  12.7.3., **14.5.4.2.**, 14.6.2., 14.7., Table
  14.14., Figures 237, 238, 240, 241, 245, 247,
  250, 251, 261, 262, 310
  angle 12.2.2.4., 12.3.8.8.
  sharp (mitred) 9.2.3.1.4., 12.3.4., Figure
    239

Bends (*continued*)
    backing pieces, *see* Erosion, wear back
        methods
    blind (blank) tees 2.5.2., 4.2.3.3., 9.3.8.,
        12.3.8.3., 13.5.5., Figures 261, 272
    effects of **9.3.2.4., 9.3.3.,** 9.3.4., 9.3.8.,
        12.2.2., 14.3.4.3.
    elbows 4.2.3.3., 9.3.8., 12.3.4.
    equivalent length, *see* Scaling
    equivalent resistance 9.3.3.
    erosion, *see* Erosion
    fabricated 9.2.3.1.5., Figure 242
    failure 2.4.5., 12.3.6.2., 12.3.6.3., 12.3.7.3.,
        13.5.5., Figure 271
        premature 12.3.6.2.
    flow pattern, (*see also* Erosion) 12.3.5.,
        Figures 265, 266
    geometry, (*see also* Pipeline geometry)
        4.2.3.3., 5.2.2.3., 9.2.3.1.4., 9.3.1.,
        9.3.2., **9.3.8.,** 12.2.2.4., 12.3.3., **12.3.4.,**
        14.3.5.2., Figure 264
    impact of particles, *see* Erosion, particle im-
        pact
    mitred, *see* Bends, angle, sharp
    number of 2.4.7., 3.3.2.4., 4.2.3., 4.2.3.3.,
        5.2.2.3., 5.3.8., 9.1., 9.2.3.1.4., 9.3.2.,
        9.3.3., 9.3.4., 10.5.2.1.1., 11.1.1., 11.1.3.,
        14.1.2., 14.2.2., 14.3.4.3., 14.3.5.2.,
        Figures 246, 248
    pressure drop, *see* Pressure drop
    radius 12.2.2.4., 14.5.4.2.
        long (large) 4.2.3.3., 2.5.2., 9.3.8., 12.3.4.,
            12.3.8.2., 12.3.8.5., 12.3.9., 13.5.5.,
            Figures 261, 262
        short (small) 3.2.9., 9.2.3.1.4., 9.3.8.,
            12.3.4., **12.3.8.3.,** 12.3.9., 13.5.5.,
            Figure 262
    replacement 10.6.3.2., 12.3.9.
    rubber **12.3.8.6.**
    scaling, *see* Scaling
    steel 12.3.6.3., 12.3.8.6., 12.3.8.8.
        mild 12.3.4., 12.3.6.1., 13.5.5.
    tee-pieces 2.5.2.
        with valve 11.3.2.
    wear, *see* Erosion
Bentonite 2.4.6., 4.2.1., 4.3.2.1., 7.5.6., 8.1.,
    8.3.3., 9.3.1., 9.3.2.1., Table 8.1., Figures
    82, 146, 206, 226, 228, 230, 231, 283
    conveying characteristics Figures 216, 217
BET methods (specific surface determination)
    15.2.2.3.3.
Blaine method (specific surface determination),
    see Specific surface
Blind tees, tee-pieces, *see* Bends
Blockage 1.1., 2.2.6.2., 2.3.2., 2.4.2., **2.4.3.,**
    2.5.3.1., 3.2.2., 3.2.5., 3.2.6., 3.2.7.5.,
    3.2.7.8., 3.2.7.9., 3.2.8., 5.2.2.6., 5.4.4.,
    6.1.3., 6.2.6., 6.6.2., Chapter 7, 10.4.3.,
    10.4.7., 10.5.2.6.1., 11.2.2.2., 11.2.3., 11.4.,
    11.5., 12.1., 12.3.7.1., 12.3.8.3., 12.3.8.8.,

Blockage (*continued*)
    12.7.1., 13.1., 13.2.1., **13.2.2.: 13.2.2.1. to**
    13.2.2.9.2., 13.3.2.2., 13.3.4., 13.4.3.,
    13.4.3.2., 13.4.3.5., 13.6.6., 13.6.8.,
    13.6.10., Table 13.1.
    blow tank discharge line 13.4.3.4.
    checklist **13.2.2.1., Table 13.1.**
    diverter valves 12.4.1., 13.6.2.
    filtration unit, *see* Filtration unit
Blow egg, *see* Blow tanks
Blow tanks (blow eggs, powder pumps, pressure
    eggs), (*see also* Air mover) 1.4.3., 1.4.10.,
    1.4.14., 1.6.1.5., 1.6.1.6., **2.3.7.,** 2.3.8.,
    2.5.2., 2.5.3., 2.5.4.2., 3.2.1., **3.2.7.:**
    3.2.7.1. to 3.2.7.11, 3.2.8., 3.2.9., **3.3.2.1.,**
    4.6.3.1., 5.2.2.1., 6.1.1., 7.4.6., 7.5.1.,
    8.3.2., 9.3.7., 10.2.2.3., 10.2.4., 10.2.5.,
    10.2.5.1.4., **10.2.5.2.5.,** 10.2.6.2.2.,
    10.2.7.2.2., 10.3.6., **10.5.: 10.5.1. to**
    10.5.4.1., 12.3.7.2., 12.7.5., **13.4.3.:**
    13.4.3.1. to 13.4.3.5., 13.4.5.4., 13.6.4.,
    14.1.1., 14.3.1., **14.4.3.: 14.4.3.1. to 14.4.4.,**
    14.5.2.1., 14.5.3.1., 14.5.3.2., **14.6.3.:**
    14.6.3.1. to 14.6.3.2., 14.6.5., Tables 3.1. to
    3.4., 14.3., 14.4., 14.5., 14.7., 14.9., Figures
    9, 59, 60, 61
    air ingress, *see* Ingress of air
    air leakage, *see* Air leakage
    air requirements **14.5.3.1.2., Table 14.9.**
    air surge 2.5.2., 10.2.5.2.5., 10.2.7.2.2.,
        13.2.7.4., 13.3.5.1., 13.4.5.4.
    blowing cycle, *see* Conveying system, batch
    capability, (*see also* Discharge capability)
        8.3.2., 14.3.1.
    coded 10.2.5.2.5., 14.4.3.1., **14.5.2.1.**
    conical membrane 3.2.7.5.
    continuously operating system, *see* Conveying
        system, continuously operating
    control 1.4.3., 1.5.3., **3.2.7.8.,** 3.2.7.9., 7.4.6.,
        10.2.5.1.4., 10.5., 10.5.2., 10.5.2.6.,
        10.5.2.6.1., 10.5.4., 13.2.2.2.2., **13.4.3.1.,**
        Table 3.2., Figure 43
    air supply proportioning 3.2.7.8.,
        13.2.2.2.2., 13.4.3.1., 13.4.3.4.,
        13.4.3.5., Table 3.2., Figure 43
    automatic 14.5.4.3.
    conveying cycle, *see* Conveying system, batch
    costs, *see* Costs
    depressurising 10.5.3.2.
    discharge 10.5.3.1., 13.4.3.3.
        bottom **3.2.7.5.,** 3.2.7.6., 10.2.5.2.5.,
            13.4.3.5., Figures 33 and 34
        capability 3.2.7.8., **13.4.3.4.,** 14.2.2.
        characteristics Figure 43
        limit **13.4.3., 13.4.3.4.,** Figure 13
        top 2.3.8., **3.2.7.5.,** 3.2.7.6., 3.2.7.11.,
            10.2.5.2.5., 10.4.7., 10.5.2., 13.4.3.3.,
            13.4.3.4., 13.4.3.5., Figures 30, 31, 32
    discharge line **3.2.7.6.,** 10.5.2., 10.5.3.1.,
        13.4.3.3.,

Blow tanks (*continued*)
 discharge line (*continued*)
  air velocity 13.4.3.4.
  blockage 13.4.3.4.
  diameter 13.4.3., 13.4.3.4.
 discharge valve, (*see also* Blow tanks, valves)
  2.3.8., 10.5.3.1.
  with **3.2.7.4.**, 3.2.9., **10.5.3.: 10.5.3.1. to
   10.5.3.3.**, 10.5.4., 12.3.7.2., 14.4.3.1.,
   14.4.3.3., 14.3.3.1.2., 14.5.3.2.,
   14.5.4.3., 14.5.5., 14.6.1., 14.6.2.,
   14.6.3.1., 14.6.3.2., Tables 14.9.,
   14.15., 14.18 and 14.20.
  without **3.2.7.3.**, 3.2.7.4., 3.2.7.10., 3.2.9.,
   7.4.6., 10.2.5.2.5., 10.4.7., **10.5.2.:
   10.5.2.1. to 10.5.2.6.1.**, 10.5.3.1.,
   10.5.3.3., 14.4.3.1., **14.4.3.2.**,
   14.5.3.1.2., 14.5.3.3., 14.5.5., 14.6.1.,
   14.6.2., 14.6.3., 14.6.3.2., Tables 14.3.,
   14.9., 14.15., 14.18. and 14.20.
 economic assessment, *see* Costs
 filling 10.5.2.2.1., 10.5.2.3., 10.5.2.5., 14.4.4.
 fluidisation, see Fluidisation
 fluidising membrane 3.2.7.3., **3.2.7.5.**,
  3.2.7.6., 10.2.5.2.5., 10.5.2., 13.4.3.2.,
  13.4.3.3.
  annular ring 3.2.7.6.
  blinding **13.4.3.2.**, 13.4.3.3.
  pressure drop, see Pressure drop
 non-coded 14.4.3.1., 14.5.2.1.
 operating pressure 2.5.2., 3.2.1., 14.5.2.1.,
  Table 3.1., Figure 12
 performance 13.4.3.2.
 plenum chamber 3.2.7.3.
 power requirements, see Power requirements
 pressure drop, see Pressure drop
 pressurising 3.2.7.3., 3.2.7.4., 3.2.7.5.,
  3.2.7.10., 3.2.7.11., 10.5.2.1., 10.5.2.2.,
  10.5.2.6., 10.5.2.6.1., 10.5.3.1., 14.4.4.
 purge 12.7.5.
 selection 1.4.10., 10.2.5.: 10.2.5.1. to
  10.2.5.1.4., 10.2.5.2.5.
 shut down transient 2.3.8., 7.4.6.
 single plug blow tank systems, *see* Conveying
  system, innovatory
 size (volume) 10.5.2.2., **10.5.4.1.**, 14.4.3.1.,
  14.5.1., 14.5.2.1., **14.6.3.1.**, 14.6.3.,
  14.6.3.2., Table 14.5.
 stalling 13.4.3.4.
 start up transient 2.3.8., 7.4.6., 10.5.2.6.1.
 twin 1.4.14., 2.3.8., **3.2.7.7.**, 10.2.5.2.5.,
  10.5.4.: 10.5.4.1., **14.4.4.**, 14.5.3.2.,
  Table 14.8., Figures 35, 62
  air requirements 14.5.3.1.3., 14.5.5., Table
   14.10.
  in parallel 10.5.1., 14.6.1., 14.6.2., **14.6.4.**,
   Tables 14.15., 14.17 and 14.18
  in series **3.2.7.11.**, 14.4.2.2.1., Tables
   14.15., 14.17. and 14.18.
  venting air loss 14.4.2.2.1.

Blow tanks (*continued*)
 valves, (*see also* Blow tanks, discharge valve)
  2.3.8., 10.5.3.2., 14.5.4.2., 14.6.3.2.
  setting 10.5.2.2.1., 10.5.2.3., 10.5.2.5.,
  vent line 2.3.8., 10.5.2.1., 10.5.3.2.
  venting 3.2.7.3., 3.2.7.4., 3.2.7.11., 3.3.2.1.,
   10.5.2., 10.5.2.1., **10.5.3.2.**, 12.3.7.2.,
   12.7.5., 13.4.5.4., 14.4.4.
Blow-through valve, *see* Rotary valve
Blower, *see* Air mover
Blower, Roots type, *see* Roots type blower
Blowing seal **2.3.2.**, 10.2.5.2.1.
Bore, *see* Pipeline bore
Boundary layer effect **7.3.1.**
British Standards
 BS 1796 15.2.2.2.
 BS 2955 15.2.2.3.1., 15.5.7
 BS 3406 15.2.2.2.
 BS 4359 **15.5.6.1.**, 15.2.2.3.3.
 BS 4550 **15.5.6.2.**
 BS 5500 14.5.2.1.
Bulk density, *see* Density
Bulk solid (material) 1.4.2., 1.6.1.3., 3.3.3.,
 3.3.3.3., 10.2.7.1., **Chapter 15,** 11.1.5.
 aeration, *see* Aeration
 compaction, (*see also* Material compressibility) 8.3.3., 15.1.3., 15.3.1., 15.5.5.2.,
  Table 15.2.
 pores
  closed **15.3.2.1.**
  open 15.3.2.1.
 properties, *see also* Material, properties,
  Material type 7.4.7., **Chapter 15, Table
  8.1.**
 storage 15.1.2., 15.1.3., 15.2.2.1.1.,
  15.2.2.2.5.
 strength, *see also* Material, strength 15.4.2.4.
 surface area, *see* Specific surface
 transport 15.1.2., 15.1.3.
 volume 15.4.3.2.

Carbon black 10.4.12., 12.7.4.
Carmen–Arnell constant 15.5.6.1.
Carmen and Arnell equation **15.5.6.1.**, 15.5.8.1.
Case studies 1.4.14., 4.4., 5.4.2., 6.2.4., 6.2.6.,
 7.5.6., 10.6.4., **Chapter 11, Chapter 14**,
 Figures 57 to 62, 83 to 87, 88 to 91, 167,
 168, 214, 215, 217, 228, 297 to 307, 308 to
 339
Catalyst 15.2.2.3.3., 15.5.6.1.
Cement 1.4.14., 2.1., 2.2.4., 2.4.2., 2.4.3.,
 2.4.6., 2.4.7., 3.2.7.3., 3.2.7.8., 3.2.7.9.,
 4.3.2.1., 5.3.8., 6.4.3., 7.3.1., 7.3.4., 7.4.4.,
 7.4.5., 7.4.6., 7.5.1., 7.5.2., 7.5.4., 7.5.5.,
 7.5.6., 8.1., 8.2.2., 8.2.3., 8.2.4., 8.3.1.,
 8.3.3., 8.4.1., 8.4.4., 8.4.4.1., 8.5., 9.3.1.,
 9.3.2.1., 9.3.2.4., 9.3.3., 9.3.4., 9.3.5.1.,
 9.3.6.1., 9.3.7., 10.2.5.2.2., 10.5.2.1.,
 10.5.2.1.1., 11.1.5., 11.2.1., 11.2.2.,

Cement (*continued*)
  11.2.2.1., 11.2.2.2., 11.2.3., 11.2.4., 11.2.5.,
  11.4., 12.3.7.1., 13.4.3.2., **Chapter 14**,
  15.5.1., 15.2.2.4., 15.3.5., 15.4.4., 15.5.8.,
  15.5.8.1., 15.5.8.2., 15.5.8.3., 15.2.3.,
  15.5.6.1., 15.5.6.2., Tables 8.1., 14.1., 15.1.
  to 15.4., Figures 38, 42, 43, 57, 58, 82, 97,
  98, 136, 137, 138, 140 to 149, 225 to 228,
  230, 231, 145, 247, 250, 251, 257, 259, 275
  to 281, 283, 288, 303, 307, 309, 310, 318
  bulk density Tables 8.1, 14.1.
  conveying characteristics 143, 145 to 149, 197
    to 205, 297, 298, 304 to 306, 313 to 316,
    319 to 328
Centrifugal (turbo) compressor 3.3.2.2., **6.6.2.**
Characteristic gas constant **1.7.1.**, 5.2.2.7.,
  6.2.3., 6.4.1., 7.2.2.
Chemical processing 12.2.1., 15.5.2.2., 15.5.6.1.
Chemical products 10.4.3., 12.4.2., 13.5.6.
Choice of conveying system, *see* Conveying system, selection
Choked flow nozzles 5.4.3., 7.4.2., 10.2.6.1.1.,
  13.2.2.3.2., 13.3.5.
Choking 1.6.1.10., **1.6.1.14.**, **2.4.3.**, 6.2.6.,
  6.4.3., 11.1.2.
Cleaning
  fabric filters, *see* Filtration unit
Closed conveying systems, *see* Conveying system, closed
Cloud, dust, *see* Dust cloud
Coal 2.4.5., 8.1., 8.3.1., 8.3.3., 8.4.1., 8.4.4.,
  8.4.4.1., 8.5., 9.3.1., 9.3.2.1., 10.4.3.,
  12.3.6.1., 12.3.8.6., 12.6.2., 12.6.3.1.,
  13.5.5., Table 8.1., Figures 221, 222, 227,
  275 to 281, 283, 293
  20 mm Figure 229
  ash, 5 mm Figure 229
  conveying characteristics Figures 221, 222
  degraded 8.1, 8.3.1., 8.3.2., 8.3.3., 8.4.1.,
    8.4.4., 8.4.4.1., **8.4.4.1.1.**, 8.5., 15.1.1,
    15.5.8., Figures 275 to 281, 283, 293
  lump 10.4.3.
  powdered 15.5.2.2.
  pulverised 2.1.
  singles 12.3.6.1., 15.5.1., 15.2.2.4., 15.3.5.,
    15.4.4., 15.5.8., 15.5.8.1., Tables 15.1. to
    15.4.
Coal mines 12.3.1.
Coarse granular materials, (*see also* Granular
  materials; Large particles) 1.4.3., 4.2.1.,
  15.5.1.
Coating
  filter fabrics **3.3.3.3.1.**
  pipeline by conveyed material, *see* Pipeline,
    coating
Cocoa, (*see also* Foodstuffs) 10.4.3., 12.6.2.,
  12.6.3.1., 15.4.1.
Coffee, (*see also* Foodstuffs) 12.6.3.2.
Cohesive materials 2.5.1, 2.5.3., 2.5.4.2., 2.5.5.,
  3.2.3., 3.2.3.4., 3.2.4., 10.2.2.7.,

Cohesive materials (*continued*)
  10.2.5.2.1., 10.2.5.2.2., **10.4.1.**, 13.4.4.3.,
  13.4.4.4., **13.6.3.**, 15.3.3.1.3., 15.4.1.,
  15.4.2.3., 15.4.3.1., 15.4.3.1.1., 15.5.2.1.,
  15.5.4.3., 15.5.4.4., 15.5.5.2.
Coke 12.3.8.6.
Collecting efficiency
  gas–solid separation device, *see* Gas–solid
    separation device; Cyclone separator;
    Fabric filter; Filtration unit; Gravity set-
    tling chamber
Combined negative and positive pressure conveying systems, *see* Conveying system, combined negative and positive pressure
Combustible materials 1.6.1.18., 2.3.5.,
  10.2.2.1., **10.4.3.**
Combustion, fliudised 15.5.2.2.
Combustion potential 12.1
Commissioning trails 13.2.2.2.: 13.2.2.2.1.,
  13.2.2.2.2., 13.2.2.2.3.
Compaction, *see* Bulk solid
Components of conveying system, (*see also* Air
  mover; Feeding device; Gas–solid separation device, individual names of components) 1.4.10., 1.4.11., 1.4.13., Chapter 3,
  6.4.5.: 6.4.5.1. and 6.4.5.2., 6.6.: 6.6.1. to
  6.7., Chapter 10, 11.1.3., 11.1.4., 11.1.5.,
  13.1., 13.2.2.7.4., **13.4.: 13.4.1. to 13.4.5.4.**,
  13.6.9., **Chapter 14**, 15.2.2.3.2., 15.4.1.
  costs, *see* Costs
  faults 13.1.
  over-rated 13.1., 13.2.2.9.1.
  power requirements, *see* Power Requirements
  problems 13.1., **13.4.: 13.4.1. to 13.4.5.4.**
  replacing **11.1.4.**, 13.2.2.4., **13.2.2.7.4.**
  selection **Chapter 10**
  specification 13.1, **13.4, 14.5.: 14.5.1. to
    14.5.5.**
  wear 1.4.13., 13.2.2.8., **13.2.2.8.1.**,
    13.2.2.9.1., 13.4.4.6.
  energy loss 13.2.2.9.1.
Compressed air (gas)
  cooling 6.4.3., 6.4.4., 6.4.5.1., 6.6.1., 6.6.6.
  heating 6.4.4.
  oil free 6.6.5., 14.5.3.2.1., 14.5.3.2.2., Tables
    14.11., 14.12.
  oil removal 6.6.3., 6.6.6., 6.6.7.
  theory and use 1.4.6., **Chapter 6**
Compressibility
  air, *see* Air compressibility
  material, *see* Material compressibility
Compression 1.4.6., **Chapter 6**, 9.2.3.1.,
  13.4.3.2.
  adiabatic **6.4.2.**
  effects
    air humidity **6.4.2.**
    volumetric flow rate **6.3.2.**
  isentropic efficiency 6.3.2., Figure 96
    mathematical model, *see* Mathematical
      models

Compression (*continued*)
  isothermal 4.6.1., 6.3.2., 6.4.2., 6.2.1.1.,
    13.6.5.
  mathematical model, *see* Mathematical
    models
  thermodynamic irreversibility 4.6.1., 5.2.2.13.,
    6.3.2.
  transmission losses 4.6.1., 5.2.2.13., 6.7.,
    10.2.6.1.1.
  work 4.6.1.
Compressor, *see* Air mover
Condensation, (*see also* Water vapour) 6.4.2.,
    6.4.3., 6.4.4., 12.5.3., 13.2.2.3.1., 13.4.3.2.,
    13.5.3., 13.5.7., 15.1.2.
  freezing 12.5.3.
  saturation point 13.4.3.2.
Conducting footwear 12.5.2.
Conducting heat transfer 13.6.9.
Controlled environment, (*see also* Conveying
    system, closed) 2.4.8., 10.2.2.2., 10.4.10.,
    10.4.11.
Conversion factors **1.8.**
Conveying
  dense phase, *see* Dense phase, *see also* Con-
    veying mode
  dilute phase, *see* Dilute phase, *see also* Con-
    veying mode
  medium phase, *see* Medium phase, *see also*
    Conveying mode
  problems 1.4.2., 10.4.1., **Chapter 12, Chapter
    13,** Figure 63
Conveying air (gas), (*see also* Air; Gas; Inert
    gas; Nitrogen; Single-phase flow) 4.2.2.1.,
    12.3.2., 13.2.2.4., 13.2.2.9.1., 13.3.1.1.,
    13.4.3.3.
  density, *see* Density
  expansion 4.5.2., 6.2.2., 6.2.6., 6.3.1., 8.2.2.,
    12.2.3.,
  heating 10.4.2., 13.6.10.
  humidification 10.4.4.
  pressure 1.6.1.1., 6.1.2., **6.2.: 6.2.1. to 6.2.6.**,
    7.2.2., 7.3.4., 10.2.7.2.2., 12.2.2.2.,
    13.2.2.2.2., Figures 85 to 91, 299
  recirculation 10.2.2.2.
  temperature, *see* Temperature
  velocity, (*see also* Free air velocity) 1.4.3.,
    1.4.6., 1.6.1.3., 1.6.1.8., 1.6.1.11.,
    1.6.1.13., 2.2.5., 2.2.6.1., 2.4.5., 2.4.7.,
    2.5.4.2., 3.2.2., 3.2.3.1., 3.3.2.3.,
    3.3.3.1., 4.2.1., 4.2.2., **4.3.2.2.**, 4.5.2.,
    4.6.3.2., 6.1.1., 6.1.2., **6.1.3.**, 6.1.5.,
    6.1.6., 6.2., **6.2.4.**, **6.2.5.: 6.2.5.1.**, 6.2.6.,
    6.8., 7.2.1., **7.2.2.**, 7.3.1., 7.3.2., 7.3.4.,
    7.3.5., 7.4.3., 7.4.4., 7.5., **7.5.1.**, 7.5.3.,
    7.5.6., 8.2.2., 9.2.1., **9.2.2.1.**, 9.2.3.1.,
    9.2.3.1.1., 9.3.4.3., 9.3.5.1., 9.3.7.,
    10.2.6.1.2., 10.5.2.1.1., 11.1.2., 11.1.3.,
    11.2.1., 11.2.2.1., 11.3.2., 11.3.3.,
    12.2.3., **12.3.6.3.**, 12.3.7.1., 12.3.7.3.,
    12.3.8.4., 12.7.2., 12.7.3., 12.7.4., 13.1.,
    13.2.2.2.1., 13.2.2.2.2., 13.2.2.3.2.,

Conveying air (*continued*)
  velocity (*continued*)
    13.2.2.8.2., 13.3.4., 13.4.5.1., 13.5.5.,
    13.5.7., 13.6.2., 13.6.7., 13.6.9., 14.2.1.,
    14.3.4.5., 14.3.5.2., 14.4.2.1., Figures 81
    to 84, 88 to 91, 270, 271, 299, 300
  entrainment 1.6.1.11., 1.6.1.19., 3.2.5., 6.5.
  high 2.4.5., 2.4.6., 6.1.3., 7.3.2., 7.3.5.,
    11.1.2., 11.2.2.1., 12.2.3., 12.3.6.3,
    12.3.8.4, 12.7.3., 12.7.4., 13.1., 13.3.4.,
    13.4.5.1., 13.5.5., 13.6.2., 13.6.7.
  increasing 2.4.7., 12.3.8.4., 13.2.2.8.2.
  low 4.2.1., 6.1.3., 12.2.3., 13.2.2.3.2.
  mathematical model, *see* Mathematical
    models
  maximum 6.2.6., 7.2.2., 9.3.5.1.
  minimum **1.6.1.10**, 1.6.1.11., 1.6.1.13.,
    2.2.6.1., 2.2.6.2., **2.4.2.**, 2.4.3., 2.4.6.,
    4.2.2.3., 4.3.2., 4.3.2.1., 4.3.3., 4.4.,
    5.1., 5.2.2.1., 5.2.2.6., 5.2.2.9.,
    5.3.2.3., 5.3.5., 5.3.7., 5.3.8., 5.4.2,
    5.4.6., 6.2.6., 7.1., 7.2.2., **7.3.4.**,
    7.5.3., 7.5.6., 8.2.1., 8.2.3., 8.4.1.,
    8.4.3., 8.4.4.1., 8.4.4.1.1., 9.2.3.,
    9.3.4.3., 9.3.5.1., 11.1.3., 11.2.3.,
    11.2.5., 11.3.3., 11.4., 12.3.7.1.,
    12.7.2., 13.2.2.2.1., 13.2.2.5., 14.2.1.,
    14.2.2., 14.3.3., Figures 139, 140, 141,
    275, 277, 303, 309
  optimum 6.2.6., 7.1.
Conveying, batch, *see* Conveying system, batch
Conveying capability, (*see also* Conveying
    potential) 1.3., 1.4.2., **2.2.: 2.2.1. to
    2.2.6.2.**, 4.3.1, **4.3.2.3**, **4.5.3.**, 5.2.3.,
    5.2.4., 7.1., 8.1., 8.2.4., **8.4.: 8.4.1 to
    8.4.4.1.3.**, **8.5.: 8.5.1. to 8.5.4.1.**,
    10.2.5.2.3., 10.3.5., 12.4.4., 13.2.2.7.1.,
    14.3.2., Figures 64, 66, 68
Conveying capacity
  pipeline **4.5.3.**, 7.3.2., 8.2.1., 10.4.12.,
    12.7.4., 13.4.3.3.
  plant 1.3., **5.2.3.**, **5.3.3.**, 12.3.8.1.
  potential 6.1.
Conveying characteristics 1.1., 1.2., **1.4.7.**,
    1.4.8., 1.4.15., 1.5.1., 3.2.7.8., 3.2.7.9.,
    4.3.3., 4.3.4., 4.6.2., 5.3.1., **5.3.2.3.**,
    5.3.2.4., 5.3.2.5., 5.3.2.6., 5.3.2.7., **5.3.3.2.**,
    5.3.3.3., 5.3.3.4., 5.3.3.5., 5.3.4., 5.3.5.,
    5.3.6., 5.3.8., 5.4.1., 5.4.2., **Chapter 7**,
    8.1., 8.2.1., 8.3.1., 8.3.2., 8.3.3., 8.3.4.,
    8.5.1., 9.1., 9.2.4., 9.3.1., 9.3.2.1., 9.3.2.4.,
    9.3.3., 9.3.4., 9.3.4.1., 9.3.5., 9.3.6.,
    9.3.6.1., 9.3.7., 9.3.8., 10.3.4., 11.1.1.,
    11.1.2., 11.1.5., 11.2.: 11.2.1. to 11.2.6.,
    11.3.2., 11.4., 11.5., **14.2.1.**, 14.2.2.,
    14.3.1., 14.3.2., 14.3.3., 14.3.4., 14.3.4.4.,
    14.3.4.5., 14.3.5., 14.3.5.1., 14.3.5.2.,
    14.3.5.3., 14.3.6., 14.4.1., 14.4.2., 14.4.2.1.,
    14.5.1., 14.5.3.1., 14.7., 15.1.1., 15.4.4.,
    A.4.,
  barytes Figures 187 to 196

Conveying characteristics (*continued*)
  bentonite Figure 216, 217
  cement Figures 143, 145 to 149, 197 to 205,
    297, 298, 304, 305, 306, 313 to 316, 319
    to 328
  coal Figures 221, 222
  computer analysis **7.5.4.**
  determination Chapter 7, **7.4.: 7.4.1. to 7.4.7.**
  flour Figure 218
  fluorspar Figure 206
  material type A Figures 150, 151, 152, 253,
    155, 157, 159, 161, 163, 165
  material type B Figures 150, 151, 152, 154,
    156, 158, 160, 162, 164, 166
  pearlite Figure 219
  p.f. ash Figures 207 to 210
  polyethylene pellets Figure 220
  pvc Figure 215
  sand Figures 211 to 214
  scaling, *see* Scaling
  steady state **7.4.6.**
  sugar, granulated
    as supplied Figure 223
    degraded Figure 224
  untypical use 5.3.5., **7.5.: 7.5.1 to 7.5.6.**,
    11.4., Figure 171
Conveying conditions 1.2., 1.4.4., **4.2.2.:**
  4.2.2.1. to 4.2.2.3., 4.3.1., 4.3.5., 5.2.4.,
  5.3.2.3., 5.3.4., 5.3.6., 5.3.8., 7.4.3., **7.4.5.**,
  7.4.6., 7.5.1., 7.5.5., 7.5.6., 8.1., 9.1.,
  9.3.1., 9.3.2.2., 9.3.2.3., 9.3.2.4., 9.3.3.,
  9.3.4., 9.3.5.1., 9.3.8., 11.1.1., **11.1.2.**,
  11.2.2.2., 11.3.2., 14.2.1., 14.3.4.2.,
  14.3.4.4., Figures 249, 252, 256
  minimum 1.4.7., 4.3.3., Chapter 7, **7.4.5.**,
    8.2.1., 8.2.3., 9.3.6.1., 14.2.2., Figures
    138 to 141, 303, 309
  optimum 1.2., 1.5.3., 7.3.6., 7.5.5., 11.3.,
    13.6.8.
Conveying, continuous, *see* Conveying system,
  continuously operating
Conveying cycle, *see* Conveying system, batch
Conveying distance 1.2., 1.3., 1.4.2., 1.4.4.,
  1.4.5., 1.4.6., 1.4.7., 1.4.9., 2.2.1., **2.2.4.**,
  2.2.5., 2.3.1., 2.3.2., 2.3.5., 2.3.7., 3.2.5.,
  3.2.7.1., **3.2.7.9.**, 4.1., 4.2.2.3., 4.2.3.,
  4.2.3.1., 4.3.1., 4.3.2.1., 4.3.3., **4.3.4.:**
  4.3.4.1 to 4.3.4.3., 4.4., 4.5.2., 4.5.3.,
  4.6.2., 4.6.3., 4.7.1., 4.7.2., 5.1., **5.2.2.3.**,
  5.2.2.13., **5.3.2.2.**, 5.3.2.3., **5.3.2.4.**,
  5.3.2.5., 5.3.3.1., 5.3.3.3., 5.3.4., **5.3.5.**,
  5.3.6., 5.3.7., 5.3.8., 5.4.1., 5.4.5., 5.4.6.,
  6.2.6., 6.6.1., 7.1., 7.2.1., 7.3.1., 7.4.1.,
  7.5.4., **7.5.5.**, 8.1., 8.3.1., 9.1., 9.2.1.,
  9.2.3.1.2., 9.2.3.1.3., 9.3.2., **9.3.2.1.**,
  9.3.2.4., **9.3.4.**, 10.1., 10.2.2.5., 10.2.2.6.,
  10.2.3., 10.2.6.2.1., 10.3.6., **10.5.2.4.**,
  11.1.2., 12.2.2.4, 13.1., 13.4.3.1., 13.4.4.2.,
  14.1.1., 14.1.2., 14.2.1., 14.2.2., **14.3.4.**,
  14.3.4.3., 14.3.4.5., 14.4.3.2., 14.7.,
  Figures 3, 64, 99, 100, 101 to 104, 105, 106,

Conveying distance (*continued*)
  107, 108 to 115, 116, 117, 118, 245, 250, 251
  change 1.4.5., 1.4.7., 1.4.9., 4.2.2.3., 4.3.1.,
    4.3.3., **4.3.4.: 4.3.4.1 to 4.3.4.3.**, 4.5.2.,
    4.5.3., **4.6.2.**, 4.7.1., 5.1., 5.3.2.3., **5.3.5.**,
    5.3.7., 5.4.1., 5.4.6., **7.5.5.**, 8.1.,
    10.2.6.2.1., 13.1., 13.2.2.2., **13.2.2.6.**,
    13.4.4.2, Tables 3.3., 3.4, Figures 101 to
    104, 108 to 115, 116, 122 to 133, 145, 149
  cement 7.5.5., 14.2.2., Figures 145, 149,
    311, 313, 315, 316
  increasing 2.2.4, **4.6.2.** 5.4.6., 7.5.5., Figures
    116, 145, 149
  long 2.2.5., 2.3.2., 2.3.5., 2.3.7., 3.2.7.,
    4.2.3.1., 4.2.3.2., 4.3.4.2., 4.3.4.3.,
    4.5.2., 6.2.6., 6.6.1., 9.1., 9.2.1.,
    9.2.3.1.2., 9.2.3.1.3., 10.2.5.2.5., 10.2.3.,
    10.5.3.6., 13.4.3., 13.4.3.1.
  medium 2.3.1., 3.2.7.
  multiple 1.4.5., 1.5.3., 4.3.4.1., 5.1., 5.4.5.,
    10.2.2.5., 10.2.6.2.1., **10.3.5.**
  pressure drop, conveying line **4.3.3., 4.3.4.3.**,
    4.5.2., 4.7.1., 5.3.5., 7.3.1., 7.5.5.,
    9.2.3.1.2., 14.3.4.4., Figures 105 to 107,
    145, 149, 312
  scaling, *see* Scaling
  short 2.2.5., 2.3.1., 2.3.2., 3.2.5., 3.2.7.,
    4.3.2.1., 4.3.4.3., 6.6.2., 7.3.3., 10.3.6.,
    13.4.3.1.
Conveying, dual negative and positive pressure
  systems, *see* Conveying system, dual negative and positive pressure
Conveying duty 1.4.14., 4.5.2., 10.2.6.2.3.,
  13.1., Chapter 14, 14.1.3.
  unable to meet 13.2.1., **13.2.2.7.: 13.2.2.7.1.**
    to 13.2.2.7.4.
Conveying gas, *see* Air; Conveying air; Gas;
  Inert gas; Nitrogen
Conveying, high pressure dense phase *see* Conveying system, high pressure, *see also*
  Dense phase
Conveying, high velocity dilute phase, *see* Dilute
  phase
Conveying, horizontal, *see* Two-phase flow, *see*
  also Pipeline length, Scaling
Conveying limits 1.2., 2.2.6.2., 2.4.3., 2.4.6.,
  7.3.2., 7.4.5., 7.5.5., 7.5.6., 8.2.1., 8.2.2.,
  8.2.3., 11.2.3., 11.2.2.2., **14.3.4.5.**,
  14.3.5.3., Chapter 5, Chapter 11, Figures
  98, 228
  minimum 9.3.4.2., 14.3.4.5., 14.3.5.3.
Conveying line, *see also* Conveying system;
  Pipeline
  blockage, *see* Blockage
  characteristics
  design, *see* Conveying system design
    case study **11.2.: 11.2.1. to 11.2.6.**
  discharge (delivery) 1.4.2., **1.4.3.**, 1.5.1.,
    2.5.2., **Chapter 3**, 5.2.2.2., 10.2.5.1.4.
  multiple discharge points 1.4.5., 1.5.3.,
    4.3.4.1., 4.4., 5.1., 5.4.1., **5.4.5.**,

Conveying line (*continued*)
  discharge (*continued*)
    multiple discharge points (*continued*)
      7.5.5., 10.2.2.3., 10.2.2.5., 10.2.6.2.1.,
      10.3.2., **10.3.3.**, **10.3.5.**, **13.3.2.1.**
  exit (outlet) 6.2., 6.2.2., 6.2.4.
  air pressure 5.2.2.13., 14.4.2.1.
  air velocity **1.6.1.12.**, 4.5.2., 6.1.2., 6.1.3.,
    6.1.5., 6.2.5.1., 6.2.6., 6.7., 11.2.1.,
    11.2.2., 11.2.2.1., 11.2.2.2., 11.5.,
    12.4.3., 12.7.5., 14.4.2.1., Table 14.2.,
    Figures 81, 82, 235, 236
  feed (pick-up), (*see also* Feeding device; indi-
    vidual names of feeding devices) 1.4.2,
    1.4.3., 1.5.1., **2.3.2.**, 2.4.3., **Chapter 3**,
    5.2.2.2., 5.2.2.13., 5.2.2.16., 5.3.3.4.,
    6.1.1., 7.4.6., 7.5., 10.2.2.6., 10.2.4.,
    10.2.5., 10.2.5.1.2., 10.2.5.1.4., **10.3.1.**,
    10.3.3., 10.4.1., 10.4.7., 11.3.3., **11.5.**,
    13.2.2.7.1., 13.4.3., 13.6.4., 13.6.10.,
    Table 13.1
    case study **11.5.**
    feed points 1.4.6., 6.2.2., 6.2.4., 6.2.5.1.,
      9.2.2.1., 9.2.2.3., 10.2.2.3., 10.2.2.4.,
      10.2.2.5., 11.3.3., 13.2.2.2.1.,
      13.2.2.2.2., 13.6.9.
    air velocity 13.4.3.4.
    overfeeding 13.2.2.2.2.
    multiple feed points 4.4., 5.4.2., **10.3.1.**,
      10.3.3., **10.3.4.**, **13.3.1.1.**
    energy loss 10.3.1.
    problems **13.4.4.3.**
    rate **3.2.2.5.**, 3.2.4., 3.2.6., 5.2.2.13.,
      5.4.4., 6.6.2., 11.1.4., 11.2.6., 11.3.2.,
      11.4., 13.1., **13.2.2.2.2.**, 13.4.4.2.,
      15.3.3.3.
      fluctuations, *see also* Surge 10.2.6.1.1.,
        11.5., **13.2.2.2.3.**
      surge, *see* Surge
      underfeeding 13.2.2.2.2.
    inlet 3.2.8., 6.2., 6.2.2., 6.2.4., 6.2.6.
      annular gap (negative pressure systems)
        3.2.8.
      primary air 3.2.8.
      secondary air 3.2.8.
    inlet air pressure 5.2.2.13., 11.2.2., 14.4.2.1.,
      14.5.2.2., 14.5.2.3., Tables 14.1. and
      14.6.
    inlet air velocity (entrainment velocity, pick-
      up velocity) 1.4.6., 1.6.1.2., **1.6.1.11.**,
      2.4.6., 3.2.2., 3.2.5., 3.2.8., 3.3.3.2., 3.3..
      4.3.2.2., 4.3.4.1., 4.5.2., 4.6.2., 4.6.3.1.,
      5.2.2.6., 5.2.2.7., **5.2.2.9.**, **5.2.3.5.**,
      5.2.3.8., **5.2.3.12.**, 5.2.3.13., 5.3.5.,
      5.3.8., 6.1.2., 6.1.3., 6.1.5., 6.2.4.,
      6.2.5.1., 7.4.5., 7.4.6., 7.5.1., 7.5.2.,
      7.5.5., 7.5.6., 8.2.2., 8.2.4., 9.2.3.1.6.,
      9.3.4.2., 10.2.5.2.4., 10.2.6.1.2.,
      11.2.2.1., 11.2.2.2., 11.2.5., 11.5.,
      12.3.7., 12.3.7.3., 12.7.5., 13.2.2.2.1.,
      13.2.2.2.2., 13.2.2.6., 14.3.3., 14.3.4.1.,

Conveying line (*continued*)
  inlet air velocity (*continued*)
    14.3.4.3., 14.3.4.5., 14.4.2.1., 14.5.3.1.2.,
    Table 14.2., Figures 81, 82, 98, 138, 231,
    310, 311
  lines of constant 14.3.4., Figure 146
  outlet, *see* Conveying line exit
  pressure drop, *see* Pressure drop
Conveying, low pressure, dilute phase, *see* Conveying system, low pressure, *see also* Dilute
  phase
Conveying, low velocity dense phase, *see* Dense
  phase
Conveying material through pipeline, *see* Two-
  phase flow, *see also* Material mass flow rate
Conveying mode, *see also* Dense phase; Dilute
  phase; Medium phase 1.4.8., **2.2.6.: 2.2.6.1.
  to 2.2.6.2.**, Chapter 8, 10.5.2.1.1., 11.1.5.,
  14.2.1., Figures 3, 64, 275, 276, 277
Conveying, open surface **10.3.6.**
Conveying parameters 5.2.2.: 5.2.2.1. to
  5.2.2.16., 5.2.3.9.
  combinations 1.3., **4.5.2.**, 4.7.2.
Conveying performance 1.4.8., 1.4.10., 1.5.1.,
  3.2.3.1., 4.2.3.3., 4.3.5., 4.4., 7.1., **Chapter
  8**, 9.3.2.1., **Chapter 11**, 13.1., 13.2.2.2.,
  13.2.2.9., 15.5.7., Tables 3.2. and 3.3.,
  Figures 167 to 170
Conveying potential, *see also* Conveying capability 4.2.2., 4.3.2.2., 4.3.3., 4.4., 4.5.1.,
  5.2.2.1., 5.2.3.10., 5.3.4., 5.3.6., 6.1.,
  7.5.6., 8.2.4., 8.5.1., 10.2.2.5., 11.1.2.,
  11.2.6., 14.3.3.
Conveying rate, *see* Material mass flow rate
Conveying system 1.4.2., 1.4.4., **Chapter 2**, 3.1.,
  4.2.2.1., 5.1., Chapter 10, **13.3.: 13.3.1. to
  13.3.5.**, **14.4.: 14.4.1. to 14.4.4.**, **14.6.:
  14.6.1. to 14.6.5.**, 14.7., 15.4.1., Figures 1,
  2, 3
  batch, (*see also* Material mass flow rate)
    1.4.3., 1.4.14., 2.3.7., **2.3.8.**, 2.5.2.,
    2.5.3., 3.2.1., 3.2.7.2., 3.2.7.3., 3.2.7.4.,
    3.2.7.7., 3.2.9., 3.3.2.1., 3.3.3.3.2.,
    4.2.2.2., 4.6.3.1., 5.3.2.1., **7.4.6.**, **10.2.4.**,
    10.2.5., 10.2.5.2.5., **10.2.7.2.2.**, 10.3.6.,
    10.5.: 10.5.1. to 10.5.4.1., 11.3.2.,
    13.4.3.2., 14.1.1., 14.5.5., 14.6.2.,
    14.6.2.1., Tables 14.18 and 14.20
    blowing cycles 10.5.2.1., **10.5.2.1.1.**,
      10.5.2.2., 10.5.3.3., 7.4.6.
    time 10.5.2.2., 10.5.2.2.1., Figure 40
    conveying cycles **2.3.8.**, 3.2.7.3., 3.2.7.4.,
      7.4.6., 10.2.5.2.5., 10.2.7.2.2., 10.5.:
      10.5.1. to 10.5.4.1., 12.3.7.2.,
      13.2.2.8.2., **13.4.5.4.**, 14.4.3.2.,
      14.4.3.3., Figures 29, 38 to 42
    analysis 1.4.10., **10.5.: 10.5.1. to 10.5.4.1.**
    frequency 14.6.3.2.
    sequencing 3.2.7.7., 10.5.4., 10.5.4.1.,
      14.4.4., Figure 37
    innovatory systems 2.5.2., 2.5.3.

Conveying system (*continued*)
  batch (*continued*)
    twin blow tanks
      conveying cycle frequency 14.4.4.
  case studies Chapter 11, **Chapter 14**
  closed 1.6.1.15., **2.4.8.**, 7.5.1., 7.5.5.,
    9.2.3.1.2., 9.2.3.1.3., 9.3.4.3., 9.3.5.,
    10.1., 10.2.2., 10.2.2.1., **10.2.2.2.**,
    10.2.2.4., 10.3.5.2.2., 10.4.3., 10.4.10.,
  closed loop, *see* Conveying system, closed
  combined negative and positive pressure
    2.3.6., 6.2.2., 6.2.5.1., 6.3.3., 6.6.2.,
    10.1., **10.2.2.5.**, **10.2.6.2.5.**, 10.3.3.,
    10.3.6., 11.3.2., 13.2.2.8.1., **13.3.3.**,
    13.3.3.1., 13.4.2., Figures 8, 88, 89
    operating pressure 13.3.3.1.
    power requirements, *see* Power require-
      ments
    system inbalance **13.3.3.1.**
  commissioning **13.2.2.2.: 13.2.2.2.1. to
    13.2.2.2.3.**
    problems, *see* Conveying problems
  comparison 1.3., **14.6.: 14.6.1. to 14.6.5.**
  components, *see* Components of conveying
    system
  considerations **3.2.2.: 3.3.2.1. to 3.3.2.5.**,
    4.6.2.1., 7.1., **10.2.7.2.: 10.2.7.2.1. to
    10.2.7.2.2.**
  continuously operating **3.2.2.**, 3.2.7.2.,
    3.3.3.3.2., 4.6.3.1., 5.2.2.2., 5.2.2.11.,
    5.2.2.12., 5.3.2.1., 10.2.2.2., 10.2.4.,
    10.2.5., 10.2.7.2.1., 14.1.1., 14.3.6.,
    14.4.2., 14.5.3.1., **14.5.3.1.1.**, 14.5.3.1.2.,
    14.5.3.2., 14.6.1., 14.6.2., Tables 14.2.,
    14.8., 14.17. and 14.19., Figures 5, 46,
    57, 59
    blow tanks **3.2.7.11.**, 10.2.5., 10.2.5.2.5.,
      14.5.3.1.1., 14.5.3.2., 14.6.1., 14.6.2.,
      Tables 14.8., 14.17. and 14.19., Figure
      36
  control 1.5.3., **7.4.2.**, 7.4.3., 11.3.1., **11.3.2.**,
    13.1.
  design 1.1., **1.2.**, 1.3., **1.4.5.**, 1.4.7., 1.4.8.,
    1.4.9., 1.4.10., **1.5.2.**, **4.5.: 4.5.1. to
    4.5.3.**, **Chapter 5**, 6.1., 6.1.5., **6.2.3.**,
    7.1., 7.3.6., 7.4.5., 7.4.6., 7.5., 7.5.4.,
    7.5.5., 7.5.6., 8.2.1., 8.2.2., 8.2.3., 8.2.4.,
    8.3.1., 8.5.1., **Chapter 9, Chapter 10**,
    12.2.3., 12.6.3.2., 13.1., 13.2.2.2.,
    13.2.2.2.2., 13.2.2.5., 13.2.2.7.,
    13.2.2.7.1., 13.2.2.8.2., **Chapter 14**,
    15.1.3., 15.2.2.3.2., **15.3.3.2.**, 15.4.3.2.,
    15.4.4., Figures 64, 65, 67
    blow tanks 7.4.6.
    case study **Chapter 14**, Figures 57 to 62, 308
      to 339
    curves **4.5.: 4.5.1. to 4.5.3.**, 5.3.7., **8.2.2.** to
      8.2.4., 8.3.2.
    data, *see* Conveying characteristics; Test
      data
    mathematical model, *see* Mathematical
      models

Conveying system (*continued*)
  design (*continued*)
    parameters **1.2.**, 4.7.1., 5.1., 5.3.7., 7.1.
    procedures **Chapter 5**
    dual negative and positive pressure **10.2.2.6.**,
      10.3.3., 10.6.
    economic assessment, *see* Costs
    energy loss 10.2.5.1.3.
    high pressure 1.4.6., **1.6.1.6.**, 2.2.5., **2.3.7.**,
      2.4.7., 2.5.1., 2.5.2., 3.2.7.1., 4.5.2.,
      4.6.3.1., 5.4.3., 6.1.3., 6.2.1.1., 6.2.6.,
      6.3.3., 6.6.1., 6.6.3., 6.6.6., 6.6.7., 7.4.4.,
      10.1., 10.2.4., 10.2.5., 10.2.5.2.5.,
      10.2.6.2.2., 12.3.7.2., 12.3.7.3., 13.3.5.1.,
      14.1.1., 14.3.3., **14.4.2.2.1.**, 14.4.3.1.,
      Figures 86, 99, 230, 231
    innovatory 1.4.2., **2.5.: 2.5.1. to 2.5.5.**, 10.1.,
      10.2.2.7., 10.3.7., 10.4.1., 10.4.3.,
      10.4.12.
    plug control systems **2.5.4.: 3.5.4.1. to
      2.5.4.2.**, Figure 47
    pulse phase systems 1.4.2., **2.5.3.**, 2.5.3.1.,
      2.5.4.2., 3.2.1., **3.2.9.**, 4.1., 4.6.2.1.,
      4.7.3., 10.2.2.7., 10.4.1., 12.2.3.,
      12.3.7.1., Figures 44, 45, 46
    single plug blow tank systems 1.4.2., **2.5.2.**,
      2.5.4.2., **3.2.7.10.**, 4.1., 10.2.2.7.,
      10.4.3., 12.3.7.2., **13.3.5.: 13.3.5.1.**,
      Figures 28, 29
    surge, 2.5.2
  intermittently operating 13.3.2.
  low pressure **1.6.1.4.**, 1.6.1.6., 2.2.5., 2.3.7.,
    3.2.1., **3.2.2.**, 3.2.7.1., 4.6.3.2., 4.7.2.,
    5.2.2.5., 5.2.2.12., 5.3.2.5., 5.4.3., 6.2.1.,
    6.2.4., 6.3.2., 6.6.2., 6.6.4., 6.6.5.,
    9.3.2.3., 10.1., 10.2.5.2.5., 10.2.5.6.3.,
    10.2.7.1.4., 11.1.1., 11.1.5., 13.4.4.1.,
    14.1.1., 14.3.6., 14.4.1., **14.4.2.2.3.**,
    14.4.3.1., 14.5.3.2.3., Figures 85, 100, 229
  medium pressure **1.6.1.5.**, 3.2.7.1, 6.2.1.1.,
    6.6.3., 6.6.6., 6.6.7., 10.2.5., **14.4.2.2.2.**
  modifying **11.1.3.**, 11.1.4.
  multiple use 1.4.5., **5.4.: 5.4.1. to 5.4.6.**,
    10.2.6.2.1.
  multiple delivery points, *see* Conveying line
    discharge
  multiple material handling, *see* Multiple
    material handling
  multiple pick-up points, *see* Conveying line
    feed
  negative pressure 1.4.6., 1.6.1.1., **1.6.1.4.**,
    1.6.1.11., 2.2.5., **2.3.5.**, 2.3.6., 2.4.8.,
    3.1., 3.2.1., 3.2.3.5., 3.2.4., 3.2.8.,
    3.3.2.2., 4.3.4.3., 5.2.2.5., 5.4.3., 6.1.1.,
    6.1.2., 6.2.1.1., 6.2.2., 6.2.4., 6.2.5.1.,
    6.3.3., 6.6.2., 6.6.5., 10.1., **10.2.2.4.**,
    10.2.2.5., 10.2.5.1.2., 10.2.5.2.1.,
    10.2.5.2.2., 10.2.5.2.4., **10.2.6.2.4.**,
    10.2.7.2.1., 10.3.1, 10.3.6., 10.4.10.,
    10.4.11., 11.1.4., 11.3.2., 12.6.2.,
    13.2.2.2.2., 13.2.2.8.1., 13.2.2.8.2.,

Conveying system (*continued*)
  negative pressure (*continued*)
    13.3.2.: 13.3.2.1. to 13.3.2.2., 13.4.2.,
      13.4.5.2., 13.4.5.3., Figures 7, 14, 49, 87
  open 10.1., 10.2.2., **10.2.2.1.**, 10.4.3.
  open surface **10.3.6.**
  operating conditions 13.1., 15.4.1.
  optimising **1.4.11., Chapter 11**, 13.2.2.7. to
    13.2.2.7.4., 14.7.
  overrated 10.2.2., 13.1., 13.2.2.9.1.
  plug (*see also* Conveying system, innovatory)
    2.2.6.2., 2.5.3., 2.5.3.1., Figures 45, 46
  positive pressure 1.4.3., 1.4.6., 1.6.1.12.,
    2.3.1., 2.3.4., 2.3.5., 2.3.6., 2.4.3., 3.1.,
    3.2.1., 3.2.2., 3.2.3.5., 3.2.4., 3.2.6.,
    6.1.1., 6.1.2., 6.2.5.1., 6.6.2., 9.2.3.1.6.,
    10.1., **10.2.2.3.**, 10.2.2.4., 10.2.5.,
    10.2.5.1.2., 10.2.5.2.1., 10.2.5.2.2.,
    10.2.5.2.4., 10.2.6., **10.2.6.2.3.**,
    10.2.7.1.2., 10.3.1., 10.3.2., 11.1.4.,
    11.1.5., 11.2.1., 12.3.7.2., 12.6.2.,
    13.2.2.2.2., 13.2.2.8.2., **13.3.1., 13.3.1.1.**,
    13.4.4.1., 13.4.5.2., 13.4.5.3., Figures 4,
    5, 6, 10, 90, 91
  requirements 1.4.10., **10.3.: 10.3.1. to 10.3.7.**
  selection 1.3., **1.4.4.**, 1.4.10., **1.5.1., 2.4.:**
    2.4.1. to 2.4.8., 2.5.1., **Chapter 4**, 7.5.4.,
    Chapter 10, Chapter 14, 15.2.2.3.2.
    considerations **2.4.: 2.4.1 to 2.4.8., 4.7.:**
      4.7.1. to 4.7.3.
  shut down 7.4.6., 12.6.3.2., 13.2.2.3.3.,
    13.5.6.
    explosion risk 12.6.3.2.
  start up 7.4.6., **10.3.7.**, 10.5.2.6.1, 12.6.3.2.,
    13.2.2.3.: 13.2.2.3.1. to 13.2.2.3.3.,
    13.4.3.2., 13.5.6.
  uprating 1.1., 1.2., 1.4.11., 1.5.3., 7.1., **Chap-
    ter 11**, 14.7., Figure 69
Conveying trials (*see also* Conveying characteristics; Test data; Test pipeline) 1.2., 1.3.,
  1.4.8., 1.4.9., 1.4.15., 5.1., 5.3.1., 5.3.2.3.,
  5.3.4., 5.3.8., 7.4.: 7.4.1. to 7.4.7., 7.5.5.,
  7.5.6., **Chapter 8**, 9.1., 9.3.1., 9.3.2.1.,
  9.3.5.2., 9.3.5.1., 9.3.6.1., 9.3.7.,
  10.5.2.1.1., 11.1.2., 11.3.2., 11.3.3.,
  12.3.6.2., 12.6.3., **14.2.: 14.2.1. to 14.2.2.**,
  14.7
Conveying unit, mobile 10.3.6
Conveying velocity 3.2.2.4., 3.3.3.1., 4.6.2.,
  4.7.3., 6.1.5., 7.3., 10.4.5., 10.4.6., 11.3.3.,
  12.3.7.1., 13.4.3.4., 14.3.3.
Conveying, vertical, (*see also* Pipeline length)
  1.6.1.14., 2.4.3., 2.4.7., 9.1., Figures 253 to
  256
  pressure drop, *see* Pressure drop
  scaling, *see* Scaling
  equivalent length, *see* Scaling
Conveyor, air-assisted gravity, *see* Air-assisted
  gravity conveyor
Correlation studies 1.4.8., 1.4.15., 5.1., 5.3.1.,
  5.3.8., Chapter 8, 9.3.3., 9.3.5.2., 15.1.1.,

Costs Chapter 10, **Chapter 14**,
  air quality, 2.4.8.
  capital 1.4.2., 1.4.10., 1.4.14., 4.1., 4.7.2.,
    4.7.3., 6.1., 10.1., 10.2.2.1., **10.6.: 10.6.1.
    to 10.6.4.**, 14.5.1., 14.6.3.: 14.6.3.1. to
    14.6.3.2., 14.6.4., 14.7., Figures 334, 335,
    337, 339
  air-assisted gravity conveyor 2.5.5.
  air drying equipment 6.4.5.1.
  air movers 10.2.6.2., **14.5.3.2.: 14.5.3.2.1.
    to 14.5.3.2.3.**, 14.6.2.2., Tables 14.11.
    to 14.13., 14.17., 14.18., Figure 335
    reciprocating compressors **14.5.3.2.1.**,
      Tables 14.11., 14.17., 14.18
    roots type blower **14.5.3.2.3.**, Tables
      14.13., 14.17., 14.18
    screw compressor **14.5.3.2.2.**, Tables
      14.12., 14.17., 14.18
  conveying line feed
    multiple feed points 10.3.1
  conveying systems, innovatory 10.2.2.7.
  feeding device **14.5.2.: 14.5.2.1. to
    14.5.2.3.**, Tables 14.5. to 14.7., Figure
    335
    blow tanks 2.3.7., 3.2.7.1., 3.2.7.3.,
      3.2.7.7., 10.5.2.2.1., **14.5.2.1.**,
      14.6.3.: 14.6.3.1. to 14.6.3.2., Tables
      14.5., 14.17., 14.18., Figure 337
      control 10.5.2.6.3.
      twin 14.6.4, Table 14.17., Figure 339
    gate lock valve 10.2.5.2.4.
    rotary valve 14.5.1., **14.5.2.3.**, Tables
      14.7., 14.17.
    screw feeder **14.5.2.2.**, Tables 14.6.,
      14.17
    venturi feeder 10.2.5.2.3.
  gas–solid separation device 3.3.2.3., 3.3.3.,
    3.3.3.2., 3.3.3.3., 10.2.7.1., **14.5.5.**,
    Table 14.16.
    filtration unit 12.2.1., **14.5.5.**, Table
      14.16., Figure 335
  oil removal 6.6.6.
  pipeline and valves **14.5.4.: 14.5.4.1. to
    14.5.4.4.**, 14.6.2., Tables 14.14.,
    14.17., 14.18., Figures 335
    bends 14.4.5.2., Table 14.14
    control valves 14.4.5.3., Table 14.14.
    diverter valves 14.5.4.4., Table 14.14.
  pipeline bore **14.6.2.: 14.6.2.1. to
    14.6.2.2.**, Tables 14.14., 14.17.,
    14.18., Figure 334
  plant air 10.2.6.2.2.
  commissioning 14.6.5., 14.7.
  comparison 1.4.6., **Chapter 14**, Figures 334,
    335, 337, 339
  construction 10.6.2., 14.5.1., 14.6.2.2.,
    14.6.5., 14.7.
  economic assessment, **14.6.5.**
    blow tanks 14.6.5.
    screw feeders 14.6.5.
  erosion

Costs (*continued*)
  erosion (*continued*)
    solutions 12.3.8.1., 12.3.8.4., 12.3.8.5.,
      12.3.8.8.,
    installation 14.5.1., 14.6.2.2., 14.6.5.
    filtration unit 14.6.2.2.
    pipeline 14.6.2.2.
  maintenance **10.6.3.2.**
  operating 1.4.2., 1.4.4., 1.4.10., 1.4.14., 4.1.,
    4.5.2., 4.7.2., 4.7.3., 5.2.2.13., 10.1.,
    10.6.: 10.6.1. to 10.6.4., 14.7.
    air-assisted gravity conveyor 2.5.5., 6.5.
    air drying equipment 6.4.5.: 6.4.5.1. to
      6.4.5.2.
    air mover 10.2.6.2.
    air supply 2.4.8.
    conveying line feed
      multiple feed points 10.3.1.
    conveying system, innovatory 10.2.2.7.
    feeding device
      blow tanks 14.5.2.1., 14.6.3.: 14.6.3.1. to
        14.6.3.2., 14.6.5.
      twin 14.6.4., Table 14.17.
    pipeline bore 4.6.3.1.
    plant air 10.2.6.2.2.
  power **6.8.**, 10.2.3., 10.6.1., 10.6.3., **10.6.3.1.**,
    14.3.5.2., 14.6.5.
    air mover 14.5.3.2.
    feeding device
      blow tank 14.5.2.1., 14.6.4., Figure 339
      screw feeder 2.3.2.
    gas–solid separation device 10.2.7.1.
    filtration unit 2.4.4.
  staff wages and number 10.6.1.
  test work 14.2.1.
  total **14.5.: 14.5.1 to 14.5.5.**
Coulter counter, Coulter principle 15.2.2.2.,
  15.2.2.4., 15.2.3.
Cross sectional area of pipe, *see* Pipeline, cross
  sectional area
Cyclone separator, *see also* Gas–solid separation
  device 1.4.3., 2.3.3., 3.1., 3.3.2., 3.3.2.2.,
  3.3.3., **3.3.3.2.**, **10.2.7.1.2.**, 10.2.7.1.3.,
  10.2.7.1.4., 10.2.7.2.1., 12.6.3.2., 13.5.6.,
  Figures 51, 53, 54
  dimensions **3.3.3.2.**, Figure 54
  explosion risk 12.6.3.2., 13.5.6.
  reverse flow **3.3.3.2.**, Figure 52

D/d ratio, *see* Bend diameter
Damp materials, (*see also* Hygroscopic materials; Moisture content; Wet materials)
  10.4.2.
Dangerous materials, *see* Hazardous materials,
  see also Combustible materials; Explosive
  materials; Radioactive materials; Toxic
  materials
Darcy's equation **7.2.1.**, 7.2.2., 9.2.1., **9.2.3.1.**,
  Figure 134

De-aeration constant 8.3.3., **15.5.5.1.**, **15.5.8.3.**
  vibrated 1.4.8., **8.4.3.**, 8.4.4.1.1., **8.5.4.**,
    15.5.5.2., **15.5.8.3.**, Table 15.4., Figures
    277, 280
Definitions 1.4.1., **1.6.: 1.6.1. to 1.6.1.22.**
Degradation, *see* Particle degradation
Deliquescent materials 15.4.2.4.
Delivery points, *see* Conveying line discharge
Delivery (supply) pressure (of air mover), *see*
  Air supply pressure
Dense phase (non-suspension flow) 1.4.8.,
  1.6.1., **1.6.1.3.**, 1.6.1.4., 1.6.1.6., **2.2.6.2.**,
  2.3.1., 2.4.2, 2.4.3., 2.4.4., 2.4.5., 2.4.7.,
  2.4.8., 2.5.1., 2.5.5., 3.2.7., 3.2.7.8., 4.2.1,
  4.3.2.1., 4.3.2.2., 4.3.4.1., 4.6.2., 4.6.2.1,
  4.6.3.1., 4.7.1., **4.7.2.**, 5.2.2.6., 5.2.2.9.,
  5.2.4., 5.3.8., 5.4.5., 5.4.6., 6.1.1., 6.1.3.,
  6.1.5., 6.2.6., 6.6.1., 7.3.3., 7.4.7., 7.5.,
  7.5.3., 7.5.5., 8.2.1., 8.2.2., 8.2.3., 8.2.4.,
  8.3.2., 8.3.4., 8.4.1, 8.4.2., 8.4.3, 8.4.4.,
  8.4.4.1., 8.4.5., 8.5.1., 8.5.2., 8.5.3., 8.5.4.,
  8.5.4.1., 9.3.3., 9.3.4.2., 9.3.5.2., 9.3.8.,
  10.2.2.7., 10.2.4., 10.2.5.2.5., 10.2.6.2.1.,
  10.4.7., 10.4.9., 14.5.2.6., 11.1.2., 11.1.5.,
  12.2.3., 12.3.6.3., 12.3.7.2., 12.3.7.3.,
  12.6.2., 12.6.3.2., **12.7.5.**, 13.2.2.2.1.,
  13.2.2.6., 13.4.3.5., 13.5.6., 14.4.1.,
  14.4.2.1., 14.7., 15.5.5.1., Figures 64, 82,
  91, 225, 275, 276, 277
Density
  air (gas) 3.3.3.2., 6.1.2., 6.2., 6.2.6., 7.2.1.,
    7.2.2., **9.2.2.2.**, 9.2.3.1., 12.3.7.3.,
    13.2.2.3.2., 13.5.2., 13.6.9., 15.1.2.,
    Figure 232
  bulk 2.5.5., 3.2.3.5., 3.3.3.2., 4.2.1., 5.2.2.1.,
    5.4.4., 8.3.1., 8.3.3., 13.2.2.7.1.,
    13.4.4.2., 14.1.4., 15.1.2., 15.1.3.,
    15.3.3.: 15.3.3.1. to 15.3.3.2., Tables
    8.1., 15.2.
    aerated **15.3.3.1.3.**
    as poured **15.3.2.1.1.**, 15.3.3.2., 15.3.4.,
      15.3.5., Table 15.2.
    cement Table 14.1
    compacted (trapped) **15.3.3.1.2.**, 15.3.3.2.,
      15.3.5., Table 15.2.
    fluidised 14.5.2.1.,
  particle 3.3.3.2., 4.2.1., 5.2.2.1, 6.5., 8.3.3.,
    8.4.5., 8.5.4.1., 10.2.7.1.3., **15.3.2.:**
    15.3.2.1. to 15.3.2.2.2., 15.3.4., 15.5.1.,
    15.5.4.3., 15.5.4.4., Tables 8.1., 15.2.,
    Figures 70, 282, 283, 285
    apparent **15.3.2.1.**, 15.3.5.
    effective **15.3.2.1.**
    relative density **15.3.2.2.1.**
    true **15.3.2.1.**
  phase, *see* Phase density
Deposition of material in pipeline 1.4.12.,
  11.3.3., 12.3.7.1., **12.7.: 12.7.1. to 12.7.5.**
  solution **12.7.3.**
Design, *see* Conveying system design
Diameter of conveying line, *see* Pipeline bore

Dilute phase (lean phase, suspension flow)
1.6.1., 1.6.1.2., 1.6.1.4., 1.6.1.10.,
1.6.1.13., **2.2.6.1.**, 2.2.6.2., 2.3.1., 2.3.7.,
2.4.3., 2.4.5., 2.4.7., 2.4.8., 2.5.1., 3.2.2.,
3.2.7., 4.2.1., 4.3.2.1, 4.5.2., 4.6.2.,
4.6.3.1., 4.7.1., 4.7.2., **4.7.3.**, 5.2.4., 5.3.8.,
5.4.6., 6.1.1., 6.1.3., 6.1.5., 6.1.6., 6.2.4.,
6.2.6., 6.3.3., 6.6.2., 6.8., 7.3., 7.3.2.,
7.3.5., 7.5.5., 8.2.1., 8.2.2., 8.2.4., 8.3.2.,
8.4.1., 8.4.2., 8.4.3., 8.4.4., 8.4.4.1., 8.4.5.,
8.5.2., 8.5.3., 8.5.4., 8.5.4.1., 9.1., 9.2.1.,
9.3.2.3., 9.3.2.4, 9.3.3., 9.3.5.2., 9.3.8.,
10.2.2.7., 10.2.4., 10.2.5.2.4., 10.2.6.2.3.,
10.3.5., 10.4.5., 10.4.8., 10.4.9., 10.5.2.6.,
10.3.1., 11.1.2., 11.1.5., 12.2.3., 12.3.6.3.,
12.3.7.1., 12.3.7.2., 12.3.8.6., 12.6.2.,
12.6.3.2., 12.7.5., 13.2.2.2.1., 13.5.6.,
14.3.6., 14.4.1., Figures 64, 81, 90, 275,
276, 277
Discharge, *see* Conveying line discharge
Discharge hopper, *see* Reception hopper
Discharge valves
blow tanks, *see* Blow tanks
Disengager, Disengaging system, *see* Gas–solid
separation device
Distance conveyed, *see* Conveying distance
Diverter valves, *see* Pipeline
Double door discharge gates, *see* Gate lock
valve
Double dump gates, *see* Gate lock valve
Double flap valves, *see* Gate lock valve
Drag force 1.6.1.2., 4.3.2.3., 5.2.2.1., 7.3.
Drop-out box 3.2.3.3.
Drop-through feeder, *see* Rotary valve
Dry materials 15.3.3.1.3.
Drying
air, *see* Air drying; Air drying equipment
materials 15.5.2.2.
Dual negative and positive pressure systems, *see*
Conveying system, dual negative and positive pressure
Duning **1.6.1.19**, 2.2.6.2.
Dust (*see also* Fine materials: Powdered materials) 2.1., 2.3.5., 3.3.1., 3.3.2., 3.3.2.2.,
3.3.2.3., 3.3.2.4., **3.3.2.5.**, **3.3.3.**, 10.2.2.4.,
10.2.7.1.2., 10.2.7.1.3.
accumulations 13.4.2, 13.4.4.5.
cloud 1.6.1.18., 2.4.8., **3.3.2.5.**, **3.2.3.**,
10.2.2.2., 12.5.1., 12.5.2., 12.6.1.,
12.6.2., 12.6.3.2., 13.5.6.
confined 12.6.2.
flame propagation 12.6.3.2., 13.5.6.
ignition energy, minimum 12.6.3.1., 12.6.4.
ignition temperature, minimum 12.6.3.1.,
12.6.4.
pressure build-up 12.6.2.
control, (*see also* Gas–solid separation device)
3.3.3.: 3.3.3.1. to 3.3.3.3.2.
emission **3.3.2.5.**, 3.3.3., 3.3.3.3.2.
explosion, *see* Explosions; Explosion risks;
Explosive materials
removal, *see* Dust control

Duty
air mover, *see* Air mover
conveying, *see* Conveying duty

Economic assessment, *see* Costs
Elbows, *see* Bends
Electrical sensing zone technique (particle size
determination) 15.2.2.2., **15.2.2.2.4.**
Electron microscope (particle size determination) 15.2.2.2., **15.2.2.2.5.**
Electrostatic charge, (*see also* Static electricity)
2.4.8., **10.4.4.**, **12.5.1**, 12.5.2., 13.5.4.,
13.5.6., 15.4.2., **15.4.2.3.**
build-up 12.1
control 12.5.2
earthing 12.5.1., **12.5.2.**, 13.5.4.
effects 15.5.4.4.
Elutriation (particle size determination)
15.2.2.2., **15.2.2.2.3.**
Empty pipeline relationships, *see* Single-phase
flow
Energy, *see* Power requirements
loss, *see* individual entries
specific 5.3.4., 6.8., **7.5.3.**, 7.5.6., 8.2.2.,
13.6.8.
lines of constant 7.5.3., Figure 148
Entrainment, (*see also* Conveying line inlet;
Conveying line inlet air velocity) 1.6.1.1.,
1.6.1.19., 6.5.
Environmental control, *see* Controlled environment
Environmental pollution, *see* Pollution, *see also*
Dust; Dust clouds
Equivalent length, *see* Scaling
Eroded surfaces
repair 12.3.8.7.
Erosion, (*see also* Abrasive materials; Particle
hardness) 1.1., 1.4.12., 1.5.4., 2.3.6., 2.3.7.,
2.4.5., 2.4.6., 2.5.1., 2.5.2., 2.5.5., 3.1.,
3.2.3.1., 3.2.3.4., 3.2.5., 3.2.6., 3.2.7.1,
3.2.7.4., 3.3.2.2., 3.3.3.2., 4.7.3. 6.1.3.,
6.2.6., 7.3.2., 8.2.2., 10.2.2.7., **10.4.5.**,
10.5.3.2., 10.6.3.2., 11.4., 12.1., **12.3.:
12.3.1. to 12.3.9.**, 13.1., 13.3.4., **13.3.5.1.**,
13.5.5., 14.1.4., 14.5.4.2., 15.2.2.3.2.,
Figure 268
aircraft 12.3.2
engines 12.3.2, 12.3.6.2.
bend geometry **12.3.4.**, Figures 264, 265
conveying air velocity exponent 2.4.5,
12.3.6.3.
flow pattern 12.3.5., Figure 266
secondary 12.3.8.2., Figure 265
particle
deflection **12.3.8.4.**, 12.3.8.8., 13.5.5.
hardness **12.3.6.1.**, 13.5.5.
impact 10.4.5., 10.4.6., 10.4.9., 12.3.2.,
12.3.5., 12.4.3., 13.5.5.
angle **12.3.3.**, **12.3.4.**, 12.3.5., 12.3.8.2.,
12.3.8.3., 13.5.5., Figures 263, 265
energy loss 10.4.9.

Erosion (*continued*)
  particle (*continued*)
    penetration 12.3.6.2., 12.3.6.3.
    size **12.3.6.2.**
  resistance 12.3.3., 12.3.8.5., 12.3.8.6.,
    12.3.8.7., 12.3.9., 14.1.4., 14.5.4.2.
  relative abrasive wear resistance **12.3.8.5.**,
    Figure 274
  secondary 12.3.7.2.
  solutions **12.3.8.: 12.3.8.1. to 12.3.8.8.,**
    12.3.9., 13.5.5., 14.5.4.2.
    air injection **12.3.8.4.**
    pipeline surface material **12.3.8.5.**,
      12.3.8.6., 12.3.8.7.
    wear back methods 12.3.5., 12.3.8.,
      12.3.8.8., 13.5.5.
      annular gap 12.3.8.8.
      concrete 12.3.8.8.
      perspex 12.3.5.
    specific 12.3.8.5., Figures 264, 267, 268, 269,
      270, 273
    mild steel bends Figure 267, 270
    straight pipeline 2.5.2., 12.3.1., 12.3.5.,
      12.3.8.2., 12.3.8.8., 12.3.9., 12.7.3.,
      13.3.5.1., 13.5.5., 14.5.4.1.
  threshold 12.3.6.1., 12.3.6.2., 12.3.6.3.
  wear **12.3.4.**, 12.3.6.2, 12.3.7.2., 12.3.8.1.,
    12.3.8.4., 12.3.8.6., 12.7.3., 13.4.4.6.,
    13.5.5., 14.5.4.1., Figures 271, 273
    mild steel bends Figure 271
    patterns **12.3.5.**, Figure 266
    pockets 12.3.5., 12.3.8.8., 12.3.9., 13.5.5.
    points 12.3.5., 12.3.8.8.
    tests 12.3.6.2.
Erosive materials, *see* Abarasive materials
Erosive wear, *see* Erosion
Exhaust pressure, (*see also* Air requirements;
  Air supply pressure) 3.2.2., 4.6.1.,
  5.2.2.13., 5.2.2.16., 5.2.3.8., 5.3.3.5., 5.4.3,
  6.1.1., 6.2.2., 6.2.4., 6.2.5.1., 6.4.4., 6.6.5.,
  10.1., 10.2.3., 10.2.5., 10.2.6.1., 13.2.2.2.1.,
  13.2.2.2.2., 13.3.3., Figures 2, 76
  case study 6.2.4.
Exhauster, (*see also* Fans; Liquid ring vacuum
  pump; Roots type exhauster; Air mover)
  3.2.2., 3.3.2.2., 6.1.2., 6.2.4., 10.2.6.2.4.,
  10.2.7.2.1., 13.3.2.
  ingress of material, *see* Ingress of material
  inlet 13.2.2.2.2.
  power requirements, *see* Power Requirements
  pressure capability 13.3.3.
Exit, *see* Conveying line exit
Explosions, (*see also* Dust cloud) 1.1., 12.1.,
  12.5.1., 12.5.2., **12.6.: 12.6.1. to 12.6.4.**,
  13.4.4.5., **13.5.6.**
  characteristics **12.6.3., 12.6.4**
  contained 13.5.6.
  effects 12.6.2.
  explosion pressure
    maximum 12.6.4.
  ignition 12.5.1., 12.5.2., **12.6.3.1.**, 13.4.4.5.,
    13.5.6.

Explosions (*continued*)
  ignition (*continued*)
    energy
      minimum 12.6.3.1., 12.6.4.
    temperature
      minimum 12.6.3.1., 12.6.4.
  oxygen concentration 12.6.4.
  quenching effect 12.6.3.2.
  risks 1.4.1.2., 1.5.4., **12.6.: 12.6.1. to 12.6.4.**,
    13.5.6.
  spark 12.1., 12.5.1., 13.5.6.
    source 12.5.1., 12.6.3.1., 13.4.4.5., 13.5.6.
  stoichiometric value **1.6.1.18.**, 12.6.3.2.
  tests 12.6.3.1., 12.6.3.2., **12.6.4.**
Explosive materials 2.1., 2.3.5., 2.4.8., 3.3.1.,
  10.2.2.2., 10.2.2.4., 10.2.7., 12.6.4., 12.7.1.
  explosible concentration 12.5.2, **12.6.3.2.**,
    12.6.4.
    explosibility limits **12.6.3.2.**, 12.6.4.,
      13.5.6.
  Group A **12.6.4.**
  Group B **12.6.4.**
Extrusion hairs (angel hairs, snake-skins,
  streamers), (*see also* Particle melting)
  12.4.1., 12.4.2., 12.4.3., 12.4.4., 13.2.2.9.2.,
  13.6.2., Figures 295 and 296
  solution **12.4.4.**

Fabric filter, *see* Filtration unit
Fans, (*see also* Aerodynamic compressor; Air
  mover) 6.1., 6.1.1., 6.1.2., 6.5., 6.6.1.,
  6.6.2., 6.7., 7.3.5., 10.2.6.2.3., 10.2.6.2.4.,
  10.2.6.2.5., 10.2.7.1.4., **13.3.4.**
  operating pressure 10.2.6.2.3., 10.2.6.2.4.,
    10.2.7.1.4.
  overfeeding 13.3.4.
  performance **13.3.4.**
  rating 6.1.2., 6.1.7., 7.3.5.
Feed hopper, *see* Supply hopper
Feed surges, *see* Surge
Feeding device, (*see also* Blow tanks; Gate lock
  valves; Rotary valve; Screw feeder; Suction
  nozles; Venturi feeder) **2.3.2.**, 2.3.5.,
  2.3.6., 2.3.7., 3.1., **3.2.: 3.2.1. to 3.2.9.**,
  4.2.2.2., 4.7.2., **5.2.2.10.**, 5.2.2.3.,
  5.2.3.10., 5.3.2.1., **5.4.4.**, 8.2.2., 9.2.1.5.,
  10.1., 10.2.2.3., 10.2.2.6., 10.2.4., **10.2.5.:**
  10.2.5.1. to 10.2.5.2.5., 10.3.4, 10.3.5.,
  10.4.5., 10.6., 10.6.3.1., 11.1.4., 12.2.2.4.,
  12.3.7.2., 13.2.2.2.2., 13.2.2.2.3., 13.2.2.7.,
  13.2.2.9.1., 13.3.1.1., 13.4.4.1., 13.5.6.,
  14.5.1., **14.5.2.: 14.5.2.1. to 14.5.2.3.**,
  14.6.2., Table 3.1
  air leakage, *see* Air leakage
  air lock 10.2.5.1.4.
  capability 5.2.3.10., 10.2.5.1., **10.2.5.1.1.**,
    10.2.5.2.3., 13.6.3.
  conveying limits Figure 13
  delivery 11.2.6.
  energy loss 10.2.5.2.1., 10.3.1.
  entrainment device **3.2.3.3.**

Feeding device (*continued*)
  flow control **5.4.4.**, 5.4.6, 10.2.5.1.,
    10.2.5.1.4., 10.2.5.2.3., 10.3.4., 10.3.5.,
    13.2.2.2.2.
  flow into 10.2.5.2.1, 13.4.4.4.
  operating characteristics 11.1.5.
  operating pressure 3.2.1., 10.2.5., 10.2.5.1.1.,
    10.2.5.2.1., 10.2.5.2.2., 10.2.5.2.3.,
    14.3.6., **14.4.2.2.**; **14.4.2.2.1. to**
    14.4.2.2.3., Table 3.1., Figure 12
  pressure drop, *see* Pressure drop
  rating **10.2.6.1.1.**, 11.1.4., Figure 13
  selection 1.4.10., 10.2.1., 10.2.4., **10.2.5.**:
    10.2.5.1. to 10.2.5.2.5., 14.4.2.2.
  sizing **13.4.5.3.**
  suitability 10.2.5.1.
  vent 13.2.2.7.1.
  venting 2.3.2., 2.5.2., 3.2.6., 10.2.5.2.1.
  wear 13.2.2.4., **13.2.2.8.1.**
Feeding the conveying line, *see* Conveying line
    feed
Feret's diameter **15.2.2.**
Fibrous materials 10.2.7.1.1., 15.4.2.2.
Fick's law of diffusion 15.5.5.1.
Filtration **13.2.2.7.2.**
  air drying equipment 6.4.5.2.
  air mover
    inlet 6.4.3, 6.6.6.
    exit 13.4.2
  problems 13.1.
  unit (*see also* Gas–solid separation device)
    1.4.3., 1.6.1.8., 2.3.3., 2.3.5., 2.3.6.,
    2.3.7., 2.4.4., 3.1., 3.2.7.4., 3.3.2.,
    3.3.2.1., 3.3.2.2., 3.3.2.3., **3.3.3.**: **3.3.3.1.**
    to 3.3.3.2. 6.2.2., 7.4.2. 10.2.2.4.,
    10.2.6.2.5., 10.2.7.2.1., 10.2.7.2.2.,
    10.6.3.1., 12.2.1., 12.2.2.4., 12.6.3.2.,
    13.1., 13.2.2.2.2., 13.2.2.7.2., 13.3.4.,
    13.4.5.: **13.4.5.1. to 13.4.5.4.**, 13.5.2.,
    13.5.6., **14.5.5.**, 14.6.1., Tables 3.5., 3.6.,
    3.7., 14.16, Figures 51, 55, 56, 332
  air to fabric ratio (face velocity) **3.3.3.3.**,
    11.1.4., 13.2.2.7.2., **13.4.5.3.**
  blockage 2.4.4., 3.1., 3.3.3.3., 12.2.1.,
    12.4.1, 13.1., 13.2.2.7.2., 13.4.5.:
    13.4.5.1. to 13.4.5.4., 13.6.2.
  capability 11.1.4., 11.2.6., 14.5.5., Table
    14.16., Figure 332
  cleaning 3.3.3.3., **3.3.3.3.2.**, 10.2.7.1.4.,
    10.2.7.2.1., 10.6.3., 13.2.2.7.2., 13.4.2.
    mechanical shaking **3.3.3.3.2.**,
      10.2.7.2.2., 14.5.5., Figure 55
    pulse jet **3.3.3.3.2.**, 10.2.7.2.1., Figure 56
    reverse air **3.3.3.3.2.**, 13.4.5.2., **14.5.5.**
  costs, *see* Costs
  depth filtration **3.3.3.3.**
  effective area 3.3.3.3., 13.4.5.3.
  effective mesh size **3.3.3.3.**
  explosion risk 12.6.3.2, 13.5.6.
  fabrics (cloths, screens) **3.3.3.3.**, **3.3.3.3.1.**,
    12.2.1., 13.2.2.7.2., 13.4.5.1., 13.4.5.3.,
    13.5.9., 14.5.5., Tables 3.5., 3.6., 3.7.

Filtration (*continued*)
  fabrics (*continued*)
    behaviour 3.3.3.3.1., Table 3.7.
    blinding **3.3.3.3.**
    calendering **3.3.3.3.1.**
    coating **3.3.3.3.1.**
    collecting efficiency 3.3.3.3.1.
    fibres 3.3.3.3., 3.3.3.3.1., 14.3.5., Tables
      3.5., 3.6., 3.7.
    flow path 3.3.3.3.
    napping **3.3.3.3.1.**
    needlefelt 3.3.3.3., 3.3.3.3.1., 3.3.3.3.2.
    non-woven 3.3.3.3.1.
    penetration **3.3.3.3.**
    porosity 3.3.3.3.1.
    sieving **3.3.3.3.**
    singeing **3.3.3.3.1.**
    woven **3.3.3.3.1.**
  failure 13.1.
  filter bags 3.3.3.3.1., 3.3.3.3.2., 10.6.3.2.,
    13.4.5.2., Figures 55, 56
  filter cake 3.3.3.3., 3.3.3.3.2.
  filter envelopes 3.3.3.3.1., 3.3.3.3.2.
  maintenance **13.4.5.2.**
  performance 13.4.5.2.
  number of, 13.3.2., 13.4.2., 14.5.5., Figure
    332
  power requirements, *see* Power requirements
  pressure drop, *see* Pressure drop
  replacing **11.1.4.**
  selection **10.2.7.1.3.**, **14.5.5.**
  size 3.3.3., 13.4.5.3., 13.5.2., 14.5.5.
  specification 12.2., 13.4.5.4., 14.5.1.
  weather cowl 14.5.5.
  worn 13.3.2.
Fine materials (particles), 'fines', *see also* Dust
  1.4.3., 2.1., 2.3.3., 2.4.4., 2.5.3., 3.2.3.2.,
  3.2.3.3., 3.2.4., 3.3.1., 3.3.2., 3.3.2.2.,
  3.3.2.3., 3.3.2.4., 3.3.3., 3.3.3.2., 4.3.2.1.,
  6.5., 9.3.7., 10.2.2.7., 10.2.7.1., 10.7.1.3.,
  10.7.2.1., 10.4.1., 10.4.2., 10.4.3., 10.4.7.,
  10.4.12., 11.2.6., 12.2.1., 12.3.6.2., 12.4.4.,
  12.6.2., 12.7.4., 13.2.2.8.2., 13.4.3.5.,
  13.5.4.1., 13.5.6., 13.6.7., 15.2.2.1.2.,
  15.3.2.2.2., 15.3.3.1.3., 15.4.3.1., 15.5.1.
Fine particles. *see* Fine materials
Fire Research Station 12.6.4.
Fire
  flash, (*see also* Explosions) 12.6.2.
  risk 12.6.4.
Fish 13.6.6.
Flame propagation, (*see also* Explosions)
  12.6.3.2., 13.5.6.
Floor, insulated 12.5.2.
Flour 8.1., 8.3.1., 8.3.2., 8.3.3., 8.4.1., 8.4.4.,
  8.4.4.1., 8.5., 9.1., 9.3.2.1., 10.4.3., 12.6.2.,
  15.1.1., 15.2.2.4., 15.2.3., 15.3.5., 15.4.4.,
  15.5.2., 15.5.8.1., 15.5.8.2., 15.5.8.3.,
  Tables 8.1., 15.1 to 15.4., Figures 218, 227,
  275 to 281, 283
  conveying characteristics Figure 218
Flow properties, *see* Two-phase flow

Flow rate, *see* Air flow rate; Air mass flow rate; Conveying air velocity; Conveying line feed; Conveying line inlet air velocity; Feeding device flow control; Feeding device flow into; Material mass flow rate; Volumetric flow rate
Flowability, *see* Two-phase flow
Fluffy materials 6.6.2., 10.2.5.2.1., 10.2.6.2.5.
Fluidisation, (*see also* Aeration; Air retention properties; Geldart's classification; Material type A; Material type B; Permeability) 3.2.7.5., 3.2.7.6., 3.2.7.8., 3.2.7.9., 3.2.7.10., 15.3.3.1.3., **15.5.: 15.5.1. to 15.5.8.3.**
  behaviour 15.5.4., 15.5.4.4.
  characteristics 8.4.2., 8.4.3., 8.5.3., 15.5.4.4.
  mechanical vibration 15.5.4.4.
  pneumatic transport **15.5.4.2.**
  stirrers 15.5.4.4.
Fluidised beds, *see* Fluidisation
Fluidised bulk density, *see* Density
Fluidised combustion 15.5.2.2.
Fluidising air 2.5.2., 3.2.7.1., 3.2.7.3., 3.2.7.8., 3.2.7.10., 10.2.5.1.4., 10.5.2.6.1., 10.5.3.1., 10.5.3.2.
  velocity 3.2.7.8., **6.5.**
    minimum 6.5., 8.3.3., **15.5.4.1.**, 15.5.4.2., 15.5.4.4., 15.5.7., Table 15.4., Figures 70, 292
    terminal Figure 70
Fluidising membrane
  air-assisted gravity conveyor, *see* Air-assisted gravity conveyor
  blow tank, *see* Blow tank
  pressure drop, *see* Pressure drop
Fluidising velocity, *see* Fluidising air velocity
Fluorspar 2.4.2., 2.4.3., 8.1., 8.2.3., 8.2.4., 8.3.3., 8.4.5., 9.3.1., 9.3.2.1., Table 8.1., Figures 82, 146, 206, 226, 228, 230, 231, 283
  conveying characteristics Figure 206
Food products, *see* Foodstuffs
Foodstuffs, (*see also* individual names of food-stuffs) 10.2.2.7., 10.4.3., 12.6.2., 12.7.1., 13.5.6., 13.6.9.
Footwear, conducting 12.5.2.
Formulae **1.9.**
Fragile materials, *see* Friable materials
Free air 1.6.1.7., 6.6.1., 13.5.2., 14.5.2.3.
  conditions (standard conditions, standard reference conditions) 1.4.6., **1.6.1.7.**, 6.1.2., 6.1.4., **6.1.7.**, 6.2.1.1., 6.2.2., 6.3.1., 6.3.2., 7.2.2., 10.2.6.1.2., 13.2.2.2.1., 14.5.3.1., Figures 88 to 91
  delivery, *see* Air mover
  requirements **7.2.2.**, 13.2.2.2.1.
  velocity, (*see also* Conveying air velocity) **1.6.1.9.**, 1.6.1.11., 1.6.1.12., 5.2.2.6.
Free moisture, *see* Moisture
Free flowing materials, *see* Two-phase flow
Friable (fragile) materials, (*see also* Particle degradation) 2.4.4., 2.5.1., 2.5.2., 2.5.5., 3.2.5., 3.3.2.6., 3.2.7.1., 4.5.2., 5.2.2.1.,

Friable (*continued*)
  6.1.3., 7.4.7. 10.2.2.7., 10.2.5.2.3. 10.2.5.2.4., 10.2.5.2.5., **10.4.6.**, 12.1., 12.2.1., 12.2.3., 12.3.7.2., 12.3.8.1. 13.4.5.1., 13.6.7., 15.2.2.1.2., 15.2.2.2.3., 15.3.2.2.2., Figure 290
Friction 4.3.2.3., 5.2.2.1.
  charge 12.5.1.
  coefficient 7.2.1., 7.3.1., **9.2.2.4.**, 9.2.3.1.4., Figures 234, 237
  resistance 2.2.4., 2.5.2., 2.3.5.1.
Fuels, *see also* individual names of fuels 10.4.3., 12.6.2., 13.5.6.
  pulverised 12.7.2., 12.3.1.

Gas, *see* Air; Conveying air; Inert gas; Nitrogen; Single-phase flow
Gas–solid flow, *see* Two-phase flow
Gas–solid separation device (separator, disengager), (*see also* Cyclone separator; Filtration unit; Gravity settling chamber) 1.4.3., 1.5.1., **2.3.3.**, **Chapter 3**, 10.1., 10.2.2.6., 10.2.5.2.5., **10.2.7.: 10.2.7.1. to 10.2.7.2.2.**, 10.6.3.1., 14.2.7.1.4.
  air lock 10.2.7.1.3.
  collection (separation) efficiency 3.3.3., 3.3.3.1., 3.3.3.2., 3.3.3.3., 3.3.3.3.1., 10.2.7.1., 10.2.7.2.1.
  considerations 3.3.2., **10.2.7.2: 10.2.7.2.1. to 10.2.7.2.2.**
  costs, *see* Costs
  failure 10.2.7.2.1.
  ingress of material, *see* Ingress of material
  selection 1.4.10., **10.2.7.1.: 10.2.7.1.1. to 10.2.7.1.4.**, 10.2.7.2.2.
  specification 10.2.7.2.1.
  venting 10.2.2.1., 10.2.7.1.1., 10.2.7.1.3.
Gas–solid suspension, *see* Explosions, *see also* Two-phase flow
Gate lock valves (double door discharge gates, double dump gates, double flap valves, gate valves), (*see also* Feeding device) 3.2.1., 3.2.2., **3.2.6.**, 4.3.4.3., 5.2.2.16., 10.2.5.: 10.2.5.1. to 10.2.5.1.4., **10.2.5.2.4.**, 13.2.2.4., Figure 27
  air leakage, *see* Air leakage
  costs, *see* Costs
  operating range Table 3.1., Figure 12
  operating sequence Figure 26
  pressure drop, *see* Pressure drop
  sealing 13.2.2.4.
  selection 10.2.5.: 10.2.5.1. to 10.2.5.1.4., 10.2.5.2.4.
  venting 3.2.6.
Gate valves, *see* Gate lock valves
Geldart, D. 2.5.5., **8.5.5.**, 15.5.4.4.
Geldart's classification of fluidisation behaviour, (*see also* Aeration; Air retention properties; Fluidisation; Material type A; Material type B; Permeability) 2.5.5., 8.1., **8.4.5.**, **15.5.4.4.**, Figures 282, 283

Geldart's classification *(continued)*
Group A materials 2.5.5., 8.4.5., 15.5.4.4., 15.5.5.
Group B materials 2.5.5., 8.4.5., 15.5.4.4.
Group C materials 2.5.5., 8.4.5., 15.5.4.4.
Group D materials 2.5.5., 8.4.5., 15.5.4.4.
Granular materials, *(see also* Coarse granular materials) 1.4.3., 2.3.3., 2.4.3., 2.5.2., 2.5.4.2., 3.2.3.2., 3.2.7.5., 3.2.8., 4.2.1., 4.3.2.1., 8.5.3., 10.2.7.1.1., **10.4.7.**, 12.6.4., **13.4.3.5.**, 13.4.4.3., 13.4.4.4., **13.6.4.**, 15.5.1.
Granulated sugar, *see* Sugar
Graphical representation of mathematical models, *see* Mathematical models
Graticule 15.2.2.2.5.
Gravity settling chambers, *(see also* Gas–solid separation device) 1.4.3., **3.3.3.1.**, **10.2.7.1.1.**, Figure 50
mesh separating screen 3.3.3.1., 10.2.7.1.1.
vent 3.3.3.

Hardness **1.6.1.21.: 1.6.1.21.1. to 1.6.1.21.3.**, **12.3.8.5.**, Figure 274
brinell 12.3.8.5., **1.6.1.21.2.**
conveying system components 13.5.5.
identation Figure 274
Moh's scale 12.3.8.5., **1.6.1.21.1.**
particle, *see* Particle
pipeline materials, *see* Pipeline materials; Pipeline surface materials
vickers 12.3.8.5., **1.6.1.21.3.**, Figure 273
Hazardous materials, *see* Combustible materials; Explosive materials; Radioactive materials; Toxic materials
Health and Safety at Work Act 1974 3.3.1.
Health and Safety Executive 12.6.2.
Heavy particles 10.2.7.1.1.
Helical lobe rotary compressor, *see* Rotary screw compressor
H M Factory Inspectorate 12.6.4.
Hopper (silo)
discharge from 10.4.1., 10.4.2., 13.6.3., 15.5.5.1., 15.5.2.2.
reception (discharge, receiving) 3.3.2., 3.3.3.1., 3.3.3.3.2., 6.2.2., 7.4.2., 10.2.7.1.3., 10.3.6., 11.3.2., 12.5.1., 12.6.2., 12.6.3.2., 13.3.2., 13.4.5.2., 13.5.4., 13.5.9., 14.1.2., 14.7., Table 13.1.
explosion risk 12.6.3.2., 13.5.6.
shut off valve 15.5.2.2.
storage 13.3.3.2.
supply 2.3.2., 2.3.7., 3.2.2., 3.2.3., 3.2.5., 3.2.6., 3.2.7.3., 3.2.7.4., 3.2.7.9., 3.2.7.11., 10.5.2., 10.5.3.2., 11.3.2.
discharge aid 13.6.3.
discharge form 13.6.10., 15.2.2.3.2.
volume 15.3.3.2.
transfer 10.3.6.

Horizontal
conveying, *see* Two-phase flow, *see also* Pipeline length
length of pipeline, *see* Pipeline length
scaling, *see* Scaling
Humidity, *(see also* Moisture) 1.4.6., **6.4.: 6.4.1. to 6.4.5.2.**
air 6.4.
control **12.5.3.**
relative **1.6.1.17.**, 6.4.1., 6.4.4., 12.5.3., 13.5.4., 13.6.5., Figure 95
saturated air 6.4.1., 6.4.2., 6.4.3.,
saturation point 6.4.2., 13.6.5.
specific **1.6.1.16.**, **6.4.1.**, 6.4.2., 6.4.4., 13.6.5.
Hygroscopic materials 2.5.6., 2.4.8., **6.4.1.**, 10.2.2.7., **10.4.8.**, 12.5.3., 12.5.4., 12.7.4., 13.2.2.8.2., 13.4.3.2., **13.6.5.**

Ideal Gas Law 5.2.2.7., **6.2.1.: 6.2.1.1.**, 6.4.1., 7.2.2., 9.2.2.1.
isothermal 6.2.1.: 6.2.1.1.
Impaction
compacted bulk density 15.3.3.1.2.
Impervious materials 15.4.2.4.
Incompressible fluid 15.5.6.1., 15.5.8.1.
Indenter, *see also* Hardness 1.6.1.21.2., 1.6.1.21.3.
Inert gas, *(see also* Air; Conveying air; Gas; Nitrogen; Single-phase flow) 2.4.8., 10.2.2.2.
Ingress of air 2.4.8., 10.2.2.4., 13.3.2.1., **13.3.2.2.**
Ingress of material
air mover 2.3.6., 10.2.2.4., 10.2.2.5., 10.2.6.2.5., 10.2.7.2.1., 13.2.2.8.1., 13.4.2
roots type blower 10.2.7.2.1.
exhauster 2.3.5., 2.3.6., 3.3.2.2., 10.2.2.4., 10.2.2.5., 10.2.6.2.5., 10.2.7.2.1.
feeding device
rotary valve 13.4.4.5.
Inlet, *see* Conveying line inlet
Innovatory systems, *see* Conveying system, innovatory
Instrumentation, *see* Conveying system, control
Insulated floor 12.5.2.
Inter-particle forces 15.4.1., 15.4.2.1., 15.5.4.4., 15.5.7.

Kozeny constant 15.5.6.1.

Lagging 13.2.2.3.1.
Large particles 12.3.8.6., **13.6.6.**
heavy 10.2.7.1.1.
Lea and Nurse method (specific surface determination) **15.5.6.2.**
Leakage, air, *see* Air leakage
Lean phase, *see* Dilute phase
Light materials 6.6.2., 10.2.6.2.5., 10.2.5.2.1.

Limits of conveyability (conveying), *see* Conveying limits
Line, *see* Conveying line; Pipeline
Liquid ring compressors, (*see also* Air mover; Exhauster) **6.6.5.**, 10.2.6.2.3., 10.2.6.2.4., Figure 78
  operating pressure Figure 72
  single stage 6.6.5.
  two stage 6.6.5.
Liquid ring vacuum pumps, *see* Liquid ring compressor
Load cells 7.4.2., 11.3.2.
Load transducer 7.3.4.
Logic diagrams
  system capability 1.4.5., 5.1., **5.2.3.: 5.2.3.1. to 5.2.3.14., 5.3.3.: 5.3.3.1. to 5.3.3.5.**, 5.3.4., 5.3.6., 10.2.4., Figures 66, 68
  system design 1.1., 1.4.5., 1.5.2., 5.1., **5.2.2.: 5.2.2.1. to 5.2.2.16.**, 5.2.4., 5.3.1., **5.3.2.: 5.3.2.1. to 5.3.2.9.**, 5.3.4., 5.3.6., 10.1., 10.2.3., 10.2.4., Figures 65, 67
  system selection 1.1., 4.7.1, 10.1.
Long radius bends, *see* Bends
Low density materials 10.2.7.1.1.
Low density polyetheylene pellets, *see* Polyethylene
Low pressure fan systems, *see* Fans
Lysholm, A. 6.6.6.
Lysholm compressor, *see* Rotary screw compressor

Maintenance 12.3.9., **13.4.5.2.**, 14.7.
Marcus, R. D. 8.4.5.
Martin's diameter **15.2.2.**
Mason, J. S. 12.3.5.
Mass flow ratio, *see* Phase density
Mass ratio, *see* Phase density
Material, (*see also* Particle; Solids; individual names of materials)
  categorisation (characterisation), (*see also* Material properties; material type; individual material properties and types) 1.4.15., **3.3.2.4.**, Chapter 8, Chapter 15
  change during conveying, (*see also* Particle degradation; Particle melting) 7.4.7., 13.6.9.
  change of in conveying system, *see* Multiple material handling compatability with conveying system, *see* Material mass flow rate, material compatability
  compressibility, (*see also* Bulk solid, compaction)
    allowance 15.5.8.1.
  conveying, *see* Two-phase flow
  conveying characteristics, *see* Conveying characteristics
  density, *see* Density
  feed, *see* Conveying line feed
  feeding device, *see* Feeding device

Material (*continued*)
  flow capabilities, *see* Material mass flow rate; Air mass flow rate
  flow rate, *see* Material mass flow rate
  ingress, *see* Ingress of material
  leakage 10.4.11.
  mass flow rate (conveying rate, system throughput), (*see also* Two-phase flow) 1.2., 1.3., 1.4.2., 1.4.4., 1.4.7., 1.4.8., 1.6.1.1., 2.2.1., 2.5.2., 3.1., 3.2.2., 3.3.2.3., 4.1., 4.3.1., **4.3.4.2.**, 4.4., 4.5.: 4.5.1. to 4.5.3., 4.6.2., 4.6.3., 4.7.1., 5.1., **5.2.2.2.**, **5.2.2.11.**, 5.2.3., **5.2.3.9.**, 5.2.3.10., 5.2.3.12., **5.2.3.13.**, **5.2.4.**, **5.3.2.1.**, 5.3.2.3., **5.3.2.5.**, 5.3.3.4., **5.3.3.5.**, 5.3.4., 5.3.7., 5.4.2., 6.1.3., 6.2.1., 6.3.3.7.1., 7.3.5., 7.3.6., 7.4.: 7.4.1. to 7.4.7., 7.5.: 7.5.1., to 7.5.6., 8.1., 8.2.: 8.2.1. to 8.2.3., 8.3.4., **8.5: 8.5.1. to 8.5.4.1.**, 9.1., 9.3.: 9.3.1. to 9.3.8., 10.1., 10.2.3., 10.2.4., **10.5.2.3.**, 11.1.1., 11.1.2., 11.1.4., 11.2.: 11.2.1. to 11.2.6., 11.3.1., 11.3.2., 11.5., 12.2.1., 13.1., **13.2: 13.2.1 to 13.2.2.9.2.**, 13.3.2.2., 13.3.3.1., 13.3.4., 13.6.7., 14.1.1., **14.1.3.**, 14.2.1., 14.4.1., 14.4.2., 14.5.3.1.2., 14.7., 15.1.1., Figures 60, 61, 62, 64, 80, 81, 82, 97, 98, 105, 106, 108 to 115, 117, 118, 119, 120, 121, 122 to 133, 136, 142, 229, 230, 231, 248, 257, 258, 278, 279, 280
  air-assisted gravity conveyor 2.5.5., 6.5.
  blow tanks, 3.2.7.: 3.2.7.1. to 3.2.7.11., 10.5.: 10.5.1. to 10.5.4.1., 13.4.3.: 13.4.3.1. to 13.4.3.5., 14.4.3.: 14.4.3.1. to 14.4.3.3., **14.4.4.**, 14.6.3.2.
  control **5.4.4.**, 5.4.6., **11.3.2.**, 13.2.2.2.2.
  conveying characteristics, *see* Conveying characteristics
  conveying distance 4.1., 4.3.1., **4.3.4.: 4.3.4.1. to 4.3.4.3.**, 4.4., 4.5.2., 4.6.2.: 4.6.2.1. to 4.6.3., 4.7., 5.3.2.3., 5.3.2.4., 5.3.2.5., 5.3.4., **5.3.5.**, 5.4.5., 5.4.6., 7.1., **7.5.5.**, **9.3.2.1.**, 9.3.2.3., 10.3.5., 11.1.2., **13.2.2.6.**, **14.3.4.: 14.3.4.1. to 14.3.4.5.**
  decreasing **13.2.2.8.: 13.2.2.8.1. to 13.2.2.8.2.**, 13.2.2.9.1.
  increasing **13.2.2.9.: 13.2.2.9.1. to 13.2.2.9.2.**
  lines of constant 9.3.2.3., Figure 243
  material compatability 1.4.2., 1.4.4., 1.4.13., **2.4.6.**, 4.2.1., **4.2.2.3.**, **4.3.2.: 4.3.2.1. to 4.3.2.3.**, 4.4., 4.6.3.1., 4.6.3.2., **4.6.3.3.**, 5.1., **5.3.4.**, 5.4.2., **5.4.6.**, 6.1.6., 6.3.3., 7.3.5., **7.5.6.**, 8.2.: 8.2.1. to 8.2.4., 8.3.: 8.3.1. to 8.3.4., 10.3.4., **11.4.**, **13.2.2.5.**, 13.6.: 13.6.1. to 13.6.10., **14.2.1.**, 14.7.
  mathematical model, *see* Mathematical models

Material (*continued*)
  mass flow rate (*continued*)
    maximum 10.2.7.1.4., 14.3.6.
    mean 10.5.2.1., 13.2.2.2.3., 14.4.4.
    optimum 5.3.5., **11.4.**, Figure 171
  phase density 2.2.2., 5.2.2.8., 5.2.3.9.,
    5.2.3.11., 5.2.4., 6.1.3., 6.1.6., 7.3.3.,
    7.3.6., 7.4.: 7.4.1. to 7.4.7., 7.5.: 7.5.1.
    to 7.5.6., 8.1., 11.1.2., **11.2.3.**, 14.4.1.,
    14.4.2.
  pipeline bore 2.2.3., 4.3.1., **4.3.5.**, 4.4.,
    4.5.3., 4.6.3.: 4.6.3.1. to 4.6.3.3., 4.7.,
    5.2.2.2., 5.2.3.3., 5.3.2.3., 5.3.2.4.,
    5.3.2.5., **5.3.2.7.**, 5.3.4., **5.3.6.**, 5.3.7.,
    6.2.6., 7.1., 9.2.3.1.3., **9.3.6.**, 9.3.6.1.,
    11.2.5., 14.3.5.: 14.3.5.1. to 14.3.5.3.,
    14.3.6., 14.4.1., 14.4.2., 14.4.3.1.,
    14.5.3.1.2.
  pipeline geometry **2.3.7.**, 5.3.2.3., **5.3.4.**,
    9.3.2.: 9.3.2.1. to 9.3.2.4.,
    9.3.3., 9.3.4., **9.3.5.: 9.3.5.1. to
    9.3.5.2., 9.3.8.**, 14.3.4.: **14.3.4.1. to
    14.3.4.5.**
  pipeline material **9.3.7.**
  plug 2.5.2.
  pressure drop, conveying line 3.2.8.,
    4.2.2.1., 4.3.1., **4.3.3.**, **4.3.4.3.**, 4.5.2.,
    5.2.2.2., 5.2.2.11., 5.2.4., 5.3.2.3.,
    5.3.7., 7.3.1., 7.3.5., 7.3.6., 7.4.: 7.4.1.
    to 7.4.7., 7.5.: 7.5.1. to 7.5.6., 8.1.,
    8.3.4., **9.3.2.3.**, **9.3.4.1.**, 10.2.5.1.3.,
    12.2.1., **13.4.3.3.**, **14.3.4.4.**, **14.3.5.1.**
  problems 13.1., **13.2.: 13.2.1. to 13.2.2.9.2.**
  ratio between time averaged mean value
    and to the maximum or steady state
    conveying rate (batch conveying)
    2.3.8., 10.2., 10.2.5.2.5., 10.5.: 10.5.1.
    to 10.5.4.1., 14.4.3.: 14.4.3.1. to
    14.4.3.3., 14.4.4., 14.5.3.2., Tables
    14.3., 14.4.
  ratio with air mass flow rate Figures 257,
    258
  scaling, *see* Scaling
  steady state conveying rate 2.3.8., 2.5.2.
    3.2.7.2., 3.2.7.3., 3.2.7.4., 4.2.2.2.,
    4.6.3.1., 7.4.3., 7.4.6., 10.4., 10.5.:
    10.5.1. to 10.5.4.1., 14.4.3.: 14.4.3.1.
    to 14.4.3.2., 14.4.4., 14.5.3.1., Table
    14.3.
    maximum 10.5.2.1.
  suction nozzles 3.2.8.
  surge, *see* Surge
  time averaged mean value 2.3.8., 3.2.7.2.,
    3.2.7.4., 4.2.2.2., 4.6.3.1., 5.2.2.2.,
    7.4.6., 10.5.2.1., 10.5.2.1.1., 13.4.3.2.,
    14.4.3.2., 14.4.3.3., 14.4.4., 14.5.3.1.,
    Tables 14.3. and 14.4.
  melting, melting point, *see* Particle melting
  properties, (*see also* Material type, individual
    material properties) 1.1., 1.4.8., 1.4.10.,
    1.4.15., 1.6.1., 1.6.1.6., 2.2.1., 2.4.3.

Material (*continued*)
  properties (*continued*)
    2.5.3.1., 2.5.5., 3.1., 3.2.3., 3.2.3.1.,
    3.2.3.2., 3.2.3.4., 3.2.7.5., 3.3.2.4.,
    3.3.3.2., **4.2.1**, **4.2.2.3.**, 4.3.1., 4.3.2.1.,
    4.7.3., **5.2.2.1.**, **5.2.3.1.**, 6.1.1., **Chapter
    8**, 10.1., 10.2.2., 10.2.3., 1.2.6.1.2., **10.4:
    10.4.1. to 10.4.1.12.**, 11.1.2., 12.1.,
    12.6.4., 12.7.2., 13.1., 13.2.2.2.1.,
    13.2.2.2.2., **13.2.2.5.**, 13.2.2.8.1., 13.4.,
    13.4.4.2., 13.4.4.4., 13.5.1., **13.6.: 13.6.1.
    to 13.6.10.**, **14.1.4.**, **Chapter 15**
  air retention, *see* Air retention properties
  case study 11.5.
  determination Chapter 8, **Chapter 15**
  quality 13.6.5., **13.6.8.**
  control 12.2.1.
  recirculation **7.4.7.**, 9.3.5.
  remaining in pipeline 12.7.5., 13.2.2.3.3.,
    13.3.5.1.
  strength, (*see also* Bulk strength) 13.4.4.3.
  type, (*see also* Material properties, individual
    material types) 2.2.5., **2.4.6.**, **4.3.2.:
    4.3.2.1. to 4.3.2.3.**, 4.5.1., 4.5.2, 4.6.3.3.,
    4.7.1., 5.2.2.13., 5.2.2.14., 5.2.4., 5.3.4.,
    5.3.5., 5.3.6., 7.5.6., Chapter 8, 11.1.2.,
    11.2.4., 12.7.2., 13.1., 13.2.2.2.1.,
    13.2.2.2.2., **13.2.2.5.**, 13.4.4.2., 13.4.4.4.,
    13.5.1., 14.7., Chapter 15, Figures 229,
    230, 231
  case study **11.4.**
Material type A (good air retention properties),
  (*see also* Aeration; Air retention properties;
  Geldart's classification of fluidisation behaviour; Fluidisation; Permeability) 1.4.4.,
  Chapter 4, **4.6.3.1.**, Chapter 5, 8.2.4.,
  8.4.1., 9.3.1., 9.3.4.2., 15.5.1., 15.5.4.4.
Material type B (poor air retention properties),
  (*see also* Aeration; Air retention properties;
  Geldart's classification of fluidisation behaviour; Fluidisation; Permeability) 1.4.4.,
  Chapter 4, **4.6.3.2.**, Chapter 5, 8.2.4.,
  8.4.1., 9.3.1., 9.3.4.2., 13.4.3.4., Chapter 15
Mathematical models 1.4.5., 4.3.1., 5.1., 7.4.1.,
  10.2.3.,
  air mass flow rate **5.2.2.7.**, 7.5.1., 9.2.4.
  compression **Chapter 6**
    isentropic **6.3.2.**
    isothermal 6.2.1., 6.3.1., 6.3.2.
  conveying air velocity 6.1.4., 6.2.5., 6.2.5.1.,
    7.2.2., 9.2.2.1., 9.2.3.1., 10.2.6.1.2.,
    13.2.2.2.1.
  conveying systems capability Figure 66
  conveying system design 1.5.2., 5.1., **5.2.:
    5.2.1. to 5.2.4.**, Figure 65
  graphical representation **6.2.1.1.**, **6.2.5.1.**,
    7.4.4.
  logic diagrams 1.5.2., **5.2.2.: 5.2.2.1. to
    5.2.2.16., 5.2.3.: 5.2.3.1. to 5.2.3.14.**
  material mass flow rate, (*see also* Ideal Gas
    Law) 5.2.4., 6.3.3.

Mathematical models (*continued*)
  power requirements 4.6.1., 5.2.2.13.,
    5.2.2.14., 10.6.3., 14.4.2.1.
  scaling **9.3.: 9.3.1. to 9.3.8.**
  single-phase flow Chapter 6, **7.2.: 7.2.1. to
    7.2.2., 9.2.: 9.2.1. to 9.2.4.**, 10.2.6.1.:
    10.2.6.1.1. to 10.2.6.1.3.
  Darcy's equation 7.2.1., 9.2.3.1., Figure 134
  pressure drop 7.2.1., 9.2.1., 9.2.3.: 9.2.3.1.
    to 9.2.3.1.6., 9.2.4.
  system design **5.2.: 5.2.1. to 5.2.4.**
  venturi feeder
    throat 3.2.5.
  volumetric flow rate 5.2.2.16., 5.2.3.7., 6.1.4.,
    6.2.1., 6.2.5., 6.3.1., 7.2.2., 9.2.2.1.,
    10.2.6.1.2., 14.5.3.1.,
Mean particle size, *see* Particle size
Mechanical conveying systems 1.3., 10.6.1.
Medium phase **8.4.5.**
Metal powders 10.4.3., 12.6.2., 13.5.6.
Microscopy, electron transmission and light
  (particle size distribution) 15.2.2.2.,
  15.2.2.2.5., 15.2.3.
Mine shafts, (*see also* Coal mines; Mine work-
  ings) 10.2.5.1.1.
Mine workings, (*see also* Coal mines; Mine
  shafts) 9.3.5.2.
Mined materials, (*see also* Coal) 12.3.8.8.
Minimum conveying air velocity, *see* Conveying
  air velocity
Mode of conveying, *see* Conveying mode; Dense
  phase; Dilute phase; Medium phase
Mode of operation, *see* Conveying system, mode
  of operation
Moist materials, (*see also* Damp materials; Hygroscopic materials; Wet materials)
  13.2.2.8.2., 15.4.2., 15.5.4.4.
Moisture, (*see also* Condensation; Humidity;
  Water vapour) **6.4.: 6.4.1. to 6.4.5.2.**
  conveying air **6.4.: 6.4.1. to 6.4.5.2.**,
    Figure 95
  conveying line **13.2.2.3.1.**
  effect on flowability of material **15.4.2.4.**
  free, 5.2.2.1., **15.4.2.4.**
  inherent 15.4.2.4.
Moisture content
  conveying air, (*see also* Humidity) **6.4.: 6.4.1.
    to 6.4.5.2.**, 10.4.8., **13.4.3.2.**, 13.6.5., Fi-
    gure 95
  material, (*see also* Damp materials; Deliques-
    cent materials; Hygroscopic materials;
    Moist materials; Wet materials) 6.3.3.,
    6.4., 8.3.3., **10.4.2.**, 13.6.5., 13.6.10.
Moody chart **9.2.2.1.**, Figure 234
Multiple delivery points *see* Conveying line discharge
Multiple material handling 1.1., 1.4.5., 1.5.3.,
  4.4., 5.1., 5.2.2.15., 5.2.3.10., 5.4.1., **5.4.2.**,
  7.4.5., 7.5.6., 10.2.6.2.1., **10.3.4.**, 13.2.2.5.
  case study 4.4., 5.4.2., 5.4.6.
Multiple pick-up points, *see* Conveying line feed

Negative pressure (vacuum) conveying systems,
  see Conveying system, negative pressure
Nitrogen, (*see also* Air; Conveying air; Gas;
  Inert gas; Single-phase flow) 2.4.8., 6.2.3.,
  10.2.2.2., 10.4.3.
Nitrogen absorption (BET methods) (specific
  surface determination) 15.2.2.3.3.
Nomenclature 1.4.1., **1.7.: 1.7.1. to 1.7.4.**
Non-abrasive (erosive) materials 3.2.3.
Non-conducting materials 12.5.1.
Non-suspension flow, *see* Dense phase
Nozzles, suction, *see* Suction nozzles
Null point **1.6.1.15.**, 2.4.8.
Nylon 13.6.2.
  pellets 10.4.9., 13.6.2.

Oil-free air from air mover 14.5.3.2.1.,
  14.5.3.2.2.
Oil injection, air mover, (*see also* Air mover,
  cooling 6.6.3., 6.6.4.)
Oil-rig 14.5.4.4.
Oil separation (removal)
  compressed air 6.6.3., 6.6.6., 6.6.7.
Open conveying system, *see* Conveying system,
  open
Open surface conveying **10.3.6.**
Operating pressure (range)
  air mover, *see* Air mover, individual names of
    air movers
  conveying system, *see* Conveying system
  exhauster, *see* individual names of exhausters
  feeding device, *see* Feeding device; individual
    names of feeding devices
Operating range, *see* Operating pressure
Operational problems, *see also* individual names
  of problems 1.1., 1.4.12., 1.4.13., 1.5.4.,
  Chapter 12, Chapter 13
  solutions 1.1., 1.4.12., 1.4.13., **Chapter 12,
    Chapter 13**
Optical microscope (particle size distribution)
  15.2.2.2., **15.2.2.2.5.**
Optimising conveying systems, *see* Conveying
  system, optimising
Orifice plate 7.4.2.
Outlet, *see* Conveying line exit
Oxygen level of conveying air 10.4.3., 13.5.6.
  minimum to prevent explosion 12.6.4.

Paddle device 3.2.8.
Particle, (*see also* Material; Solids)
  angular 12.3.6.1.
  coarse, *see* Coarse granular materials
  degradation, (*see also* Friable materials) 1.1.,
    1.4.12., 1.5.4., 2.3.6., 2.3.7., **2.4.4.**,
    2.4.6., 2.5.1., 2.5.3., 2.5.5., 3.1.,3.2.5.,
    3.2.6., 3.2.7.1., **3.2.2.3.**, 3.3.3.3., 4.7.3.,
    6.1.3., 6.2.6., 7.3.2., 8.2.2., 8.3.1.,
    10.2.2.7., 10.4.6., 11.4., 12.1., **12.2.:
    12.2.1. to 12.2.3.**, 12.3.2., 12.3.8.1.,

Particle (*continued*)
degradation (*continued*)
13.1., 13.3.4., **13.4.5.1.**, **13.6.7**,
15.2.2.1.3., 15.2.2.2.3., 15.2.2.3.2.,
Figures 289, 290, 293, 294
coal Figure 293
sugar Figure 294
density, *see* Density
diameter 15.2.2.
equivalent 15.2.2.
statistical 15.2.2.
Feret's **15.2.2.**
Martin's **15.2.2.**
Stokes **15.2.2.2.2.**, 15.2.2.2.3.
fine, *see* Fine materials
forces, *see* Inter-particle forces
hardness, (*see also* Abrasive materials; Erosion) 2.4.5., 5.2.2.1., 10.4.5., 12.1.,
12.2.2.1., **12.3.6.1.**, 13.5.5., 14.1.4.,
Figure 267
heavy, *see* Heavy particles
impact, *see* Bends; Erosion
interaction with fluids 15.2.2.2.5.
large, *see* Large particles
mass 3.3.3.1., 3.3.3.2.
melting 1.4.12., **10.4.9.**, 12.2.2.3., 12.3.5.,
12.4.: **12.4.1.** to **12.4.4.**, 13.6.9.
number of **15.2.2.2.4.**
packing arrangement 15.2.2.2.5., 15.3.4.,
15.5.4.
spacing Figure 285
properties, (*see also* Material properties;
Material type; individual particle properties) **15.2.3.**
shape 2.4.4., 4.2.1., 5.2.2.1., 6.3.3., 8.3.1.,
8.3.3., 12.1., 12.2.1., 12.2.2.1., 12.3.6.1.,
12.3.6.3., 13.6.6., 13.6.8., **15.2.**, 15.2.1.,
15.2.2., 15.2.2.2.5., **15.2.2.3.**: **15.2.2.3.1.**
to **15.2.2.3.3.**, 15.2.3., 15.3.4., 15.4.2.,
15.4.2.2., 15.5.7., Table 15.1.
descriptive terminology 15.2.2.3.,
15.2.2.3.1., 15.2.2.3.2.
factor 8.3.3., **15.2.2.3.2.**, **15.5.7.**, **15.5.8.2.**,
Table 15.4
sphericity **15.2.2.3.2**, 15.5.7.
size 3.3.3.2., 6.3.3., 6.5., 8.3.1., 8.3.3., 8.4.4.,
8.4.4.1., 12.2.2.1., **12.3.6.2.**, 12.6.2.,
13.5.6., 13.6.8., 15.1.3., **15.2.**: **15.2.1.** to
15.2.2.2.5., 15.2.3., 15.4.1., **15.4.2.1.**,
15.5.4.8., 15.4.4., 15.5.6.3.
analysis 1.4.8., **15.2.**: **15.2.1.** to **15.2.3.**
determination **15.2.2.2.**: **15.2.2.2.1.** to
15.2.2.2.5.
electrical sensing zone technique
15.2.2.2., **15.2.2.2.4.**
electron microscope 15.2.2.2., **15.2.2.2.5.**
elutriation 15.2.2.2., **15.2.2.2.3.**
microscopy 15.2.2.2., **15.2.2.2.5.**, 15.2.3.
sedimentation 15.2.2.2., **15.2.2.2.2.**
sieving 15.2.2.2., **15.2.2.2.1.**
distribution 1.4.8., 2.4.2., 2.4.3., 2.4.4.,

Particle (*continued*)
size (*continued*)
distribution (*continued*)
3.3.2.4., 4.2.1., 5.2.2.1., 8.3.3., 8.4.4.,
8.4.4.1., 8.5.4.1., 12.2.1., 13.4.5.1.,
14.1.4., 15.1.3., 15.2.1., **15.2.2.1.**:
15.2.2.1.1. to **15.2.2.1.2.**, **15.2.2.**:
15.2.2.1. to **15.2.2.2.5.**, 15.2.3.,
15.4.2.1.
cumulative 12.2.3., 15.2.2.1., **15.2.2.1.1.**,
Figures 286, 287, 289
cement Figure 288
fractional percentage frequency curve
8.4.4.1.1., 12.2.3., 15.2.2.1.,
15.2.2.1.2., Figure 290
Gaussian 8.4.4.1., 8.5.4.1.
irregular 8.4.4.1., 8.5.4.1.
mean, *see* Particle size, median value
median value 2.4.2., 2.5., 4.2.1., 8.3.3.,
8.4.4.1. 8.4.5., 10.2.7.2.2., 12.2.3.,
12.3.6.2., 13.6.6., 14.1.4., **15.2.2.1.1.**,
15.2.2.3.3., 15.2.3., 15.5.7., 15.5.8.2.,
Tables 8.1 and 15.1., Figures 70, 268,
269, 281 to 284
range 3.3.2.5., 3.3.3., 8.4.4., **8.4.4.1.**,
8.5.4.1., 10.2.7.1., 15.1.3.
strength, 12.2.2.1.
structure 15.2.2.2.5., 15.2.2.3.2.
surface moisture 15.4.2.4.
velocity 2.4.4., 10.4.9., 12.2.2.1.
terminal 6.5., Figure 267
Particulate material Figure 284
Pearlite 8.1., 8.3.1., 8.3.2., 8.3.3., 8.4.1., 8.4.4.,
8.4.4.1., **8.4.4.1.3.**, 8.5., **8.5.4.1.**, 9.3.1.,
9.3.2.1., 15.1.1., 15.2.2.4., 15.3.5., 15.4.4.,
15.5.8., 15.5.8.1., 15.5.8.2., 15.5.8.3.,
Tables 8.1., 15.1 to 15.4., Figure 219, 227,
275 to 281, 283
conveying characteristics Figure 219
Pellets 3.2.3., 3.2.3.2., 3.3.2.4., 4.3.2.1.,
10.2.5.2.1., 13.4.4.3.
agricultural feed 2.1.
nylon, *see* Nylon
plastic, *see* Plastic
polyester, *see* Polyester
polyethylene, *see* Polyethylene
Permeability, (*see also* Aeration; Air retention
properties; Fluidisation; Geldart's classification of fluidisation behaviour; Material type
A; Material type B) 1.4.8., 4.2.1., 5.2.2.1.,
8.5.4.1., 13.4.3.4., 13.4.3.5., 15.2.2.3.3.,
15.5.3.: **15.5.3.1.** to **15.5.3.2.**, 15.5.6.1.,
15.5.6.3., 15.5.8.1., Figure 292
cell 15.5.6.2.
characteristics 8.4.1., 8.5.4.1.
data 8.5.3., 15.5.6.1.
factor 1.4.8., 8.3.3., **8.4.1.**, 8.4.2., 8.4.3.,
8.4.4.1.: **8.5.2.**, 8.5.4., **15.5.3.2.**, 15.5.8.,
Tables 15.4., Figures 275, 278, 291, 292
granular materials **13.4.3.5.**
poor 13.4.3.4.

Permeameter **15.5.3.**: **15.5.3.1. to 15.5.3.2.**,
  15.5.4., 15.5.5., 15.5.2., 15.5.6.1., 15.5.6.2.,
  15.5.8., 15.5.8.1., Figure 291
air flow rate 15.5.3.1., 15.5.3.2.
air velocity 15.5.3.1.
bed 15.5.3.8., 15.5.3.2., **15.5.4.**, 15.5.6.1.,
  Figures 291, 292
pressure drop, *see* Pressure drop
Permeametry 8.4.2., 8.5.4., **15.2.3.**, **15.5.3.**:
  15.5.3.1. to 15.5.3.2., 15.5.6.3., 15.5.7.,
  Figure 292
coal Figure 293
sugar Figure 294
Pervious materials 15.4.2.4.
Petrochemical industry 12.3.1.
P.f.ash, *see* Pulverised fuel ash
Pharmaceutical products 10.4.3., 12.6.2.,
  13.5.6., 15.2.2.3.3.
Phase density (mass flow ratio, mass ratio, solids
  loading ratio) **1.6.1.1.**, 1.6.1.2., 1.6.1.3.,
  1.6.1.10., **2.2.2.**, 2.2.3., 2.2.4., 2.2.5.,
  2.2.6., 2.2.6.1., 2.2.6.2., 2.3.2., 2.3.7.,
  2.4.2., 2.4.3., 2.4.6., 2.4.7., 3.2.7.8., 4.2.2.,
  4.2.2.3., 4.3.2., 4.3.2.1., 4.3.2.2., 4.3.3.,
  4.3.4., **4.3.4.1.**, 4.5.2., 4.6., 4.6.3.1., 5.1.,
  5.2.2.6., 5.2.2.7., **5.2.2.8.**, 5.2.2.9., 5.2.3.8.,
  5.2.3.9., **5.2.3.1.**, 5.2.3.11., 5.2.3.13.,
  5.2.4., 5.3.2.4., 5.3.5., 5.3.6., 5.4.5., 5.4.6.,
  6.1.1., 6.1.3., 6.1.6., 6.3.3., **7.3.3.**, 7.3.4.,
  7.3.5., 7.3.6., 7.4.: 7.4.1. to 7.4.7., 7.5.:
  7.5.1. to 7.5.6., 8.1., 8.2.3., 8.4.5., 9.3.2.3.,
  9.3.2.4., 9.3.4., 9.3.4.2., 9.3.5.1., 9.3.5.2.,
  9.3.6.1., 10.2.4., 10.5.2.1.1., 11.1.2.,
  11.2.2., **11.2.3.**, 11.2.5., 11.4., 12.2.2.1.,
  12.3.7.1., 12.4.3., 12.6.3.2., 13.2.2.2.1.,
  13.2.2.6., 14.2.1., 14.2.2., 14.3.4.5.,
  14.3.5.3., 14.3.6., 14.4.1., 14.4.2.,
  14.5.3.1.2., 14.7., Table 14.2.,
  Figures 93, 94, 98, 99, 100, 101 to 104, 137,
  138, 139, 140, 141, 167 to 170, 225, 226, 228
  to 230, 231, 154, 255, 256, 285, 295, 296,
  303, 305, 309
conveying characteristics, *see* Conveying characteristics
lines of constant 11.1.2.
Photosedimenometer 15.2.3.
Pick-up, *see* Conveying line inlet
points, *see* Conveying line feed
velocity, see Conveying line inlet velocity
Pigments 2.4.6.
Pipeline, (*see also* Conveying line) **Chapter 14**
angle 13.3.8.8.
bends, *see* Bends
blockage, *see* Blockage
bore (diameter, size) 1.2., 1.3., 1.4.4., 1.4.6.,
  1.4.7., 1.4.9., 1.4.14., 2.2.1., **2.2.3.**,
  2.3.7., 2.4.3., 4.1., 4.2.3., 4.3.4., 4.4.,
  4.5.2., 4.5.3., **4.6.3.**: **4.6.3.1. to 4.6.3.3.**,
  4.7.1., 5.1., 5.2.2.2., 5.2.2.3., **5.2.2.4.**,
  5.2.2.6., **5.2.2.12.**, 5.2.2.13., 5.2.2.14.,
  5.2.2.15., **5.2.3.3.**, 5.2.4., 5.3.2.3.,

Pipeline (*continued*)
bore (*continued*)
  5.3.2.4., 5.3.2.5., **5.3.2.7.**, **5.3.2.8.**,
  5.3.3.1., 5.3.3.3., 5.3.4., **5.3.6.**, 5.3.7.,
  5.3.8., 6.1.2., 6.1.3., **6.1.4.**, 6.1.5., 6.1.7.,
  6.2.5.: 6.2.5.1., 7.1., 7.2.1., 7.4.1., 7.5.5.,
  8.3.1., 9.1., 9.2.1., **9.2.3.1.3.**, 9.3.2.,
  9.3.4.3., **9.3.6.**: **9.3.6.1.**, 10.1., 10.2.3.,
  10.2.4., 10.2.5.1.1., **10.5.2.5.**, 11.1.2.,
  11.2.6., 11.3.2., 12.2.2.4., 12.3.7.3.,
  12.7.2., 13.3.3.1., 13.6.6., 14.1.1.,
  14.2.1., 14.2.2., 14.3.4.3., 14.3.4.4.,
  14.3.5.: **14.3.5.1. to 14.3.5.3.**, **14.3.6.**,
  14.4.2.: 14.4.2.1. to 14.4.2.2.3., 14.5.1.,
  14.5.2.2., 14.5.2.3., 14.5.3.1.2., 14.5.4:
  14.5.4.1., 14.5.4.2., 14.6.1., **14.6.2:**
  14.6.2.1. to 14.6.2.2., 14.7., Tables 14.2.,
  14.6 to 14.10., 14.14., 14.17 to 14.19.,
  Figures 57, 58, 59, 60, 64, 83, 84, 88, 89,
  90, 91, 101 to 104, 105, 106, 107, 108 to
  115, 117, 118, 119, 120, 121, 122 to 133,
  153 to 166, 236, 333, 334
air leakage
rotary valve 3.2.3.1.
blow tanks 2.3.7., 3.2.7.2., 10.2.4.,
  10.2.5.2.5., 10.5.1., **10.5.2.5.**, 14.4.3.1.,
  14.4.3.2., 14.4.3.3., 14.4.5., **14.6.3.:**
  14.6.3.1. to 14.6.3.2., 14.6.5.,
  twin 14.4.4., 14.6.4.
changing 1.3., 1.4.4., 4.1., 4.2.3., **4.2.3.2.**,
  4.3.4., **4.5.3.**, **4.5.2.**, **4.5.3.**, 4.6.3.:
  4.6.3.1. to 4.6.3.3., **5.3.6.**, 5.4.2.,
  6.1.4., 6.2.5.: 6.2.5.1., 9.3.2., 11.1.1.,
  11.1.4., **11.2.5.**, 11.2.6., 11.3.2.,
  13.2.2.7.4., 14.2.2., 14.4.1., 14.4.2.:
  14.4.2.1. to 14.4.2.2.3., 14.5.2.2.,
  14.5.2.3., 14.5.4.: 14.5.4.1. to 14.5.4.2.,
  14.6.2.: **14.6.2.1. to 14.6.2.2.**, Tables
  14.2., 14.6., 14.7. to 14.10., 14.14.,
  14.17. to 14.20., Figures 88 to 91, 108
  to 115, 119 to 121, 122 to 133
conveying system, combined positive and
  negative 2.3.6.
costs, *see* Costs
large 10.2.5.1.1., 11.1.4., 12.3.9., 12.7.2.
material mass flow rate, *see* Material mass
  flow rate
pressure drop, *see* Pressure drop
ratio to bend diameter (D/d), *see* Bend
  diameter
scaling, *see* Scaling
sizing 2.2.4., 2.3.7., 3.3.7.2., 6.1.2., **6.1.4.**,
  10.2.5.1.1.
small 4.3.4.3., 5.2.4., 10.2.5.1.1.
branches 2.4.5., 12.3.1.
case study Chapter 14
coating by conveyed material 9.3.7., 10.4.3.,
  10.4.12., **12.7.4.**, 13.2.2.8., **13.2.2.8.2.**,
  13.6.10.,
contraction section **9.2.3.1.5.**
cross section 3.3.3.3., 3.2.5.

Pipeline (*continued*)
  cross sectional area 1.6.1.8., 6.1.4., 9.3.6.1.,
    9.3.7., 10.4.12., 12.7.4., 13.2.2.8.2.,
    15.3.5.2.
  design, *see* Conveying system design
  diameter, *see* Pipeline bore
  diverter
    sections 9.2.3.1.5., 12.4.1., 13.6.2. Figure
      242
    valves 2.4.5., 5.4.5., 10.2.2.5., 10.3.1.,
      12.2.2.4., 12.3.1., 13.6.2., **14.5.4.4.**,
      14.6.2., Table 14.14.
  dog-leg sections 9.2.3.1.5., Figure 242
  ductwork 13.3.2.1.
  erosion, *see* Erosion
  external 13.2.2.3.1., 13.5.3.
  expansion (enlargement) section **9.2.3.1.5.**,
    9.3.4.3., 12.2.2.4.
  fabricated bends 9.2.3.1.5., Figure 242
  features, (*see also* individual names of fea-
    tures) 9.2.1., **9.2.3.1.5.**
  flexible 10.4.12., 12.7.4.
    sections 13.3 2.2.
  geometry (layout), (*see also* Pipeline length;
    Bend geometry) 1.1., 1.3., 1.4.9., **2.4.7.**,
    3.3.2.3., 3.3.2.4., **4.2.3.: 4.2.3.1. to
    4.2.3.3.**, 5.2.2.3., 5.3.2.3., 5.3.3.1.,
    5.3.3.3., 5.4.1., 7.4.1., 7.5.4., 8.1., 9.1.,
    9.2.3.1.5., 9.3.1., **9.3.2.: 9.3.2.1. to
    9.3.2.4.**, 9.3.6., 10.1., 10.2.1., 10.2.2.,
    10.2.3., 11.1.1., **12.2.2.4.**, 12.2.3.,
    12.2.2.8.2., 12.3.4., 13.3.2.1., 13.5.3.,
    14.1.2., 14.2.1., 14.2.2., **14.3.4.**
    scaling, *see* Scaling
  heating
    trace 13.2.2.3.1.
  influence on conveying **5.3.4.**
  length, (*see also* Conveying distance; Pipeline
    geometry)
    equivalent length of horizontal pipeline, *see*
      Scaling
    horizontal sections 1.6.1.13., 2.4.3.,
      4.2.3.1., 5.2.2.3., 7.4.2., 9.2.3.1.,
      9.3.4.: 9.3.4.1. to 9.3.4.3., 9.3.5,
      9.3.5.1., 11.3.3., 12.7.3., 12.7.5.,
      13.4.3.5., 14.3.4.3., Figures 252, 254,
      255
    scaling *see* Scaling
    vertical sections 1.3., 1.4.9., 5.3.2.4., 7.4.2.,
      9.1., **9.3.5.: 9.3.5.1. to 9.3.5.2.**, 10.3.7.,
      11.3.3., 14.1.2., **14.3.4.2.**
      down 2.4.7., 4.2.3.1., 5.2.2.3., 9.3.5.,
        9.3.5.2., Figure 256
      up 1.6.1.14., 2.4.3., 4.2.3.1., 5.2.2.3.,
        9.3.5., **9.3.5.1.**, 13.2.2.3.3., 14.3.4.2.,
        Figures 253, 254, 255
  material, (*see also* Pipeline surface material)
    9.3.2., **9.3.7.**, 10.2.6.2.3., **12.2.2.3.**,
    12.3.2., **12.3.3.**, **12.3.8.5.**, **12.3.8.6.**,
    12.3.9., 13.2.2.8.2., 13.3.2.2., 13.5.5.,
    Figures 259, 260

Pipeline (*continued*)
  material (*continued*)
    hard 12.3.8.5., 12.3.9.
    hard metal 13.3.2.2.
    hardness **12.3.8.5.**, 12.3.8.6.
    polyurethane **12.3.8.6.**
    rubber 1.4.9., **9.3.7.**, **12.3.8.6.**, Figures 259,
      260
    steel 9.3.7., Figures 259, 260
  material remaining after conveying 12.7.5.,
    13.2.2.3.3., 13.3.5.1.
  misaligned sections 12.3.1., 12.3.8.2., 13.5.5.,
    14.5.4.1.
  orientation, *see* Pipeline geometry; Bend
    geometry
  scaling, *see* Scaling
  single bore 1.6.1.11., 1.6.1.12., 4.5.2.,
    4.6.3.2., 6.2., 6.2.5.1., 6.2.6., 7.5.5.,
    9.3.4.3., 12.3.7.3.
  sizing 6.2.2.
  stepped 1.4.6., 2.4.7., 4.2.3.2., 4.5.2.,
    5.2.2.4., **6.2.6.**, 9.2.3.1.5., 9.3.2.,
    9.3.4.3., 10.2.6.2.2., 11.1.3., 12.2.3.,
    12.3.7.3., 12.3.8.4., 13.3.3.1., 13.5.5.
  surface
    coatings 12.3.8.5., **12.3.8.7.**, 13.5.5.
    hardfacing metal alloy 12.3.8.7.
    oxide ceramics 12.3.8.7.
    irregularities 12.3.1.
    material, (*see also* Pipeline material)
      12.3.8.5., **12.3.8.6.**, 13.5.5.
    properties 12.3.3., 12.3.8.5., 12.3.8.6.,
      13.5.5.
      brittle 12.3.3., 12.3.4., 12.3.8.3.,
        12.3.8.4., 13.5.5., 14.5.4.2.
      ductile 12.3.3., 12.3.4., 12.3.5.,
        12.3.8.2., 12.3.8.3.
      hard **12.3.8.5.**, 13.5.5.
      hardness Figures 273, 274
      resilient **12.3.8.6.**
    removal 12.3.3.
    sandblasting 12.4.4., Figures 295, 296
    types 12.3.3., **12.3.8.5.**, **12.3.8.6.**, **12.3.8.7.**,
      aluminium 12.3.3, 12.4.4.
      aluminium alloy 12.3.3.
      annealed 12.3.8.5.
      basalt 12.3.4., 12.3.8.5., 13.5.5., 14.5.4.2.
      ceramics 12.3.3., 12.3.4., **12.3.8.5.**,
        12.3.8.7., 13.3.2.2., 13.5.5.
      concrete 12.3.3.
      copper 12.3.3.
      glass 12.3.3.
      metal alloy 12.3.8.7.
      nickel-hard cast iron 12.3.4., **12.3.8.5.**,
        12.3.8.7., 13.5.5.
      perspex 12.3.5.
      polyurethane 12.3.8.7.
      steel
        alloy 12.3.3.
        annealed low carbon 12.3.3.
        carbon 12.3.3.

Pipeline (*continued*)
 surface (*continued*)
  types (*continued*)
   steel (*continued*)
    chromium, 11 per cent 12.3.3.
 toughened 12.3.9.
 wall
  roughness **9.2.2.4.**, 9.2.3.1.4., 10.4.9.,
   12.4.4., 13.2.2.9.2., 13.6.2., Table 9.1.
  thickness 12.3.9., 14.5.4.1.
  wear, (*see also* Erosion; Plant wear)
   13.2.2.9.2.
Pipelines used in conveying trials, *see* Test pipelines
Plant, *see also* Components of conveying system; Conveying system; Pipeline; individual
 names of components)
 air supply, *see* Air Supply
 components, *see* Components of conveying
  system, individual names of components
 wear, (*see also* Erosion) 13.2.2.8., **13.2.2.8.1.**,
  13.2.2.9.1.
  energy loss 13.2.2.9.1.
Plastic 10.4.3., 10.4.9., 12.6.2., 13.2.2.9.2.,
 13.5.6.
 anti-vibration 12.5.2.
 pellets 3.2.3.1., 10.4.9., 12.4.1., 12.4.2,
  12.4.3., 12.4.4., 13.6.2.
Plastic coating processes 15.5.2.2.
Plug control systems, *see* Conveying system,
 innovatory
Plugs, (*see also* Conveying) plug **2.5.2.**, 2.5.3.,
 2.5.4.: 2.5.4.1. to 2.5.4.2., 3.2.4., 3.2.9.,
 13.3.5., 13.3.5.1., 15.5.4.4., Figures 45, 46
 length **2.5.3.**
Pneumatic conveying, *see* Conveying
 applications **2.1.**
Pneumatic stowing 12.3.1.
Pollution, (*see also* Dust) 3.3.1., **3.3.2.5.**,
 3.3.3.3.2., 10.2.2.1., 10.2.7.
Polyester
 pellets 10.4.9., 12.4.1., 13.6.2.
Polyethylene 12.6.3.2.
 low density, Figures 295, 296
  degradation Figures 295, 296
  pellets 12.4.3.
 pellets 8.1., 8.3.1., 8.3.2., 8.3.3., 8.4.1.,
  8.4.4., 8.4.4.1., 8.4.5., 8.5.2., 9.3.1.,
  9.3.2.1., 10.4.9., 12.4.1., 12.4.3., 13.6.2.,
  15.1.1., 15.2.2.4., 15.3.5., 15.4.4.,
  15.5.8., 15.5.8.1., 15.5.8.2., 15.5.8.3.,
  Tables 8.1., 15.1., 15.2., 15.3., Figures
  220, 227, 275 to 281, 283
 conveying characteristics Figure 220
Polymers 15.4.2.3.
Polypropylene
 powder 12.7.2.
Polytetrafluorethylene rings 6.6.7.
Polyvinyl chloride 2.1., 2.4.6., 5.3.5., 7.5.6.,
 8.1., 8.2.2., 8.2.4., 8.3.3., 9.3.1., 9.3.2.1.,
 15.4.2.3., Table 8.1., Figures 81, 215, 225,

Polyvinyl chloride (*continued*)
 229, 230, 231, 283
 conveying characteristics Figure 215
 Porosity **15.3.4.1.**, 15.3.5., 15.5.6.3.
Positive displacement compressor, (*see also* Air
 mover; Reciprocating compressor; Screw
 compressor) 6.6.1., 6.6.2., Figure 73
Positive pressure conveying systems, *see* Conveying system, positive pressure
Powder pump, *see* Blow tank
Powdered materials, (*see also* Fine materials)
 3.2.7.5., 3.2.8., 4.2.1., 4.3.2.1., 9.3.8.,
 10.4.12., 12.6.4., 12.7.4., 13.4.3.5.,
 15.2.2.3.1., 15.3.2.2.2., 15.3.3.1.2.,
 15.3.3.1.3., 15.5.1., 15.5.7., 15.5.6.1.
Power costs, *see* Costs
Power requirements 1.4.4., 1.4.7., 1.5.3., 4.1.,
 4.3.4.1., 4.3.5., 4.5.2., **4.6.: 4.6.1. to
 4.6.3.3.**, 5.1., 5.2.2.6., **5.2.2.13.**, 5.2.2.14.,
 5.2.3.10., **5.3.2.6.**, **5.3.2.7.**, **5.3.4.**, **5.3.5.**,
 5.3.7., **5.4.2.**, 5.4.6., 7.5., **7.5.2.**, 7.5.3.,
 7.5.6., 9.3.5.2., 10.2.6.2.1., 13.1.,
 13.2.2.2.3., 13.2.2.9.1., 14.5.1., 14.6.2.,
 14.6.2.1., 14.6.5., 14.7., Figures 117, 118,
 167, 168
 air-assisted gravity conveyor 6.5.
 air mover 4.6.1., **5.2.2.13.**, 5.2.2.14., **5.3.2.6.**,
  5.4.2., 5.4.3., 5.4.6., **6.7.**, **6.8.**, 10.2.3.,
  10.2.6.2., 10.2.6.2.5., 10.6.3.1., 11.2.2.,
  11.2.2.1., 11.2.2.2., **11.2.4.**, 11.4., 11.5.,
  14.5.3.2., 14.6.2.1., 14.6.3.1., Tables
  14.11., 14.12., 14.13., 14.17., 14.18.
  drive power **14.4.2.1.**
  lines of constant 11.2.4., 11.4., Figures 302
  mathematical model 5.2.2.13., 10.6.3.,
   14.4.2.1.,
  reciprocating compressor 7.5.2., 14.3.5.2.1.,
   Tables 14.11., 14.19., 14.20., Figures
   77, 79
  roots type blowers 6.7., 7.5.2., 14.5.3.2.3.,
   Tables 14.13., 14.19., 14.20., Figures
   77, 78, 301, 302
  screw compressors 14.5.3.2.2., Tables
   14.12., 14.19., 14.20.
 components **14.5.: 14.5.1. to 14.5.5.**, 14.6.1.,
  14.6.2., Tables 14.19., 14.20.
 conveying distance 4.6.2.: 4.6.2.1., 4.6.3.,
  5.2.2.13, 10.2.3., Figures 116, 117, 118,
  123, 125, 127, 129, 131, 133, 167 to 170
 conveying system, combined negative and
  positive pressure 10.2.2.5., 10.2.6.2.5.,
  13.3.3.
 costs, *see* Costs
 feeding device 10.6.3.1., 14.4.2.1.
  blow tanks 14.4.2.2.1., 14.5.3.1.2., 14.6.3.:
   14.6.3.1. to 14.6.3.2., 14.6.4., Tables
   14.8., 14.9. and 14.20., Figures 58, 336
  batch size Figure 58
  twin 14.4.2.2.1., 14.6.3., 14.6.4., Tables
   14.8., 14.10., 14.20., Figures 338, 339
  rotary valve 14.4.2.2.3., 14.5.1., 14.5.2.3.,

Power requirements (*continued*)
  feeding device (*continued*)
    rotary valve (*continued*)
      Tables 14.7., 14.8., 14.19.
    screw feeder 2.3.2., 14.4.2.2.2., 14.5.2.2.,
      Table 14.6., 14.8., 14.19.
      constant pitch 10.2.5.2.2.
      decreasing pitch 10.2.5.2.2.
  gas–solid separation device 10.6.3.1.
  filtration unit 14.4.2., 14.5.5., Table 14.16.
  lines of constant 7.5.2., 7.5.6., 11.2.4., 11.4.,
    Figures 147, 153 to 166, 171, 297, 302
    curve shape 11.4.
  material
    compatability 4.6.3.1., 4.6.3.2., 4.6.3.3.
    mass flow rate 5.3.7., **7.5.2.**
    type 5.2.2.13.
  mathematical model, *see* Mathematical models
  minimum 1.3., 1.5.3., 4.7., 8.2.2., 14.6.2.1.
  pipeline bore 4.6.3.: 4.6.3.1. to 4.6.3.3.,
    5.2.2.13., 6.7., 14.4.2.1., 14.5.3.1.2.,
    10.2.3., Tables 14.2., 14.8., 14.19.,
    14.20., Figures 57, 58, 17, 77, 118, 119,
    333
  specific energy, *see* Energy
  total 10.2.3., 10.6.1., 10.6.3., **10.6.3.1.**,
    14.4.2.1., Tables 14.2., 14.7.
Pressure
  absolute 6.3.2.
  air (gas), (*see also* Ideal Gas Law) 6.2.1.,
    Figure 232
  air supply, *see* Air supply pressure
  ambient 1.6.1.15., 6.2.5.1., Figure 232
  atmospheric 6.6.1., 13.4.5.3., 13.5.2.,
  delivery, *see* Air supply pressure
  conveying air (gas), *see* Conveying air press-
    ure
  conveying line inlet, *see* Conveying line inlet
    air pressure
  exhaust, *see* Exhaust pressure
  null point **1.6.1.15.**, 2.4.8.
  operating, *see* Operating pressure
  partial
    air 1.6.1.17., 6.4.1.
    water vapour 6.4.1.
  relief venting 10.4.3., 11.3.2., 13.5.6.
  volumetric flow rate, *see* Volumetric flow rate
Pressure drop
  bulk solid 15.5.4.2.
  conveying line
    single-phase flow (air only, empty pipeline)
      1.4.9., 2.2.4., 5.2.4., **7.2.: 7.2.1. to
      7.2.2.**, 7.3.1., 7.4.3., 7.4.4., 7.5.5.,
      8.2.4., 91., **9.2.: 9.2.1. to 9.2.4.**,
      11.1.3., 11.2.2.2., 13.2.2.3.3.,
      13.2.2.8.2., 13.4.5.2., 14.3.4., Figures
      97, 107, 134, 136, 137, 235, 236, 312,
      317
      bends 9.2.3.1.4., 9.3.8., 14.3.4.
      Darcy equation **7.2.1.**, 7.2.2., 9.2.1.,
      9.2.3.1., Figure 134

Pressure drop (*continued*)
  conveying line (*continued*)
    single-phase flow (*continued*)
      pipeline bore 2.2.4., 7.2.1., 7.2.2.,
      9.2.3.1.3., 9.3.6.: 9.3.6.1., 10.2.3.,
      14.3.4., **14.3.5.1.**, Figures 236, 317
      pipeline length 7.2.1., 7.5.5., **9.2.3.1.2.**,
      9.3.2.3., 9.3.2.4., 9.3.4., 14.3.4.,
      14.3.4.4., Figures 235, 312
    two-phase flow (gas–solid flow, material
      conveying), (*see also* Pressure drop,
      total) 1.4.4., 1.4.8., 1.6.1., 2.2.1.,
      2.2.4., **2.2.5.**, 2.3.5., 2.3.7., 2.4.6.,
      2.4.7., 3.1., 3.2.7.8., 4.1., 4.2.2.,
      4.2.2.1., 4.2.2.3., 4.3.1., 4.3.2.2.,
      4.3.3., 4.3.4.: 4.3.4.1., 4.3.4.2.,
      4.3.4.3., 4.3.5., 4.4., 4.5.2., 4.5.3.,
      4.6.: 4.6.1. to 4.6.3.3., 4.7.1., 5.2.2.2.,
      5.2.2.5., **5.2.2.10.**, 5.2.2.11., 5.2.2.13.,
      5.2.3.4., 5.2.3.8., 5.2.3.10., 5.2.4.,
      5.3.2.5., 5.3.3.4., **5.3.7.**, 5.4.6., 6.1.3.,
      6.2., 6.2.4., 6.2.6., 6.6.2., 7.3.: **7.3.1.**
      to 7.3.6., 7.4.2., 7.4.3., 7.4.4., 7.4.7.,
      7.5.1., 7.5.2., 7.5.6., 8.1., 8.2.: 8.2.1.
      to 8.2.4., 8.3.4., 8.5.2., 8.5.3., 8.5.4.,
      9.1., **9.3.2.3.**, 9.3.4.: **9.3.4.1.** to
      9.3.4.3., 10.2.3., **10.2.5.1.3.**,
      10.2.6.1.1., 10.5.2.1.1., 11.1.3., 11.1.4.,
      11.2.2.: 11.2.2.1. to 11.2.2.2., 11.3.2.,
      11.4., 11.5., 12.2.1., 12.7.3., 12.7.4.,
      13.2.2.2.2., 13.2.2.3.3., 13.2.2.7.1.,
      13.6.3., 13.6.9., 14.2.1., 14.2.2., 4.3.:
      14.3.1. to 14.3.6., 14.4.3.2., 14.4.3.3.,
      14.4.4., Tables 3.4., 14.2., Figures 3,
      64, 97, 98, 101 to 104, 105, 106, 108 to
      115, 117, 118, 122 to 133, 136, 137,
      142, 144, 252, 254, 255, 278, 279, 280
      bends 2.4.7., 9.2.1., **9.2.3.1.4.**, 9.3.2.4.,
      9.3.3., 9.3.8., 11.1.3., 12.3.8.3.,
      12.7.3., 13.5.5., 14.4.3.2. Figures
      237, 238, 239, 240, 246, 248, 249,
      261, 262
      blind (blank) tees 13.5.5.
      lines of constant 9.3.3., Figure 249
      number of Figures 246, 248
      pipeline features **9.2.3.1.5.**, Figures
      240, 241, 242, 259, 260
      conveying distance 2.2.4., 2.2.5., **3.2.7.9.**,
      4.2.2.3., **4.3.3.**, **4.3.4.3.**, **4.5.2.**,
      4.6.2.: 4.6.2.1., 4.7.1., 5.3.2.5.,
      5.3.5., 5.3.7., **7.5.5.**, 9.3.2.3.,
      10.2.3., 14.3.4.: 14.3.4.1. to
      14.3.4.5., Tables 3.3., 3.4., Figures
      105, 106, 108 to 115, 117, 118, 122 to
      133, 145, 149, 243 to 245, 318
      conveying characteristics, *see* Conveying
      characteristics
      material compatability, *see* Material mass
      flow rate, material compatability
      pipeline bore 2.2.4., **4.3.5.**, **4.5.3.**, **4.6.3.:**
      4.6.3.1. to 4.6.3.3., 4.7.1., 5.2.2.2.,

Pressure drop (*continued*)
conveying line (*continued*)
pipeline bore (*continued*)
5.2.2.4., **5.2.2.12.**, 5.2.4., 5.3.2.5.,
5.3.6., 5.3.7., 9.3.2.1., 9.3.2.2.,
9.3.6.: **9.3.6.1.**, 10.2.3., 14.2.2.,
14.3.5.: 14.2.5.1. to 14.3.5.2., 14.6.,
14.4.1., 14.4.3.2., 14.4.3.3., 14.4.4.,
Table 14.2., Figures 59 to 62, 117,
118, 120, 121, 122 to 133, 317
pipeline
material 9.3.7.
surface 12.4.4., 13.2.2.9.2., Figures
295, 296
pulse phase system **2.5.3.1.**
purge 13.2.2.3.3.
stepped pipeline 6.2.6., 9.3.4.3.
test line Chapter 9
vertical 9.3.5.
down 2.4.7., 9.3.5.2., Figure 256
up 9.3.5.1., 14.3.4.2., Figures 253, 254,
255
feeding device 3.1, 3.2.2., 10.2.2.4., 10.2.5.1.,
10.2.5.1.2., 10.2.5.1.3., 10.2.6.1.1.,
11.1.3., 11.1.4., 12.3.7.2., 13.2.2.2.2.,
13.2.2.4., 13.6.7., 14.4.2.1., 14.5.1.
blow tank 2.3.7., 3.2.7.1., **3.2.7.6.**, 3.2.9.,
6.1.1., 6.4.3., 10.2.5.1.3., 10.2.5.1.4.,
10.2.5.2.5., **13.4.3.3.**, 14.5.3.1., 14.7.
discharge line 6.4.3.
fluidising membrane 10.2.5.2.5.,
13.4.3.2., 13.4.3.3.
twin 14.4.2.2.1.
gate lock valve 10.2.5.
rotary valve 3.2.2.1., 3.2.3.4., 10.2.2.5.,
10.2.5., 13.4.4.4., 14.4.2.2.3., 14.5.1.,
14.5.3.1.
screw feeder 3.2.4., 14.4.2.2.2., 14.5.3.1.
venturi feeder 10.2.5.2.3.
gas–solid separation device 10.2.6.1.1.,
10.2.7.1.4.
filtration unit 2.4.4., 3.3.2.3., 3.3.3.3.,
3.3.3.3.2., 5.2.2.13., 6.1.1., 6.6.1.,
7.4.2., 10.2.6.1.1., **10.2.7.1.4.**, 11.1.3.,
12.2.1., 13.2.2.7.2., 13.4.2., 13.4.5.1.,
13.4.5.2., 13.6.7.
lines of constant 5.3.2.3., 5.3.8., 5.4.2., 5.4.5.,
7.3.5., 7.4.4., 7.5.1., 7.5.6., 8.1., 8.2.1.,
8.2.2., **8.2.3.**, **8.2.4.**, 8.3.6., 8.5.2.,
9.2.4., 9.3.3., **9.3.4.1.**, 9.3.5., 9.3.5.1.,
11.2.2.1., 11.2.2.2., 11.2.4., 11.4.,
14.3.2., 14.3.4.4., 14.3.4.5, 14.3.5.1.,
14.3.5.2., Figure 252
curve limits **8.2.3.**, 8.3.2.
curve shape **8.2.2.**, 8.3.2., 11.4.
curve spacing **8.2.4.**, 8.3.2.
mathematical model, *see* Mathematical models
permeameter bed 15.5.3.1., **15.5.3.2.**, 15.5.4.,
15.5.4.2., 15.5.6.1., Figures 292, 293, 294
pipeline, rough wall surface 12.4.4.
scaling, *see* Scaling

Pressure drop (*continued*)
total (*see also* Pressure drop conveying line)
1.4.10., 9.2.3.1.6., 11.1.3.,
Pressure egg, *see* Blow tanks
Pressure gauge, 7.4.2., 11.3.2., 13.2.2.2.2.,
13.2.2.3.3., 13.2.2.8.1., 13.2.2.8.2., 13.4.3.,
13.4.3.3., 13.4.5.2.
Bourdon 7.4.2.
Pressure gradient, *see* Pressure drop
Pressure relief vents 10.4.3, 11.3.2.
Pressure tappings 7.4.2., 9.3.5.
Pressure transducer 7.5.4.
Product, *see* Material; Solids, *see also* individual
names of materials
Properties of conveyed material, *see* Material
properties, individual material properties
Protective clothing 12.5.2.
P.t.f.e., *see* Polytetrafluoroethylene
Pull-push systems, *see* Conveying system, com-
bined negative and positive pressure
Pulsation
air mover, *see* Air mover
two-phase (gas–solid) flow, *see* Two-phase
flow
Pulse phase systems, *see* Conveying system, innovatory
Pulsing device **2.5.3.**, **3.2.9.**
Pulverised fuel ash 2.1., 2.4.6., 4.2.1. 4.3.2.1.,
5.3.8., 6.4.3., 8.1., 8.2.2., 8.2.3., 8.2.4.,
8.3.1., 8.3.2., 8.3.3., 8.4.1., 8.4.4., 8.4.4.1.,
8.5., 9.3.1., 9.3.2.1., 9.3.5.1., 9.3.8.,
10.2.5.2.7., 10.5.2.1.1., 12.3.6.1., 12.3.7.1.,
13.4.3.2., 15.2.3., 15.1.1., 15.2.2.4., 15.3.5.,
15.4.4., 15.5.8.: 15.5.8.1. to 15.5.8.3.,
Tables 8.1., 15.1., 15.2., 15.3., 15.4.,
Figures 81, 82. 207 to 210, 225, 227, 229,
230, 231, 255. 261, 262, 275 to 281, 283
conveying characteristics Figures 207 to 210
Purge 10.5.3.2., 12.7.3., 13.2.2.3.3., 13.4.5.2.
after conveying 10.2.6.1.2., 10.5.3.2.,
12.3.7.2., 12.3.8.3., 13.2.2.3.3.,
13.2.2.8.2., 13.4.5.4.
before conveying 13.2.2.3.3.
blow tank 12.7.5.
drying conveying line 13.2.2.3.1.
pressure drop, *see* Pressure drop
P.v.c. resin, *see* Polyvinyl chloride resin
Pycnometer **15.3.2.2.2.**, 15.3.5.

Quarried materials, (*see also* Coal; Fuel)
12.3.8.6., 12.3.8.8.
Quartz, *see also* Silica 12.3.8.5.
particles Figure 273

Raask, E. 12.3.8.5.
Radial flow compressor, *see* Aerodynamic com-
pressor
Radioactive materials, 10.2.2.2., **10.4.10.**
Radius, of bends, *see* Bends

Ratio of bend diameter to pipeline bore (D/d),
  see Bend diameter
Ratio between the time averaged mean material
  flow rate and value to be achieved (batch
  conveying), see Material mass flow rate
Ratio between the time averaged mean material
  flow rate to the maximum, or steady state
  conveying rate (batch conveying), see Material mass flow rate
Receiver, see Gas–solid separation device; Hopper
Reciprocating compressor, (see also Air mover)
  6.1.1., 6.3.2., 6.3.3., 6.6.1., **6.6.7.**, **6.7.**,
  7.5.2., 10.2.6.2.3., 14.4.3.1., 14.5.3.2.,
  14.5.3.2.1., 14.6.1., Tables 14.11., 14.17. to
  14.20., Figure 329
  capability Figure 329
  operating pressure 6.6.7., 14.4.3.1.,
    14.5.3.2.1., Table 14.11., 10.2.6.2.3.,
    Figures 72, 79, 329
Recovery of conveyed material, solids, see Gas–
  solid separation device
Re-entrainment 1.6.1.19., 11.3.3., 12.3.5.,
  12.7.3.
Reference conditions, see Free air conditions
Reynold's Number 7.2.1., 9.2.2.4., Figure 234
Richmond, R. A. 15.5.5.1., 15.5.5.2.
Roots 6.6.4.
Roots type blower, (see also Air mover)
  1.6.1.4., 3.2.5., 6.3.2., 6.3.3., 6.5., 6.6.3.,
  6.6.4., 6.7., 6.8., 7.5.2., 9.2.1., 9.2.3.1.3.,
  10.2.6.2.3., 10.2.7.2.1., 11.1.1., 11.1.5.,
  11.2.: 11.2.1. to 11.2.6., 14.3.6., 14.4.2.2.3.,
  14.4.3.1., 14.5.3.2., **14.5.3.2.3.**, Table
  14.13., Figures 77, 331
  capability Figure 331
  characteristics 6.6.4., 11.1.4., **11.2.: 11.2.1. to
    11.2.6.**, 11.5., Figures 76, 301, 302
  surge Figure 307
  conveying systems, combined 10.2.6.2.5.,
    13.3.3.
  operating pressure 1.6.1.4., 1.6.1.20., 2.3.7.,
    10.2.6.2.3., 11.2.5., 14.4.2.2.3., Tables
    14.11. to 14.13., Figures 72, 77, 331
  operating principle Figure 75
  thermodynamic efficiency 10.2.6.2.3.
Roots type exhauster, (see also Exhauster)
  3.3.2.2., 10.2.6.2.4., 13.3.2.,
  characteristics 6.6.4., Figure 76
  operating pressure 10.2.6.2.4.
Rotameter 7.4.3., 11.3.2.
Rotary compressor, see Roots type blower;
  Roots type exhauster; Rotary screw compressor; Sliding vane rotary compressor
Rotary screw (helical lobe rotary, Lysholm)
  compressor, (see also Air mover) 6.1.1.,
  6.3.3., 6.6.1., **6.6.6.**, 6.6.7., 6.7.,
  10.2.6.2.3., 14.4.3.1., 14.5.3.2., **14.5.3.2.2.**,
  14.6.1., Tables 14.12., 14.17 to 14.20.,
  Figure 330
  capability Figure 330

Rotary screw (continued)
  oil-free **14.5.3.2.2.**
  operating pressure 6.6.6., 10.2.6.2.3., Figures
    72, 330
Rotary valve, (see also Feeding device) 1.4.3.,
  1.4.14., 1.6.1.4., 1.6.1.5., 1.6.1.20., 2.3.2.,
  2.3.4., 2.3.5., 2.3.7., 2.3.8., 2.5.4., 3.2.1.,
  3.2.2., **3.2.3.: 3.2.3.1. to 3.2.3.5.**, 3.2.6.,
  3.2.7.1., 4.3.4.3., 5.2.2.1., 5.2.2.16., 5.4.4.,
  7.3.6., 9.2.3.1.5., 10.2.2.3., 10.2.2.4.,
  10.2.2.5., 10.2.5., **10.2.5.2.1.**, 10.2.5.2.2.,
  10.2.6.2.3., 10.3.1., 10.4.1., 10.4.2., 10.4.5.,
  10.4.7., 10.6.3.1., 11.1.4., 12.3.7.2., 13.4.1.,
  13.4.4.: 13.4.4.1. to 13.4.4.6., 13.6.4.,
  14.3.6., 14.4.2.2.3., 14.5.1., **14.5.2.3.**,
  14.5.3.1., 14.5.3.2., 14.6.5., Tables 14.7.,
  14.8., 14.15., Figures 14, 17, 59
  air ingress, see Ingress of air
  air leakage, see Air leakage
  blow through 3.2.3., 10.2.5.2.1, 10.4.1.,
    10.4.2., 13.4.4.3., 13.6.3., Figure 16
  conveying limits Figure 13
  costs, see Costs
  drop through 3.2.3., 10.2.5.2.1., 13.4.4.3.,
    14.5.2.3., Figure 15
  energy loss 10.2.5.2.1.
  entrainment device **3.2.3.3.**, Figure 19
  feed 3.2.3.2., 3.2.3.3.
    problems **13.4.4.3.**
    rate **3.2.3.5.**
  flow control 10.2.5.1.4., 13.2.2.2.2., **13.4.4.2.**
  off set 3.2.3., 10.2.5.2.1., 10.4.7., 13.4.4.3.,
    Figure 16
  operating pressure 1.6.1.4., 1.6.1.5., 3.2.1.,
    10.2.5.1.1., 10.2.5.2.1., 14.4.2.2.3.,
    14.5.2.3., Tables 3.1., 14.7., 14.8., Figure
    12
  power requirements, see Power requirements
  pressure drop, see Pressure drop
  rotor Figures 20, 21
    design **3.2.3.4.**, 10.2.5.2.1.,
    displacement volume 3.2.3.5.
    pockets 3.2.3.4., 13.4.4.3., Figure 21
    speed 13.4.4.2., 14.5.2.3.
  seizure **13.4.4.5.**
  twin 1.6.1.5.
  venting **3.2.3.2.**, 13.4.4.4., Figure 18
  vibration 13.4.4.3.
  wear 7.3.6., 12.3.7.2., 13.1., 13.2.2.4.,
    13.2.2.8.1., 13.4.4.3., **13.4.4.6.**
Rubber
  anti-vibration 12.5.2.
  pipeline, see Pipeline

Safety precautions 10.2.2.4., 10.4.10., 12.6.4.,
  13.5.6.
  features 10.2.2.1., 10.4.3.
Saltation 1.6.1.10., **1.6.1.13.**, 1.6.1.14., **2.4.3.**,
  6.2.6., 11.1.2.
Sand 2.1., 2.4.2., 2.4.5., 4.2.1., 4.3.2.1., 5.3.8.,

Sand (*continued*)
  7.5.6., 8.1., 8.2.3., 8.2.4., 8.3.3., 8.4.5.,
  9.3.1., 9.3.2.1., 12.3.3., 12.3.4., 12.3.6.1.,
  12.3.6.2., 12.3.6.3., 12.3.8.6., 15.4.1.,
  15.4.2.4., Table 8.1., Figures 140, 211 to
  214, 226, 230, 231, 143, 244, 248, 270, 271,
  283
  conveying characteristics Figures 211 to 214
Saturated materials, *see* Wet materials; *see also*
  Damp materials; Hygroscopic materials;
  Moist materials; Moisture content of materials
Scaling 1.1., 1.3., 1.4.9., 1.4.14., 1.5.2.,
  5.3.2.3., **5.3.3.3.**, **5.3.4.**, 5.3.8., 7.3.6.,
  7.4.1., 7.5., 7.5.4., 7.5.5., 8.3.1., 9.1., **9.3.:**
  9.3.1. to 9.3.8., **14.3.: 14.3.1. to 14.3.6.**.
  Figures 149, 311 to 328
bends 1.4.9., 6.1.3., 7.3.6., 7.4.1., 7.4.2.,
  7.5.5., 8.3.1., 9.1. 9.3.2.4., **9.3.3.**, **9.3.8.**,
  14.3.4., **14.3.4.1.**
  number of Figure 311
  constant **14.3.4.3.**, 14.3.4.5., Figure 311
  distance 1.4.9., 5.3.2.3., **5.3.2.4.**, 5.3.3.3.,
    5.3.4., **5.3.5.**, 5.3.8., 7.4.1., **7.5.5.**, 8.3.1.,
    9.1., **9.3.2.1.**, 9.3.4., 9.3.4.2., 14.2.1.,
    14.3.4.: 14.3.4.1 to 14.3.4.5.. Figure 311
  equivalent length of horizontal pipeline
    bends **9.2.3.1.4.**, 9.2.4., **9.3.2.4.**, **9.3.3.**,
    9.3.4., 9.3.8., 14.3.4., 14.3.4.1.,
    14.3.4.3., Figures 247,. 310
  horizontal pipeline 9.3.2.4., 9.3.4., 9.3.4.1.,
    14.3.4.3.
  total pipeline 14.3.4.3.
  vertical pipeline 14.3.4., 14.3.4.2.
    down 9.3.5.2.
    up 9.3.5.1.
horizontal pipeline **9.3.4.: 9.3.4.1 to 9.3.4.3.**
limits 9.1., **9.3.4.2.**, **14.3.4.5.**, **14.3.5.3.**
mathematical model
  distance, orientation and geometry 9.3.2.4.,
    9.3.4., 14.3.4.3.
  pipeline bore 9.3.6., 14.3.5.2.
pipeline bore (diameter, size) 1.4.9., 5.3.2.3.,
  5.3.2.4., **5.3.2.7.**, 5.3.3.3., 5.3.4., **5.3.6.**,
  7.3.6., 7.4.1., 8.3.1., 9.1., 9.3.2.2., **9.3.6.:**
  9.3.6.1., 14.2.1., 14.2.2., 14.3.4., **14.3.5.:**
  14.3.5.1. to 14.3.5.3., 14.3.6., Figures
  316, 318, 319 to 328
pipeline geometry and orientation 5.3.3.3.,
  7.5.4., 9.1., 9.3.1., **9.3.2.: 9.3.2.1. to**
  9.3.2.4. 14.2.1., **14.3.4.**, **14.3.4.1. to**
  14.3.4.5.
pressure drop 9.3.2.1., **9.3.2.3.**, **9.3.4.1.**,
  14.3.4.4., 14.3.5.1.
rubber hose pipeline 1.4.9., **9.3.7.**
vertical pipeline 1.4.9., **9.3.5.: 9.3.5.1. to**
  9.3.5.2., **14.3.4.2.**
  down **9.3.5.2.**
  up **9.3.5.1.**
Screw compressor, *see* Rotary screw compressor
Screw feeder, (*see also* Feeding device) 1.4.3.,

Screw feeder (*continued*)
  1.4.14., 1.6.1.5., 2.3.2., 2.3.8., 2.5.4.,
  3.2.1., 3.2.2., **3.2.4.**, 3.2.7.1., 9.2.3.1.5.,
  10.2.2.3., 10.2.5., **10.2.5.2.2.**, 10.4.5.,
  10.4.6., 10.6.3.1., 13.4., 14.3.6., 14.5.1.,
  14.5.2.2., 14.5.3.1., 14.5.3.2., 14.6.5.,
  Tables 14.6., 14.8., 14.15., 14.17., 14.19.,
  Figures 14, 59
  air leakage, *see* Air leakage
  air nozzles 14.5.2.2.
  constant pitch (simple) **3.2.4.**, 10.2.5.2.2.,
    Figure 22
  conveying limits Figure 13
  costs, *see* Costs
  decreasing pitch **3.2.4.**, 10.2.5.2.2., Figure 23
  drive power 14.5.1.
  flow control 2.3.2., 3.2.4., 10.2.5.1.4.,
    13.2.2.2.2.
  operating pressures 2.3.2, 10.2.5., 10.2.5.2.2.,
    14.4.2.2.2., 14.5.2.3., Table 3.1., Figure
    12
  material mass flow rate 3.2.4.
  power requirements, *see* Power requirements
  pressure drop, *see* Pressure drop
  wear 13.2.2.4., **13.2.2.8.1.**, 14.5.2.2.
Sea level 6.6.1.
Selection of conveying system, *see* Conveying
  system selection
Separator, *see* Gas–solid separation device
Settling chamber, *see* Gravity settling chamber;
  Hopper
Shearing 15.4.1., 15.4.2.4.
  forces 4.3.2.3., 5.2.2.1.
  material 10.4.7.
  tester 15.4.3.
Short (small) radius bends, *see* Bends
Shot blast rig 12.3.6.2.
Shut down
  blow tank, *see* Blow tank
  explosion risk 12.6.3.2.
  conveying system, *see* Conveying system shut
    down
Sight glasses 7.4.4., 11.3.3., Figures 135, 175
Silica, *see also* Quartz
  impurity 12.3.6.1., 13.5.5.
Silica sand, *see* Sand
Silo, *see* Hopper
Single blow tank, *see* Blow tank
Single-phase flow (air only, empty pipeline),
  (*see also* Air mass flow rate) 1.4.7., 1.4.9.,
  7.2.: 7.2.1. to 7.2.2., 7.4.1., 9.1., **9.2.:**
  9.2.1. to 9.2.4., 9.3.1., 11.1.3., 15.1.2.
  mathematical model, *see* Mathematical models
  pressure drop, *see* Pressure drop
Single plug blow tank systems, *see* Conveying
  systems, innovatory
Site constraints 2.3.7., 10.1., 14.6.5., 14.7.
Size of pipeline, *see* Pipeline bore
Sliding vane rotary compressor, (*see also* Air
  mover) **6.6.3.**, 10.2.6.2.3., Figure 74
  cooling 6.6.3.

Sliding vane rotary compressor (*continued*)
    operating pressure 6.6.3., 10.2.6.2.3., Figure
    72
Sliding vane rotary exhauster, (*see also* Exhaus-
    ter) 10.2.6.2.4.
Slurry 15.4.2.4.
Snake skin, *see* Extrusion hairs
Smith, B. V. 12.3.5.
Solids, *see also* Material; Particle
Solids feeding devices, *see* Feeding device
Solids loading ratio, *see* Phase density
Solids remaining in conveying line 12.7.5.,
    13.2.2.3.3., 13.3.5.1.
Soluble materials 15.3.2.2.2.
Spark, *see* Explosions
Specific energy, *see* Energy
Specific erosion, *see* Erosion
Specific heat 15.1.2., Table 6.1.
    air 3.2.4., 3.2.5., 6.3.2., 6.3.3.
    ratio 3.2.4., 6.3.2.
    material Figures 93, 94
    water 6.3.3.
Specific humidity, *see* Humidity
Specific surface, 1.4.8., 8.3.3., **8.4.2.**, 8.4.3.,
    8.4.4.1., **8.5.3.**, 8.5.4., 8.5.4.1., **15.2.2.3.3.**,
    15.2.3., **15.5.6.: 15.5.6.1. to 15.5.6.3.**,
    15.5.7., **15.5.8.1.**, 15.5.8.2., Table 15.4.,
    Figures 276, 279, 281
    Carmen and Arnell equation 15.5.6.1.,
    15.5.8.1.
    methods **15.5.6.: 15.5.6.1. to 15.5.6.3.**
    BET 15.2.2.3.3.
    Blaine **15.5.6.3.**
    British Standard **15.5.6.1.**
    Lea and Nurse **15.5.6.2.**
Sphericity **15.2.2.3.2.**, 15.5.7.
Spillage 10.3.6.
Standard reference conditions, *see* Free air con-
    ditions
Starch 15.4.1.
Start up
    blow tank, *see* Blow tank
    conveying system, *see* Conveying system
Static electricity, (*see also* Electrostatic charge)
    1.4., 1.4.12., **12.5.: 12.5.1. to 12.5.3.**,
    13.5.4., 13.5.6.
    control **12.5.3.**, 13.5.4.
    earthing **12.5.2.**
Steady state conveying, *see* Material mass flow
    rate
    rate, *see* Material mass flow rate
Steam
    thermodynamic tables 6.4.1.
Stepped pipelines, *see* Pipeline, stepped
Stock piles 10.3.6.
Stoichiometric value, *see* Explosions
Storage, *see* Bulk solids
Streamers, *see* Extrusion hairs
Suck-blow systems, *see* Conveying system, com-
    bined negative and positive pressure
Suction nozzles 3.2.1., **3.2.8.**, 9.3.7., 10.2.2.4.,

Suction nozzles (*continued*)
    10.2.5., 10.3.6., Figure 49
    mechanical dredging device 3.2.8.
    operating pressure Table 3.1., Figure 12
Sugar 12.6.5., 12.6.3.1., 15.4.2.4.
    degraded 8.1., 8.3.1., 8.3.3., 8.4.1., 8.4.4.,
    8.4.4.1., **8.4.4.1.1.**, 8.5., 9.3.1., 9.3.2.1.,
    15.1.1., 15.5.8., Table 8.1., Figures 224,
    275 to 281, 286, 294
    conveying characteristics Figure 224
    granulated 4.3.2.1., 8.1., 8.3.1., 8.3.2., 8.3.3.,
    8.4.1., 8.4.4., 8.4.4.1., 8.5., 9.3.1.,
    9.3.2.1., 10.4.3., 15.1.1., 15.2.2.4.,
    15.3.5., 15.4.4., 15.5.8., 15.5.8.1.,
    15.5.8.2., 15.5.8.3., 15.4.1., 15.5.8.,
    Tables 8.1., 15.1. to 15.4., Figures 223,
    227, 275 to 281, 283, 294
    conveying characteristics, Figure 223
Superficial air velocity **1.6.1.8.**, 1.6.1.10.,
    1.6.1.11., 1.6.1.12., **15.5.3.1.**,
    filter fabric **3.3.3.3.**
    fluidisation 15.5.4.,: 15.5.4.1. to 15.5.4.4.
    permeameter 15.5.3.1., 15.5.3.2., Figure 292
    to 294
Supply pressure of air mover, *see* Air supply
    pressure
Surface coatings, *see* Pipeline
Surge
    air
    blow tanks, *see* Blow tanks
    conveying characteristics
        cement Figure 306
    material feed 3.2.2., 11.5., 13.2.2.2.3., Figure
    306, 307
    Roots type blower performance Figure 307
    single plug blow tank systems 2.5.2.
Suspension flow, *see* Dilute phase
Sutton, H. M. 15.5.5.1., 15.5.5.2.
Synthetic materials 10.4.3., 12.6.2.
System, *see* Conveying system
System design, *see* Conveying system design
System selection, *see* Conveying system selection
System throughput, *see* Material mass flow rate

Tee-piece, *see* Bends
Temperature, *see also* Ideal Gas Law
    absolute 6.3.2, 5.2.2.7.
    air 6.3.3., 13.2.2.3.2., Figures 92, 95, 232, 233
    lines of constant 6.3.3., Figure 95
    air mover
    air supply 6.3., 6.3.2., 13.2.2.3.2., Figure 96
    ambient 6.3.3., 13.2.2.2.2., 13.5.7.
    conveying air (gas). 1.4.6., 1.6.1.8., 3.3.2.,
    6.3.: 6.3.1. to **6.3.3.**, 6.4.1., 6.4.2.,
    7.2.2., 10.2.7.1.3., 12.2.2.2., **13.2.2.3.2.**,
    13.4.5.2., 13.5.7., 13.6.9.
    conveying line inlet Figure 93, 94
    conveyed material 3.3.3., **6.3.3.**, 10.2.7.1.3.,
    10.4.9., **13.6.9.** Figures 93, 94
    plastic pellets 12.4.3.

Temperature (*continued*)
mathematical models, *see* Mathematical models; *see also* Ideal Gas Law
pipeline 12.4.3, 13.2.2.3.1., 13.5.3., 13.6.9.
two-phase flow
equilibrium temperature 13.6.9., Figure 93
volumetric flow rate, *see* Volumetric flow rate
Tenders 1.4.14., 1.5.1.
Test line, *see* Test pipeline
Test data, (*see also* Bench scale tests; Conveying trials) 1.3., 1.4.14., 5.1.
conveying characteristics, *see* Conveying characteristics
conveying system design 1.2., 1.3., 1.4.5., 1.4.7., 1.4.14., 1.5.2., **5.3.: 5.3.1. to 5.3.8.**, 9.3.: 9.3.1. to 9.3.8., 10.2.3., 14.2.: 14.2.1. to 14.2.2., 14.3.: 14.3.1. to 14.3.6., 14.7.
erosion 12.3.: 12.3.1. to 12.3.8.8.
explosions 12.6.3.: 12.6.3.1. to 12.6.3.2., 12.6.4.
logic diagrams 5.3.: 5.3.1. to 5.3.8.
material properties Chaper 8, **Chapter 15**
particle degradation 12.2.1., 12.2.3., Figures 223, 224, 289, 290
Test pipeline 1.3., 7.4.1., **7.4.2.**, 7.5.5., 9.1., 9.3.2.1., 9.3.2.2., 14.2.1., **14.2.2.**, 14.3.4.4., Figures 135, 172 to 186, 308
instrumentation and control **7.4.2., 11.3.2.**
rubber Figure 180
Thermal conductivity 6.3.3., 13.6.9.
Thermal transient effects 6.3.3., 13.6.9.
Thermodynamic and transport properties tables 9.2.2.3.
Thermodynamic property tables for steam 6.4.1.
Tilly, G. P. 12.3.3., 12.3.6.2.
Throughput of conveying system, *see* Material mass flow rate
Titanium dioxide 10.4.12., 12.7.4.
Total pipeline, *see* Pipeline
equivalent length, *see* Scaling
Toxic materials, 2.1., 2.2.5., 2.4.8., 3.3.1., 10.2.2.4., 10.2.7., **10.4.11.**
Time averaged mean flow rate (value), *see* Material mass flow rate
Trade names 1.1.
Transmission losses 10.2.1.1.
Trouble shooting 1.1., 1.4.13., 1.5.4, Chapter 12, **Chapter 13**
Tungsten carbide 12.3.8.7.
Turbo blower, *see* Centrifugal compressor
Twin blow tanks, *see* Blow tanks
Two-phase flow (gas–solid flow, material conveying), (*see also* Material mass flow rate) 1.4.7., 3.2.3.3., 3.3.2.3., 3.3.3.1., 3.3.3.3., 4.2.2.: 4.2.2.1. to 4.2.2.3., 4.3.: 4.3.1. to 4.3.5., 5.3.4., 5.4.6, 6.1.6., 6.2., **7.3.: 7.3.1. to 7.3.6.**, 7.4.1., **9.3.: 9.3.1. to 9.3.8.**, 10.2.4., 10.2.7.1.2., 11.1.3., 15.1.2.
agglomerates (lumps) 15.4.1.
characteristics 2.4.4., 9.2.2., **15.4.: 15.4.1. to 15.4.4.**

Two-phase flow (*continued*)
free flowing materials 3.2.3.4., 3.2.5., 6.5., 10.2.5.2.3., 15.4.1., 15.5.2.3., 15.4.3.1., 15.5.2.1.
flowability **15.4.: 15.4.1. to 15.4.4.**
material compatability, *see* Material mass flow rate, material compatability
material concentration 3.3.2.3., 3.3.3.3., 7.3.1., 13.2.2.2.2.
material influences, *see* Material mass flow rate, material compatability
pressure drop, *see* Pressure drop
pulsating **1.6.1.20.**, 3.2.3.3., 7.4.2., 10.2.6.2.3.
turbulent **7.2.1.**, 12.3.8.2., 12.7.3.
Types of conveying system, *see* Conveying system; individual names of conveying systems

Uprating conveying systems, *see* Conveying system, uprating

Vacuum 10.2.6.2.4., 13.3.2.
Vacuum conveying systems, *see* Conveying system, negative pressure
Vacuum pump, *see* Exhauster, individual names of exhausters
Valve 11.3.3., 13.5.6., **14.5.4.: 14.5.4.1. to 14.5.4.4.**, 14.6.2., Table 14.15
control **14.5.4.3.**
butterfly 14.5.4.3., 14.5.4.4, 14.5.5, Table 14.14.
costs, *see* Costs
diverter, *see* Pipeline
isolating
blow tank, *see* Blow tank
multiple discharge points 13.3.2.1.
multiple feed points 10.3.1.
shut off
hopper 15.5.2.2.
tee-piece 11.3.2.
Van der Waal's forces 3.3.3.3.
Velocity
conveying, *see* Conveying velocity
conveying air, *see* Conveying air velocity
conveying line exit, *see* Conveying line exit air velocity
conveying line inlet, *see* Conveying line inlet air velocity
free air, *see* Free air velocity
open duct, 1.6.1.8.
superficial, *see* Superficial air velocity
Velocity head **9.2.3.1.4.**
Venting
blow tank, *see* Blow tank
conveying line feed, *see* Feeding device; individual names of feeding devices
gas–solid separation, *see* Gas–solid separation device; individual names of gas–solid separation devices
rotary valve, *see* Rotary valve

Venturi feeder, (*see also* Feeding device) 1.4.3.,
  2.3.2., 3.2.2., **3.2.5.**, 3.2.6.,4.3.4.3.,
  9.2.3.1.5., 10.2.2.3., **10.2.5.2.3.**, 10.2.6.2.3.,
  11.1.4., 13.2.2.2.2., Figures 14, 24, 15
conveying limits Figure 13
entrainment device 3.2.3.3.
flow control 3.2.5., 10.2.5.1.4., 10.2.5.2.3.,
  13.2.2.2.2.
material mass flow rate 3.2.5.
operating pressure 3.2.5., 10.2.5.2.3., Table
  3.1., Figure 12
pressure drop, *see* Pressure drop
throat **3.2.5.**
  mathematical model **3.2.5.**
Vertical
  conveying, *see* Conveying, vertical; *see also*
    Pipeline, length
  equivalent lengths of horizontal pipeline, *see*
    Scaling
  flow, *see* Pipeline length; Two-phase flow
  pressure drop, *see* Pressure drop
  sections of pipeline, *see* Pipeline length
Vibration 15.3.3.1.2., 15.4.3.1.3., 15.5.5.2.
Vibrators 15.5.4.4.
Vibratory feeder 3.2.5.
Viscosity
  air (gas) **9.2.2.3.**, 15.1.2., Figure 233
  material 15.1.2.
Voidage 8.3.3., **15.3.4.**, 15.3.4.1., 15.3.5., Table
  15.2.
Volumetric feeder, (*see also* Rotary valve; Gate
  lock valve) 5.4.4.
Volumetric (air) flow rate, (*see also* Air flow
  rate; Air mover; Air requirements; Air
  supply pressure) 1.4.6., 2.3.7., 3.2.7.3.,
  3.2.7.4., 3.3.2.1., 4.4., **5.2.2.7.**, 5.2.2.16.,
  5.2.3.7., 5.2.3.8., 5.3.2.9., 5.4.3., 6.1.,
  6.1.2., 6.1.3., 6.1.4., 6.1.5., 6.1.6., 6.1.7.,
  6.2.: 6.2.1. to 6.2.6., 6.3.: 6.3.1. to 6.3.3.,

Volumetric (air) flow rate (*continued*)
  6.4., 6.4.1., 6.5., 6.6.1., 6.6.2., 6.7., 7.2.2.,
  7.3.6., 7.4.5., 7.5.5., 7.5.6., 8.2.3., 9.2.2.1.,
  9.2.3.1.1., 10.2.3., 10.2.5.1., 10.2.6.,
  10.2.6.1., **10.2.6.1.2.**, 10.2.6.2.1.,
  10.2.6.2.3., 11.1.1., 11.1.4., 11.2.5.,
  12.3.7.3., 13.2.2.2.1., 13.2.2.2.2.,
  13.2.2.3.2., 13.2.2.4., 13.2.2.7.2., 13.2.4.,
  13.3.5., 13.4.3., 13.4.5.3., 13.5.2., 14.5.2.1.,
  14.5.5., 15.1.2., 15.5.3.1., Figures 77, 79, 83
  to 92, 95, 329 to 331
humidity **6.4.**
mathematical model, *see* Mathematical models
permeameter 15.5.3.1., 15.5.3.2.
pressure **6.2.: 6.2.1. to 6.2.6.**, 15.1.2.
temperature **6.3.: 6.3.1. to 6.3.3.**, 15.1.2.

Warren Spring Laboratory 1.1., 2.5.3.
Water
  cooling
    air mover, *see* Air mover
    removal from (compressed) air, *see* Air drying
    specific heat, *see* Specific heat
  Water vapour, 1.6.1.16., 1.6.1.17., 6.4.1.,
    6.4.2., 13.4.3.2.
  condensation, *see* Condensation
  partial pressure, *see* Pressure
Weighing mechanism 11.3.2.
Wet materials, (*see also* Damp materials; Hygroscopic materials; Moist materials) **10.4.3.**,
  13.6.10., 15.3.3.1.3., 15.4.2.4.
  surface tension 15.4.2.4.
Wood 10.4.3, 12.6.2.
  chips 12.3.6.1., 13.5.5.

Zenz, F. A. 2.4.3.

Index

Abbreviated Guide

Main entries and definitions are given in bold type. The numbers refer to Sections in the text.

Abrasive materials, particles, (*see also* Erosion) 1.2.8., 1.3.2.1., 1.3.4.1.2., 1.3.4.8.1., 1.4.4.2.1., 1.4.4.2.3., 1.4.4.2.4., 1.4.4.2.5.
Air, *see also* Conveying air; Gas; Inert gas; Nitrogen; Single-phase flow
Air (gas) compression, (*see also* Compression) 1.3.2., 1.3.4.8.1.
Air drying equipment 1.2.8.
Air extraction lines, pressure drop, *see* Pressure drop
Air flow rate, (*see also* Air mass flow rate; Conveying air velocity; Conveying line inlet air velocity; Single-phase flow; Superficial air velocity; Volumetric flow rate) 1.3.4.4.7., 1.3.4.5., 1.3.4.7.2., 1.3.4.7.4., 1.4.4.2.5., 1.4.6.4., 1.4.6.5.2., 1.3.4.1.2., 1.3.4.4.6.
Air ingress, *see* Ingress of air
Air leakage (losses) 1.4.5.
  feeding devices 1.3.2.2., 1.3.2.4., **1.3.4.9.2.**, 1.3.4.9.3., 1.4.4.1.
  blow tanks **1.3.4.9.2.**
  gate lock valves 1.4.2.2.4.
  rotary valves 1.2.4., **1.3.4.9.2.**, 1.4.4.2.1.
  screw feeders
    constant pitch (simple) 1.4.4.2.2.
    decreasing pitch 1.4.4.2.2.
Air line, *see* Air supply line
Air losses, *see* Air leakage
Air mass flow rate (*see also* Air flow rate; Air requirements; Single-phase flow), 1.3.3.1., 1.3.4.1.2., 1.3.4.3.1., **1.3.4.5.**, 1.3.4.7.4., 1.3.4.7.5., 1.3.4.9.1., 1.3.6.2., Figures 3, 4, 5, 8, 9, 11
  minimum 1.3.4.5.
Air mover (blower, compressor) (*see also* Fans; Blow tanks; Reciprocating compressors; Rotary screw compressors; Roots type blowers; Sliding vane rotary compressor; Exhauster) 1.2.7., **1.3.4.6.**, 1.3.4.10.,

Air mover (blower, compressor) (*continued*) 1.3.6.1., 1.3.6.3., 1.4.1., 1.4.6.5.1.
  air supply pressure, *see* Air supply pressure control 1.4.5.2., **1.4.5.3.**
  costs, *see* Costs
  delivery pressure, *see* Air supply pressure
  distance from conveying system 1.3.4.10.1.
  drive motor 1.3.5.1., 1.3.6.1.
    power 1.3.6.1.
  duty 1.4.5., 1.4.5.2.
  free air delivery, (*see also* Air supply pressure; Volumetric flow rate) 1.4.5.1.
  operating pressure **1.3.5.**, **Figure 13**
  power requirements, *see* Power requirements
  rating 1.3.1., 1.3.4.8.
  selection 1.1.2., **1.3.5.**, **1.3.5.1.**, **1.4.5.1. to 1.4.5.7.**
  specification **1.3.4.9.3.**, **1.3.4.10.5.**, 1.3.6.3., **1.4.5.1. to 1.4.5.7.**
  supply pressure, *see* Air supply pressure
  volumetric flow rate, *see* Volumetric flow rate
Air pressure
  conveying, *see* Conveying air pressure
  conveying line inlet, *see* Conveying line inlet air pressure
  supply, *see* Air supply pressure
Air requirements, (*see also* Air velocity; Air flow rate; Air mass flow rate; Air supply pressure; Exhaust pressure; Pressure drop; Volumetric flow rate) 1.1.2., 1.1.3., 1.2.4., 1.3.1., 1.3.3.1., 1.3.4., 1.3.4.4.8., 1.3.4.4.9., 1.3.4.7.5., **1.3.4.9.1. to 1.3.4.9.3.**, 1.3.6., 1.3.6.2., 1.3.6.3., 1.4.4.2.5., 1.4.5., 1.4.5.3., Figure 1
Air retention properties, (*see also* Material type A; Material type B)
  good 1.3.3.1., 1.3.4.3.1., 1.3.4.3.2., 1.3.4.4.9., Figures 2, 11
  poor 1.3.3.1., 1.3.4.3.1., 1.3.4.3.2., 1.3.4.4.9., Figures 2, 11

Air-solid flow, *see* Two-phase flow
Air supply, (*see also* Air flow rate; Air mass
  flow rate; Air requirements; Air supply
  pressure; Conveying air velocity; Conveying
  line inlet air velocity; Single phase flow;
  Superficial air velocity; Volumetric flow
  rate
  air mover, *see* Air mover
  control 1.3.6.2.
  plant **1.4.5.4.**
Air supply line
  pressure drop, *see* Pressure drop
Air supply (delivery, exhaust) pressure, (*see also*
  Air requirements; Conveying line inlet air
  pressure; Exhaust pressure; Volumetric flow
  rate) 1.1.2., 1.1.3., 1.3.1., 1.3.2.3., 1.3.2.4.,
  1.3.4.2.1., 1.3.4.4.7., 1.3.4.4.8., 1.3.4.7.3.,
  1.3.4.8.1., 1.3.4.9., **1.3.4.10.1. to
  1.3.4.10.5.**, 1.3.5.1., 1.3.6.1., 1.4.1., 1.4.2.,
  1.4.5., 1.4.5.1., 1.4.5.3., **Figure 13**
  high 1.3.4.8.1.
Air velocity
  conveying, *see* Conveying air velocity, (*see
    also* Conveying velocity)
  conveying line exit (outlet), *see* Conveying
    line exit air velocity
  conveying line inlet, *see* Conveying line inlet
    air velocity
  superficial, *see* Superficial air velocity
Area, cross sectional of pipe, *see* Pipeline, cross
  sectional area

Barytes 1.3.4.3., 1.3.4.3.2., Figure 5
Batch conveying, *see* Conveying system, batch
Batch size 1.4.6.5.2.
Bend diameter
  ratio to pipeline bore (D/d) 1.3.4.2.,
    1.3.4.4.4.
Bends
  blind tees 1.3.4.4.4.
  elbows 1.3.4.4.4.
  erosion, *see* Erosion
  geometry, (*see also* Pipeline geometry)
    1.3.4.2., 1.3.4.7.2.
  long (large) radius 1.3.4.4.4.
  number of 1.3.4.2., 1.3.4.2.1., 1.3.4.7.2.
  pressure drop, *see* Pressure drop
  scaling, *see* Scaling
    equivalent length, *see* Scaling
  short (small) radius 1.3.4.4.4.
Bentonite 1.3.4.3., 1.3.4.3.2.
Blind tees, *see* Bends
Blockage 1.3.2.1., 1.3.2.4., 1.3.6.2., 1.3.4.10.5.
Blow eggs, *see* Blow tanks
Blow tanks (blow eggs, powder pumps, pressure
  eggs), (*see also* Air mover) 1.2.4.,
    1.3.4.1.1., 1.4.3., 1.4.4., **1.4.4.2.5.**, 1.4.5.4.,
    1.4.6.5.2.
  air ingress, *see* Ingress of air
  air leakage, *see* Air leakage

Blow tanks (*continued*)
  air surge 1.4.2.2.5., 1.4.6.5.2.
  bottom discharge 1.4.4.2.5.
  coded 1.4.4.2.5.
  discharge valve, without 1.4.4.2.5.
  fluidising membrane 1.4.4.2.5.
    pressure drop, *see* Pressure drop
  low pressure 1.3.4.1.2.
  operating pressure 1.3.4.1.2., 1.4.4.2.5., Fi-
    gure 12
  pressure drop, *see* Pressure drop
  single plug blow tank systems, *see* Conveying
    system, innovatory
  top discharge 1.4.4.2.5.
  twin 1.3.4.1.1.
    operating pressure 1.3.4.1.2.
    in series 1.4.4.2.5.
Blower, *see* Air mover
Blower, roots type, *see* Roots type blower
Bore, *see* Pipeline bore
Bulk density, *see* Density
Bulk solid (material) 1.4.6.1., 1.4.6.2.

Cement 1.3.4.3., 1.3.4.3.2., 1.4.4.2.2., Figure 5
Choice of conveying system, *see* Conveying sys-
  tem selection
Cleaning
  fabric filters, *see* Filtration unit
Closed conveying systems, *see* Conveying system
  closed
Coal 1.3.4.3.
Coarse granular materials, (*see also* Granular
  materials) 1.3.4.3.2.
Cohesive materials, 1.2.8., 1.4.4.2.1., 1.4.4.2.2.
Collecting efficiency
  gas–solid separation device, *see* Gas–solid
    separation device; cyclone separator; Fil-
    tration unit; Gravity settling chamber
Combined negative and positive pressure conveying systems, *see* Conveying system, combined negative and positive pressure
Combustible materials 1.2.3.
Components of conveying system, (*see also* Air
  mover; Feeding device; Gas–solid separation device; individual names of components) 1.1.1., **1.4.**
  specification **1.1.4.**, **1.4.1. to 1.4.6.5.2.**
Compressibility
  air, *see* Air compressibility
Compression
  isothermal 1.3.4.6.
Compressor, *see* Air mover
Controlled environment, (*see also* Conveying
  system, closed) 1.2.2., 1.2.3.
Constraints
  selection of system or components 1.1.1.
  site 1.1.1., 1.1.2.
Conversion factors **A.3.**

Conveying
dense phase, *see* Dense phase
dilute phase, *see* Dilute phase
Conveying air (gas), (*see also* Air; Gas; Inert
gas; Nitrogen; Single-phase flow)
pressure 1.3.2., **1.3.2.3.**, 1.3.2.4.
recirculation 1.2.2.
temperature, *see* Temperature
velocity **1.3.2.1. to 1.3.2.4.**, 1.3.4.4.2.,
1.3.4.7.4.
high 1.3.4.8.1.
minimum 1.3.2.1., 1.3.3.1., **1.3.4.3.1.**,
1.3.4.3.2., 1.3.4.4.8., 1.3.4.7.3.,
1.3.4.7.4., 1.3.5.1., Figure 2
Conveying, batch, *see* Conveying system, batch
Conveying capability, (*see also* Conveying
potential) 1.3.4.3.1., 1.3.4.4.8., 1.3.4.7.4.,
1.4.4.2.3.
Conveying characteristics **1.3.3.1.** 1.3.4.,
1.3.4.1.2., **1.3.4.3.1 to 1.3.4.3.2.**, 1.3.4.4.,
1.3.4.4.2., 1.3.4.4.9., 1.3.4.5., 1.3.4.7.,
1.3.4.7.4., **1.3.4.7.5.**, 1.3.6.1., 1.3.6.2.,
1.3.6.3., Figure 6
design points 1.3.4.5.
dicalcium phosphate Figures 4, 9
for logic diagrams 1.3.3., 1.3.4.
scaling, *see* Scaling
sodium sulphate Figures 3, 8
Conveying conditions 1.3.4.4.3., 1.4.2.
Conveying continuous, *see* Conveying system,
continuously operating
Conveying cycle, *see* Conveying system, batch
Conveying distance, 1.1.2., 1.2.7., 1.3.3.,
1.3.4.1.1., **1.3.4.2.1.**, 1.3.4.3., **1.3.4.4.1. to
1.3.4.4.9.**, 1.3.4.5., 1.3.4.6., 1.3.4.7.1.,
1.3.4.7.5., 1.3.6., Figures 10, 11
change 1.3.4.3., 1.3.6., **1.3.4.4.5. to
1.3.4.4.9.**, 1.3.4.5., 1.3.4.8., **1.3.6.2.**, Figures 3 and 8, 4 and 9, 10, 11
long 1.4.4.2.5.
multiple **1.3.6.2.**
scaling *see* Scaling
Conveying, dual negative and positive pressure
systems, *see* Conveying system, dual negative and positive pressure
Conveying duty 1.1.1., 1.3.1., 1.3.4.6., 1.3.4.7.,
1.4.4.2.5., 1.4.5.
Conveying gas, *see* Air; Conveying air; Gas;
Inert gas; Nitrogen
Conveying, high velocity dilute phase, *see* Dilute
phase
Conveying, horizontal, *see* Two-phase flow, *see
also* Pipeline length
Conveying limits **1.3.4.3.1.**, Figure 10
non-availability of data **1.3.4.3.2., 1.3.4.4.9.**
Conveying line, *see also* Conveying system;
Pipeline
blockage, *see* Blockage
design, *see* Conveying system design
discharge (delivery),
multiple discharge points 1.2.4., 1.2.6.

Conveying line (*continued*)
exit (outlet) air velocity 1.3.4.4.6., 1.3.4.7.2.
feed (pick-up), (*see also* Feeding device; individual names of feeding devices) 1.1.2.,
1.2.7.
feed points 1.3.2.1., 1.3.2.3.
overfeeding 1.3.6.2.
multiple feed points 1.2.4., 1.2.5., 1.2.6.
rate 1.3.4.10.5., 1.3.6.2.
high 1.3.6.2.
low 1.3.6.2.
underfeeding 1.3.6.2.
inlet air pressure **1.3.2.3.**, 1.3.4.8.1.,
1.3.4.10.2.
inlet air velocity (entrainment velocity, pick-
up velocity) **1.3.2.1.**, 1.3.2.4., 1.3.4.3.1.,
1.3.4.4.4., 1.3.4.4.6., 1.3.4.4.9.,
1.3.4.7.2., 1.3.5.1., Figures 7, 10
high 1.4.4.2.4.
lines of constant 1.3.4.4.9.
outlet, *see* conveying line exit
pressure drop, *see* Pressure drop
resistance 1.3.4.2.1.
Conveying, low velocity dense phase, *see* Dense
phase
Conveying material through pipeline, *see* Two-
phase flow, *see also* Material mass flow rate
Conveying mode, *see* Dense phase; Dilute phase
Conveying parameters **1.3.4.7.5.**
Conveying potential, (*see also* Conveying capability) 1.2.7., 1.3.6., 1.3.6.3.
Conveying rate, *see* Material mass flow rate
Conveying system 1.1.1., Figure 1
batch, *see also* Material mass flow rate
1.3.4.1.1., 1.3.4.5., 1.3.4.7.5., 1.4.3.,
1.4.4., 1.4.4.2.5., **1.4.6.5.2.**
conveying cycles 1.3.4.1.1.
closed 1.1.2., 1.2.1., **1.2.2.**, 1.2.3., 1.2.5.
closed loop 1.4.4.2.2.
combined negative and positive pressure
1.1.2., **1.2.6.**, 1.2.7., **1.4.5.7.**
power requirements, *see* Power requirements
components, *see* Components of conveying
system
continuously operating 1.3.4.1., 1.3.4.1.1.,
1.3.4.5., 1.3.4.7.5., 1.4.3., 1.4.4.2.5.,
1.4.6.5.1.
design 1.1.1., **1.1.3.**, 1.1.4., 1.2.1., **1.3.1. to
1.3.6.3.**, 1.4.1., 1.4.5., 1.4.6.5., Figure 6
decision stages **1.1.1.**
procedure 1.3.4.7.1.
study 1.4.2.
dual negative and positive pressure **1.2.7.**
economic assessment, *see* Costs
high pressure 1.1.2., 1.4.3., 1.4.4., 1.4.4.2.5.
innovatory **1.2.8.**
plug control systems 1.2.8.
pulse phase systems 1.2.8.
single plug blow tank systems 1.2.8.
low pressure 1.1.2., 1.3.4.10.4., 1.4.4.2.5.

Conveying system (*continued*)
  mode of operation 1.1.2., 1.1.4., 1.4.1.,
    1.4.3., Figure 1
  multiple use
    multiple delivery points, *see* Conveying line
      discharge
    multiple material handling, *see* Multiple
      material handling
    multiple pick-up points, *see* Conveying line
      feed
  negative pressure 1.1.2., **1.2.5.**, 1.2.6., 1.2.7.,
    1.3.2.2., 1.3.4.9.2., 1.3.4.9.3., 1.3.5.,
    1.4.4., 1.4.4.2.1., 1.4.4.2.2., 1.4.4.2.5.,
    1.4.5.6., 1.4.6.5.1.
    applications 1.2.5.
  open 1.1.2., 1.2.1., **1.2.3.**
  operating pressure 1.1.2., 1.2.6.
  over-rated 1.3.1.
  positive pressure 1.1.2., **1.2.4.**, 1.2.5., 1.2.6.,
    1.2.7., 1.3.2.2., 1.3.4.9.2., 1.3.4.9.3.,
    1.3.5., 1.4.4., 1.4.4.2.1., 1.4.4.2.2.,
    1.4.4.2.3., 1.4.4.2.4., **1.4.5.5.**, 1.4.6.5.1.
  requirements 1.3.4.3.
  selection **1.1.2.**, 1.1.4., **1.2.1. to 1.2.8.**,
    1.3.4.1.2., **1.3.6.**, 1.4.2
    constraints 1.1.1.
  shut down 1.2.4.10.5.
  start up
    cold 1.3.2.4.
  under-rated 1.3.1.
  uprating 1.3.5.1., **1.3.6.1.**
Conveying trials, (*see also* Conveying characteristics; Test data; Test pipeline) 1.1.3.,
  1.3.4.3.
Conveying velocity 1.2.8.
Conveying, vertical, (*see also* Pipeline length)
  1.3.4.4.1.
  scaling, *see* Scaling
  equivalent length *see* Scaling
Costs 1.1.1.
  capital 1.1.2., 1.1.4., 1.2.3., 1.2.8., 1.3.4.6.,
    1.4.2., 1.4.4.2.4., 1.4.4.2.5., 1.4.5.2.,
    1.4.5.4., 1.4.6.1.
  maintenance 1.3.4.6., 1.4.4.2.5.
  operating 1.1.2., 1.1.4., 1.3.4.6., 1.4.2.,
    1.4.5.4., 1.4.6.1.
  power 1.2.8., **1.3.4.6.**, 1.4.2.
  total 1.3.4.6., 1.3.6.1., **1.4.2.**
  economic assessment 1.2.8., 1.3.4.6., 1.4.2.
Cross sectional area of pipe, *see* Pipeline, cross
  sectional area
Cyclone separator, (*see also* Gas–solid separation device) **1.4.6.3.**, 1.4.6.4., 1.4.6.5.1.

D/d ratio, *see* Bend diameter
Dangerous materials, (*see* Hazardous materials,
  see also Combustible materials; Explosive
  materials; Radioactive materials; Toxic
  materials)
Degradation, *see* Particle degradation

Delivery points, *see* Conveying line discharge
Delivery (supply) pressure (of air mover), *see*
  Air supply pressure
Dense phase (non-suspension flow) 1.2.8.,
  1.3.3.1., 1.3.4.3.2., 1.3.4.4.3., 1.3.4.4.4.,
  1.2.4.4.8., 1.2.4.4.9., 1.3.6.2., 1.4.4.2.5.
Density
  bulk 1.3.4.3.2., 1.4.6.2.
  particle 1.4.6.4
  phase, *see* Phase density
Design, *see* Conveying system design
Diameter of conveying line, *see* Pipeline bore
Dicalcium phosphate 1.3.3.1., 1.3.4.3.1.,
  1.3.4.3.2., 1.3.4.4.9., 1.3.6.2., Figures 2, 10,
  11
  conveying characteristics Figures 4, 9
Dilute phase (lean phase, suspension flow)
  1.2.8., 1.3.3.1., 1.3.4.3.2., 1.3.4.4.3.,
  1.3.4.4.4., 1.3.4.4.9., 1.4.4.2.4.
Discharge, *see* Conveying line discharge
Discharge valves
  blow tanks, *see* Blow tanks
Disengager, disengaging system, *see* Gas–solid
  separation device
Distance conveyed, *see* Conveying distance
Diverter valves, *see* Pipeline
Double door discharge gates, *see* Gate lock
  valve
Double dump gates, *see* Gate lock valve
Double flap valves, *see* Gate lock valve
Drop-through feeder, *see* Rotary valve
Dual negative and positive pressure systems, *see*
  Conveying system, dual negative and posi-
  tive pressure
Dust, *see also* Fine materials 1.4.6.2.
  accumulations 1.2.5.
  cloud 1.2.2.
Dusty materials 1.4.6.3., 1.4.6.4.
Duty
  air mover, *see* Air mover
  conveying, *see* Conveying duty

Economic assessment, *see* Costs
Elbows, *see* Bends
Empty pipeline relationships, *see* Single-phase
  flow
Energy, *see* Power requirements
Entrainment, *see* Conveying line inlet, (*see also*
  Conveying line inlet air velocity)
Environmental control, *see* Controlled environ-
  ment
Equivalent length, *see* Scaling
Erosion, (*see also* Abrasive materials) 1.3.2.1.,
  1.3.4.8.1., 1.2.8., 1.3.4.4.4.
Erosive wear, *see* Erosion
Exhaust pressure (*see also* Air requirements;
  Air supply pressure) 1.3.4.9., 1.4.5.1.
Exhauster, (*see also* Fans; Liquid ring vacuum
  pump; Roots type exhauster; Air mover)
  1.2.5., 1.2.6., **1.4.5.6.**, 1.4.6.5.1.

Exhauster (*continued*)
   ingress of material, *see* Ingress of material
   power requirements, *see* Power requirements
Exit, *see* Conveying line exit
Explosive materials 1.2.2., 1.2.5., 1.4.6.

Fabric filter, *see* Filtration unit
Fans, (*see also* Air mover) 1.4.5.7.
   low pressure systems 1.3.4.10.4.
   negative pressure systems 1.4.5.6.
Feed surges, *see* Surge, material feed
Feeding devices, (*see also* Blow tanks; Gate lock
      valves; Rotary valve; Screw feeder; Suction
      nozzles; Venturi feeder) 1.2.4., 1.2.5.,
      1.3.4.10.2., **1.4.4.2.**, 1.3.6.1., 1.3.6.2.,
      1.3.6.3., 1.4.1.
   air leakage, *see* Air leakage
   capability 1.3.6.1., 1.4.4.1.
   flow control 1.4.4.1.
      adjustable 1.3.6.2., 1.3.6.3.
      automatic 1.3.6.2., 1.3.6.3.
   flow into 1.4.4.2.1.
   operating pressure 1.3.4.1.2., **Figure 12**
   pressure drop, *see* Pressure drop
   pressure rating 1.4.4.1.
   selection 1.1.2., 1.4.3., **1.4.4.1. to 1.4.4.2.5.**,
      1.4.5.4.
   specification 1.3.6.3., **1.4.4.1. to 1.4.4.2.5.**
   suitability 1.4.4.1.
Feeding the conveying line, *see* Conveying line
      feed
Fibrous materials 1.4.6.2.
Filtration 1.4.5.7.
   requirements 1.3.2.1.
   unit (*see also* Gas–solid separation device)
      1.2.5., 1.3.6.1., 1.3.6.3., 1.4.6.3., **1.4.6.4.**
   cleaning
      mechanical shaking 1.4.6.5.2.
      pulse jet 1.4.6.5.1.
   selection 1.4.6.4.
   specification 1.3.6.3., 1.4.6.5.1.
Fine granular materials, (*see also* Granular
      materials) 1.3.4.3.2.
Fine materials (particles), 'fines', (*see also* Dust;
      Dusty materials) 1.2.8., 1.4.4.2.1.,
      1.4.4.2.2., 1.4.6.1., 1.4.6.2., 1.4.6.4.,
      1.4.6.5.1.
Fine particles, *see* Fine materials
Flour 1.3.4.3., 1.3.4.3.2., Figure 5
Flow properties, *see* Two-phase flow
Flow rate, *see* Air flow rate; Air mass flow rate;
      Conveying air velocity; Conveying line feed;
      Conveying line, inlet air velocity; Feeding
      device, flow control; Feeding device, flow
      into; Material mass flow rate; Volumetric
      flow rate
Fluffy materials 1.4.4.2.1., 1.4.5.7.
Fluidising membrane
   pressure drop, *see* Pressure drop

Fluorspar 1.3.4.3.
Food products, *see* Foodstuffs
Foodstuffs 1.2.8.
Formulae **A.4**
'Free air' 1.3.2.2.
   conditions (standard conditions, standard re-
      ference conditions) 1.3.2., 1.3.4.9.
   delivery, *see* Air mover
   requirements 1.3.2.
Free flowing materials, *see* Two-phase flow
Friable materials, (*see also* Particle degradation)
      1.2.8., 1.3.2.1., 1.3.4.8.1., 1.4.4.2.3.,
      1.4.4.2.4., 1.4.4.2.5.

Gas, *see also* Air; Conveying air; Inert gas;
      Nitrogen; Single-phase flow
Gas–solid flow, *see* Two-phase flow
Gas–solid separation 1.2.3.
Gas–solid separation device (separator, disenga-
      ger), (*see also* Cyclone separator; Filtration
      unit; Gravity settling chamber) 1.1.2.,
      1.2.5., 1.3.6.1., 1.4.4.2.5.
   collection (separation) efficiency 1.4.6.1.
   considerations **1.4.6.5.1. to 1.4.6.5.2.**
   costs, *see* Costs
   design, 1.4.6.5.
   ingress of material, *see* Ingress of material
   selection **1.4.6.1. to 1.4.6.5.2.**
   specification **1.4.6.1. to 1.4.6.5.2.**
Gate valves, *see* Gate lock valves
Gate lock valves (double door discharge gates,
      double dump gates, double flap valves, gate
      valves), (*see also* Feeding device) 1.4.4.,
      1.4.4.2.4.
   operating pressure Figure 12
   pressure drop, *see* Pressure drop
Granular materials, (*see also* Coarse granular
      materials; Fine granular materials)
      1.3.4.3.2., 1.4.4.2.1.
Granulated sugar, *see* Sugar
Gravity settling chamber, (*see also* Gas–solid
      separation device) **1.4.6.2.**
   mesh separating screen 1.4.6.2.

Hazardous materials, (*see also* Combustible
      materials; Explosive materials; Radioactive
      materials; Toxic materials) 1.4.6.
Heavy particles 1.4.6.2.
Hopper (silo)
   collection 1.4.6.4.
Horizontal
   conveying, *see* Two-phase flow, *see also* Pipe-
      line length;
   length of pipeline, *see* Pipeline length
   scaling; *see* Scaling
Hygroscopic materials 1.2.8.

Ideal Gas Law 1.3.4.7.7., **A.4.**

Inert gas, (*see also* Air; Conveying air; Gas; Nitrogen; Single-phase flow) 1.2.2.
Ingress of air 1.3.2.2.
feeding device **1.3.4.9.2.**, 1.3.4.9.3.
Ingress of material
conveying system 1.2.5.
exhauster 1.2.5., 1.2.6., 1.4.6.5.1.
Inlet, *see* Conveying line inlet
Innovatory systems, *see* Conveying system innovatory

Large particles 1.4.6.2.
Leakage, air, *see* Air leakage
Lean phase, *see* Dilute phase
Light fluffy material 1.4.4.2.1., 1.4.5.7.
Limits of conveyability (conveying), *see* Conveying limits;
Liquid ring vacuum pumps, (*see also* Air mover; Exhauster) 1.3.5.
operating pressure 1.4.5.6., Figure 13
single stage 1.4.5.6.
two-stage 1.4.5.6.
Logic diagrams 1.1.2., **1.3.3.**
use of, **1.3.4.1 to 1.3.4.10.5.**, 1.4.2., **Figure 6**
Low pressure fan systems, *see* Fans
Long radius bends, *see* Bends
Lysholm compressor, *see* Rotary screw compressor

Maintenance 1.1.2.
Mass flow ratio, *see* Phase density
Mass ratio, *see* Phase density
Material, (*see also* Particle; Solids; individual names of materials)
change in conveying system 1.3.6., **1.3.6.3.**
conveying, *see* Two-phase flow
conveying characteristics, *see* Conveying characteristics
density, *see* Density
feed, *see* Conveying line feed
feeding device, *see* Feeding device
flow capabilities, *see* Material mass flow rate; Air mass flow rate
flow rate, *see* Material mass flow rate
mass flow rate (conveying rate, system throughput) 1.1.2., 1.3.1., 1.3.2.1., 1.3.3., 1.3.3.1., **1.3.4.1.1. to 1.3.4.1.2.**, 1.3.4.2.1., 1.3.4.3.1., 1.3.4.4.5., 1.3.4.4.8., 1.3.4.4.9., **1.3.4.5.**, 1.3.4.7., 1.3.4.7.1., 1.3.4.7.4., 1.3.4.7.6., 1.3.4.7.7., 1.3.6., 1.3.6.2., 1.3.6.3., 1.4.3., Figure 3, 4, 5, 8, 9, 10, 11
achievement **1.3.6.5.**
conveying characteristics, *see* Conveying characteristics
conveying cycle 1.3.4.1.1.

Material (*continued*)
ratio between time averaged mean value and to the maximum or steady state conveying rate (batch conveying) **1.3.4.1.1.**, 1.4.4.2.5.
single blow tank **1.3.4.1.1.**
twin blow tank system **1.3.4.1.1.**
scaling, *see* Scaling
steady hourly rate 1.3.4.1., 1.3.4.1.1.
steady state conveying rate 1.4.4.2.5.
surge, *see* Surge
time averaged mean value 1.3.4.1.
properties, (*see also* Material type, individual material properties) 1.1.2., 1.2.1.
air retention, *see* Air retention properties
type, (*see also* Material properties; individual material types) 1.3.4.4.9., 1.3.4.6., 1.3.4.7.
Material type A (good air retention properties), (*see also* Air retention properties) 1.3.3.1., 1.3.4.3.1., 1.3.4.3.2., 1.3.4.4.9., 1.3.3.1., 1.3.4.3.2., Figures 2, 11
Material type B (poor air retention properties), (*see also* Air retention properties) 1.3.3.1., 1.3.4.3.1., 1.3.4.3.2., 1.3.3.4.9., 1.3.3.1., 1.3.4.3.2., Figures 2, 11
Mathematical models
logic diagrams 1.3.3.
pipeline design 1.1.3.
power requirements
air mover **1.3.4.6.**, 1.3.5.1.
scaling *see* Scaling
Minimum conveying air velocity, *see* Conveying air velocity
Mode of conveying, *see* Dense phase; Dilute phase
Mode of operation, *see* Conveying system, mode of operation
Multi ejectors 1.4.5.6.
Multiple delivery points *see* Conveying line discharge
Multiple material handling, **1.3.6.3.**
Multiple pick-up points, *see* Conveying line feed

Negative pressure (vacuum) conveying systems, *see* Conveying system , negative pressure
Nitrogen, (*see also* Air; Conveying air; Gas; Inert gas; Single-phase flow) 1.2.2.
Nomenclature **A.2.1. to A.2.4.**
Non-suspension flow, *see* Dense phase

Open conveying system, *see* Conveying system, open
Operating pressure (range) 1.2.6.
air mover, *see* Air mover, individual names of air movers
conveying system, *see* Conveying system
exhauster, *see* individual names of exhausters

Operating pressure (range) (*continued*)
  feeding device, *see* Feeding devices, individual
    names of feeding devices
Operating range, *see* Operating pressure
Outlet, *see* Conveying line exit

Particle, *see also* Material; Solids
  degradation, (*see also* Friable materials)
    1.2.8., 1.3.2.1., 1.3.4.8.1.
  density, *see* Density
  fine, *see* Fine materials
  heavy, *see* Heavy particles
  large, *see* Large particles
  size
    distribution 1.3.4.3.2.
    median value (mean) 1.4.6.5.2.
    range 1.4.4.1.
Pearlite 1.3.4.3., Figure 5
Pellets 1.4.2.2.1.
  polyethylene, *see* Polyethylene
Phase density (mass flow ratio, mass ratio, solids
    loading ratio) 1.3.3.1., 1.3.4.1.2., 1.3.4.3.1.,
    1.3.4.4.2., 1.3.4.4.3., 1.3.4.4.8., 1.3.4.4.9.,
    1.3.4.7.7., 1.4.3., Figures 2, 3, 4, 8, 9
  conveying characteristics, *see* Conveying char-
    acteristics
P.f.ash, *see* Pulverised fuel ash
Pick-up, *see* Conveying line inlet
  points, *see* Conveying line feed
  velocity, *see* Conveying line inlet velocity
Pipeline, *see also* Conveying line
  bends, *see* Bends
  blockage, *see* Blockage
  bore (diameter, size) 1.1.3., 1.3.1., 1.3.3.,
    1.3.4., 1.3.4.1.2., 1.3.4.2., 1.3.4.3.,
    1.3.4.4., 1.3.4.5., 1.3.4.6., **1.3.4.7.1, to
    1.3.4.7.7., 1.3.4.8.1.** 1.3.6.1., 1.4.4.
    estimation **1.3.4.7.7.**
    ratio to bend diameter (D/d) *see* Bend
      diameter
  cross sectional area 1.3.4.7.2., 1.3.4.7.4.
  design, *see* Conveying system design
  diameter, *see* Pipeline bore
  diverter valves 1.2.4.
  erosion, *see* Erosion
  geometry (layout), (*see also* Pipeline length;
    Bend geometry) 1.3.4.2., 1.3.4.3.,
    1.3.4.4.5., 1.3.4.7.1.
    scaling, *see* Scaling
  length, *see also* Conveying distance; Pipeline
    geometry
    equivalent length of horizontal pipeline, *see*
      Scaling
    horizontal sections 1.3.4.2., 1.3.4.4.
    scaling *see* Scaling
    vertical sections 1.3.4.4.
      down 1.3.4.2., **1.3.4.4.3.**
      up 1.3.4.2, **1.3.4.4.2.**
  orientation, *see* Pipeline geometry; Bend
    geometry

Pipeline (*continued*)
  routing 1.3.4.2., **1.3.4.2.1.**
  single bore 1.3.4.8.1.
  stepped 1.2.6., **1.3.4.8.1.**, 1.4.5.4.
Pipelines used in conveying trials, *see* Test pipelines
Plant, (*see also* Components of conveying systems; Conveying system; Pipeline, individual names of components)
  air supply, *see* Air supply
  components, *see* Components of conveying
    system, individual names of components
Plug control systems, *see* Conveying system,
  innovatory
Pneumatic conveying, *see* Conveying
Pollution, *see also* Dust 1.4.6.
Polyethylene
  pellets 1.3.4.3., Figure 5
Polyvinyl chloride resin 1.3.4.3.
Positive pressure conveying systems, *see* Conveying system, positive pressure
Powder pump, *see* Blow tanks
Power costs, *see* Costs
Power requirements 1.2.6., 1.3.2.1.
  air mover **1.3.4.6.**, 1.3.4.7., **1.3.5.1.**, 1.4.5.2.,
    1.4.5.3.
  drive power **1.3.4.6.** 1.3.5.1
  mathematical model **1.3.4.6.**, 1.3.5.1.
  conveying system, combined negative and
    positive pressure 1.4.5.7.
  feeding device
    rotary valve 1.4.4.2.2.
    screw feeder
      constant pitch 1.4.2.2.2.
      decreasing pitch 1.4.2.2.2.
    minimum 1.1.4., 1.4.2.
Pressure
  air supply, *see* Air supply pressure
  delivery, *see* Air supply pressure
  conveying air, *see* Conveying air pressure
  conveying line inlet, *see* Conveying line inlet
    air pressure
  exhaust, *see* Exhaust pressure
  operating, *see* Operating pressure
Pressure drop
  air supply lines 1.3.4.10., **1.3.4.10.1.**,
    1.3.4.10.5
  air extraction lines 1.3.4.10., **1.3.4.10.1.**,
    1.3.4.10.5.
  available for conveying material 1.3.4.4.6.,
    1.3.4.4.7., 1.3.4.4.8., 1.3.4.7.3.
  bends 1.3.4.4.4.
    blind tees 1.3.4.4.4.
    elbows 1.3.4.4.4.
    short (small) radius 1.3.4.4.4.
  conveying line
    single-phase flow (air only, empty pipeline)
      1.3.4.4.6., **1.3.4.4.7.**, 1.3.4.4.8.,
      1.3.4.4.9., 1.3.4.7.2., **1.3.4.7.3.**,
      1.3.4.7.4.

Pressure drop (*continued*)
two-phase flow (gas–solid flow, material conveying), (*see also* Pressure drop, total) 1.3.3., 1.3.3.1., 1.3.4.1.2., 1.3.4.3.1., 1.3.4.4.6., 1.3.4.4.7., 1.3.4.4.8., 1.3.4.5., 1.3.4.7., 1.3.4.7.2., 1.3.4.7.5., 1.3.4.10., **1.3.4.10.3.**, Figures 3, 4, 8, 9 and 10
  test line 1.3.4.4.6.
  vertically down 1.3.4.4.3.
feeding device 1.2.5., 1.3.2.3., 1.3.4.10., **1.3.4.10.2.**, 1.3.4.10.5., 1.4.4.1.
  blow tank 1.3.4.10.2., **1.4.4.2.5.**
  fluidising membrane **1.4.4.2.5.**
  gate lock valve 1.3.4.10.2.
  rotary valve 1.2.6., 1.3.4.10.2., 1.3.4.10.3.
  screw feeder 1.3.4.10.2.
  venturi feeder 1.3.4.10.2.
gas–solid separation device 1.3.4.10., **1.3.4.10.4.**, 1.3.4.10.5.
lines of constant, on conveying characterstics 1.3.3.1., 1.3.4.4.9.
scaling, *see* Scaling
total, (*see also* Pressure drop, conveying line) 1.3.4.10., 1.3.4.10.4., 1.3.4.10.5.
Pressure egg, *see* Blow tanks
Pressure gradient, *see* Pressure drop
Product, *see* Material; Solids, *see also* individual names of materials
Properties of conveyed material, *see* Material, properties; individual material properties
Pulse phase systems, *see* Conveying system, innovatory
Pulverised fuel ash 1.3.4.3.2., 1.3.4.3., 1.4.4.2.2., Figure 5
P.V.C. resin, *see* Polyvinyl choride resin

Radioactive materials 1.2.2.
Radius of bends, *see* Bends
Ratio of bend diameter to pipeline bore (D/d), *see* Bend diameter
Ratio between the time averaged mean material flow rate and value to be achieved (batch conveying), *see* Material mass flow rate
Ratio between the time averaged mean material flow rate to the maximum, or steady state conveying rate (batch conveying), *see* Material mass flow rate
Reciprocating compressor, (*see also* Air mover) operating pressure 1.3.5., Figure 13
Recovery of conveyed material, solids, *see* Gas–solid separation device
Reference conditions, *see* 'Free air' conditions
Roots type blower, (*see also* Air mover) 1.3.5., 1.4.6.5.1.
  operating pressure 1.3.5., Figure 13
Roots type exhauster, (*see also* Exhauster) 1.2.5., 1.4.5.6., 1.4.5.7.
  operating pressure 1.4.5.6.

Rotary compressor, *see* Roots type blower; Roots type exhauster; Rotary screw compressor; Sliding vane rotary compressor
Rotary screw (helical lobe rotary, Lysholm) compressor, *see also* Air mover
operating pressure 1.3.5., Figure 13
Rotary valve, (*see also* Feeding device) 1.2.4., 1.2.5., 1.3.4.10.3., 1.4.4., **1.4.4.2.1.**, 1.4.4.2.3.
  air ingress, *see* Ingress of air
  air leakage, *see* Air leakage
  blow through 1.4.2.2.
  drop through 1.4.2.2.1.
  off set 1.4.2.2.1
  operating pressure 1.3.4.1.2., **1.4.4.2.1.**, Figure 12
  power requirements, *see* Power requirements
  pressure drop, *see* Pressure drop
  venting 1.4.4.2.1.

Safety precautions
features 1.2.3.
Sand 1.3.4.3.
Scaling 1.3.4.3., 1.3.4.4., Figures 8, 9
  bends **1.3.4.4.4.**
  distance **1.3.4.4.** to **1.3.4.4.9.**, 1.3.6.2.
  effects **1.3.4.4.8.**, **1.3.4.7.4.**
  equivalent length of horizontal pipeline bends **1.3.4.4.4.**, **Figure 7**
  horizontal pipeline **1.3.4.4.1.**
  test pipeline **1.3.4.4.5.**
  total pipeline **1.3.4.4.5.**
  vertical pipeline 1.3.4.4.1.
    down **1.3.4.4.3.**
    up **1.3.4.4.2.**
  horizontal pipeline **1.3.4.4.1.**
  material flow rate 1.3.4.4.5.
  mathematical model
    distance, orientation and geometry **1.3.4.4.4. to 1.3.4.4.9.**
    pipeline bore **1.3.4.7.1. to 1.3.4.7.7.**
    pipeline bore (diameter, size) **1.3.4.7.1. to 1.3.4.7.7.**
    pipeline geometry and orientation **1.3.4.4.1. to 1.3.4.4.9.**, 1.3.4.7.1.
  pressure drop 1.3.4.4.
  requirements **1.3.4.4.6. .1.3.4.7.2.**
  vertical pipeline
    down **1.3.4.4.3.**
    up **1.3.4.4.2.**
  procedure 1.3.4.
Screw compressor, *see* Rotary screw compressor
Screw feeders, (*see also* Feeding device) 1.2.4., **1.4.4.2.2.**, 1.4.4.
  constant pitch (simple) 1.4.4.2.2.
  decreasing pitch 1.4.2.2.2.
  operating pressures 1.3.4.1.2., 1.4.4.2.2., Figure 12
  pressure differential 1.4.4.2.2.
  pressure drop, *see* Pressure drop

Selection of conveying system, *see* Conveying system selection
Separator, *see* Gas–solid separation device
Settling chamber, *see* Gravity settling chamber
Shearing, material 1.4.4.2.1.
Short (small) radius bends, *see* Bends
Shut down, *see* Conveying system shut down
Silo, *see* Hopper
Single blow tank, *see* Blow tank
Single-phase flow (air only, empty pipeline), (*see also* Air mass flow rate) **1.3.4.4.7.,** **1.3.4.7.3.**
  pressure drop, *see* Pressure drop
Single plug blow tank systems, *see* Conveying systems, innovatory
Site constraints 1.1.1., 1.1.2.
Size of pipeline, *see* Pipeline bore
Sliding vane rotary compressor, (*see also* Air mover) 1.3.5.
  operating pressure Figure 13
Sliding vane rotary exhauster, (*see also* Exhauster) 1.4.5.6.
Sodium sulphate 1.3.3.1., 1.3.4.3.1., 1.3.4.3.2., 1.3.4.4.9., 1.3.6.2., Figures 2, 11
  conveying characteristics Figures 3, 8
Solids, *see also* Material; Particle
Solids feeding devices, *see* Feeding device
Solids loading ratio, *see* Phase density
Spillage 1.2.5.
Standard reference conditions, *see* 'Free air' conditions
Start up, *see* Conveying system
Steady state conveying, *see* Material mass flow rate
  rate, *see* Material mass flow rate
Stepped pipelines, *see* Pipeline, stepped
Stopping and re-starting during operation 1.2.8.
Suck-blow systems, *see* Conveying system, combined negative and positive pressure
Suction nozzles 1.2.5., Figure 12
Sugar, Figure 5
  granulated 1.3.3.1., 1.3.4.3.
Superficial air velocity 1.3.2.1.
Supply pressure of air mover, *see* Air supply pressure
Surge
  air, blow tanks, *see* Blow tanks
  material feed 1.3.2.3., 1.3.2.4., 1.3.4.10.5.
  material mass flow rate 1.3.5.1.
Suspension flow, *see* Dilute phase
System design, *see* Conveying system design
System selection, *see* Conveying system selection
System throughput, *see* Material mass flow rate

Temperature, *see also* Ideal Gas Law
  conveying air (gas) 1.3.2., 1.3.2.4., 1.4.6.4.
  conveyed material 1.4.6.4.

Test line, *see* Test pipeline
Test data, (*see also* Conveying trials) 1.3.4.3.1.
  for logic diagrams 1.3.3.
Test pipeline 1.3.4.3., 1.3.4.4., 1.3.4.4.5., 1.3.4.4.6., 1.3.4.4.7., 1.3.4.7.2., 1.3.4.7.3.
Total pipeline
  equivalent length, *see* Scaling
Toxic materials 1.2.5., 1.4.6.
Throughput of conveying system, *see* Material mass flow rate
Time averaged mean flow rate (value), *see* Material mass flow rate
Twin blow tanks, *see* Blow tanks
Two-phase (gas–solid flow, material conveying), (*see also* Material mass flow rate) 1.3.4.9.3., 1.3.4.10.3., 1.4.3.
  free flowing materials 1.4.4.2.3.
  pressure drop, *see* Pressure drop
Types of conveying system, *see* Conveying system; individual names of conveying systems

Uprating conveying systems, *see* Conveying system, uprating

Vacuum conveying systems, *see* Conveying system, negative pressure
Velocity
  conveying, see Conveying velocity
  conveying air, *see* Conveying air velocity
  conveying line exit, *see* Conveying line exit air velocity
  conveying line inlet, *see* Conveying line inlet air velocity
  superficial, *see* Superficial air velocity
Venting 1.2.3.
  exhaust 1.2.5.
  rotary valve, *see* Rotary valve
Venturi feeder, (*see also* Feeding device) 1.2.4., 1.3.4.10.2., 1.4.4., **1.4.4.2.3.**
  flow control 1.4.4.2.3.
  operating pressure 1.4.4.2.3., Figure 12
  pressure drop, *see* Pressure drop
Vertical
  conveying, *see* Conveying, vertical, *see also* Pipeline length
  equivalent lengths of horizontal pipeline, *see* Scaling
  sections of pipeline, *see* Pipeline length
  flow, *see* Conveying, vertical
  pressure drop, *see* Pressure drop
Volumetric (air) flow rate, (*see also* Air flow rate; Air mover; Air requirements; Air supply pressure) 1.1.3., 1.3.1., 1.3.2., **1.3.2.2.,** 1.3.2.4., 1.3.4.7.2., 1.3.4.7.7., 1.3.4.9., **1.3.4.9.1.,** 1.3.4.9.2., **1.3.4.9.3.,** 1.3.5.1., 1.3.6.2., 1.4.5.3., Figure 13

23569398R00052

Made in the USA
Columbia, SC
09 August 2018